Understanding
Aleister Crowley's
THOTH
TAROT

THEREFORE I SAY UNTO THEE: COME FORTH UNTO ME FROM THINE ABODE IN THE SILENCE, UNUTTERABLE WISDOM, ALL-LIGHT, ALL-POWER! THOTH, HERMES, MERCURY, ODIN, BY WHATEVER NAME I CALL THEE, THOU ART STILL UN-NAMED AND NAMELESS TO ETERNITY! COME THOU FORTH, I SAY, AND AID AND GUARD ME IN THIS WORK OF ART.[1]

UNDERSTANDING
ALEISTER CROWLEY'S
THOTH
TAROT

LON MILO DUQUETTE

WEISERBOOKS
Boston, MA/York Beach, ME

First published in 2003 by
Red Wheel/Weiser, LLC
York Beach, ME

With offices at:
368 Congress Street
Boston, MA 02210
www.redwheelweiser.com

Library of Congress Cataloging-in-Publication Data

DuQuette, Lon Milo
    Understanding Aleister Crowley's thoth tarot / Lon Milo DuQuette.
        p. cm.
    Includes bibliographical references.
      ISBN 1-57863-276-5
      1. Tarot. 2. Crowley, Aleister, 1875–1947. I. Title.
    BF1879.T2D873 2003
    133.3'2424—dc22   2003014475

Typeset in the United States

Printed in Canada
TCP

10 09 08 07 06 05 04

8 7 6 5 4 3 2

THIS WORK IS LOVINGLY DEDICATED
TO BETTY LUNDSTED.

CONTENTS

PART TWO
THE CARDS 79

FIGURES

TABLES

ACKNOWLEDGMENTS

The author wishes to recognize and thank the following individuals for their friendship, wisdom, and support: Constance Jean DuQuette, Judith Hawkins-Tillirson, Rick Potter, Jody Breedlove, Hymenaeus Beta, Sabazius, James Wasserman, Bill Heidrick, Carolyn Tillie, Donald Weiser, Clive Harper, Tim Maroney, Kat Sanborn, and Donald Kraig. And to the brightest stars in the firmament of tarot:

Janet Berres, Dr. Arthur Rosengarten, Stuart Kaplan, Mary Greer, Rachel Pollack, Thalassa, Ruth Ann and Wald Amberstone, Linda Walters, Robert Place, and Bob O'Neil. Finally, I give special (and most humble) thanks to my dear Brother, Dathan Biberstein, who revealed to me the mystery of the Kerubic emblems of the Thoth Tarot—a mystery that taunted me for over thirty years.

PART I

*Little Bits of Things You Should
Know Before Beginning to Study
Aleister Crowley's Thoth Tarot*

CHAPTER ZERO

THE BOOK OF THOTH— A MAGICK BOOK?

The Tarot is a pack of seventy-eight cards. There are four suits, as in modern playing cards, which are derived from it. But the Court cards number four instead of three. In addition, there are twenty-two cards called "Trumps," each of which is a symbolic picture with a title to itself.

At first sight one would suppose this arrangement to be arbitrary, but it is not. It is necessitated, as will appear later, by the structure of the universe, and in particular the Solar System, as symbolized by the Holy Qabalah. This will be explained in due course.[1]

These are the brilliantly concise opening words of Aleister Crowley's *The Book of Thoth*. When I first read them, I was filled with great expectations. At last, I thought, the great mysteries of the Thoth Tarot are going to be explained to me—"in due course."

At the time, I considered myself a serious student of tarot, having spent three years studying the marvelous works of Paul Foster Case and his *Builders of the Adytum*[2] tarot and Qabalah courses. As dictated in the B.O.T.A. curriculum, I painted my own deck of trumps and dutifully followed the meditative exercises outlined for each of the twenty-two cards. Now, with Aleister Crowley's Thoth Tarot and *The Book of Thoth* in hand, I knew I was ready to take the next step toward tarot mastery and my own spiritual illumination.

It took a bit of bravado on my part to arrive at this threshold. My first introduction to Crowley had not been particularly satisfying. In fact, I came very close to shunning the Thoth Tarot and *The Book of Thoth* as seductive works of the devil. I wrote about this embarrassing episode in my book, *My Life with the Spirits:*[3]

Eventually, I came upon an early edition of Aleister Crowley's Thoth Tarot deck. I had never seen anything so beautiful in my life. The name Aleister Crowley sounded familiar and I vaguely recalled seeing his name footnoted in a Qabalah book that I had read by Frater Achad. I referred to my occult dictionary and discovered to my horror—"Aleister Crowley—famous Scottish Satanist."

I may have been a wild and crazy heretic, but I sure didn't want anything to do with Satanism. Knowing my brother owned a copy of *The Book of Thoth* (the companion text), I promptly gave the cards to him. Good riddance!

I was soundly disabused of this notion a few days later by our dear friend Mad Bob (a name that only begins to describe his bizarre and wonderful character), who had returned briefly from a Central American adventure. Bob had read Crowley's autobiography[4] and insisted I would love the man if I gave him a chance. When I showed him what the occult dictionary had to say, he brushed it off saying, "It doesn't matter if Crowley was a Satanist, he was a good kind of Satanist. You'll just love him! Trust me."

That was the strangest thing I had ever heard, but I respected Mad Bob's opinion and took the cards back from my brother and asked to borrow his *Book of Thoth*. Bob was right. Even though I didn't understand most of what I read, I could see that Aleister Crowley was brilliant, funny, and everything I was looking for. I bought everything I could by or concerning the man (precious little in those days) and eventually wrote to Crowley's Ordo Templi Orientis (O.T.O.) at the address published on the Caliph card included in the Thoth Tarot to ask for initiation.

And so began what (for good or ill) I must call my magical career. The Thoth Tarot being not only the catalyst that triggered my metamorphosis from dilettante to magician, but also the talisman that obligingly provided the mailing address of the Holy Order that would remain my spiritual home and university for the next quarter century.

Please don't think that by relating the above story I am suggesting that everyone who wishes to understand more about the Thoth Tarot or *The Book of Thoth* need run right out and join the O.T.O. or any other group, magical or otherwise. Occult societies are not for everybody, and no matter what any of them may suggest to new or potential members, no organization has yet cornered the market on the wisdom of the ages. In fact, all the information one will ever need in order to master the subject has already been published and is readily available—more available, in fact, than at any other time in history. At the dawn of the new millennium, it is not a matter of whether or not the answers are out there, rather it is a matter of arriving at a place where one knows the right questions to ask.

Naturally, because no two individuals are alike, we should not expect to find the answers in the same places. For me, the answers most often come, not from teachers or from mystery school lectures, but from books—books, curiously enough, that I have already read (or thought I read) many times before.

Crowley's *Book of Thoth* is one such book. It seems to change miraculously as it rests on the shelf. I can say with certainty that, in the last thirty years, I have read it cover-to-cover at least a dozen times, and have referred to it hundreds of times. Yet every time I pick it up, I find something profound that I have never seen before. More often than not, this new intelligence is precisely that bit of information I have been combing my brain or library for, or else it satisfies some spiritual frustration currently gnawing at my soul.

I used to blame this phenomenon on the fact that I am a slow learner and need to have something drummed into my head many times before I start to "get it." Nevertheless, over the years, I have spoken to so many students who tell me that the same thing happens to them (especially with books by Aleister Crowley) that I believe it to be a universal experience.

Of course, I don't believe that the words on the page actually metamorphose into different words between readings. Nor can I bring myself to think that I am careless enough to leave unread great chunks of a book I passionately want to understand. Rather, I have come to realize that it is me who changes between readings, and that the magical secret to learning more than I now know lies in my ability to become someone who is more than I now am.

For this reason, I strongly recommend that, if you are truly serious about your study of the tarot, you not only read *The Book of Thoth* but reread it regularly. Leave it off the shelf and refer to it often. Keep rereading it until it falls apart in your hands, then go out and buy a new one. It will be a different book every time you pick it up. It is a magick book. Respect it. Treasure it. Let it work its magick on you— not so much for the reward of learning more than you now know, but for sake of your spiritual destiny to become someone greater than you now are.

The idea that I should write an exegetic text on the Thoth Tarot and *The Book of Thoth* was first suggested by Miss Judith Hawkins-Tillirson[5] at an informal meeting with me, Donald Weiser, and Betty Lundsted of Weiser Books. Judith's proposition came as a complete surprise to me, and I sat speechless throughout most of her pitch. She pointed out the fact that, other than *The Book of Thoth* itself, there was no book that examined the Thoth Tarot from the point of view of a Crowley "expert."

She went on for only two or three minutes. When she was finished, she sat back in her chair and grinned at me. Don and Betty agreed that the book was a good idea and that I should send them some preliminary material. That was that. I had hardly spoken a word. I went back to my hotel and stared out the window at a glorious Chicago thunderstorm and asked myself, "What in the world have I gotten myself into?"

While the definition of the term "expert" is certainly open to debate, it is probably at least partially true that my credentials to comment on the subject are as presentable as anyone's. However, I must warn the reader that my understanding of Crowley, Thelema, and tarot is constantly changing. No matter how smugly secure I may appear in my theories and opinions, please keep in mind that I am perpetually reexamining my theories and changing my opinions. I counsel you to be prepared to do the same.

CHAPTER ONE

LITTLE BITS OF THINGS
YOU SHOULD KNOW

It seems important that you should understand my motive. To me this Work on the Tarot is an Encyclopaedia of all serious "occult" philosophy. It is a standard Book of Reference, which will determine the entire course of mystical and magical thought for the next 2000 years. My one anxiety is that it should be saved from danger of destruction, by being reproduced in permanent form, and distributed in as many distant places as may be. I am not anxious to profit financially; if I had the capital available in this country, I should send (say) 200 copies to State Libraries in all parts of the world, and as many more to my principal representatives.[6]
—Aleister Crowley to Mr. Pearson, Photoengraver, May 29, 1942.

Every year since 1969, when the first color edition appeared in bookstores and specialty shops worldwide, Aleister Crowley's Thoth Tarot has remained one of the best-selling tarot decks in the world. This is not surprising. In my opinion, it is quite simply the most stunningly beautiful deck of tarot cards ever created. It took the artist, the immensely talented Frieda Harris,[7] over five years (1938–1943)[8] to complete the seventy-eight surrealistic masterpieces.

Today, the images remain as hauntingly evocative as when they were first exhibited. The popularity of the cards, however, shines in bright contrast to the black reputation of the man who designed them and who relentlessly dictated every aspect of their execution—a man maligned during his lifetime as a black magician, and branded by the press "the wickedest man in the world."

Paradoxes seem to define the life and career of Edward Alexander (Aleister) Crowley.[9] Yes, in many ways he was a scoundrel. There is no doubt that he wallowed shamelessly in his carefully cultivated persona as England's literary and spiritual bad-boy. At the same time, he took life and himself very seriously. Among

stinctions, he was a world-class mountaineer,[10] chess master, painter, poet,
an, novelist, critic, and theatrical producer. He introduced America to astrol-
sadora Duncan to the *I Ching*, and the poet Victor Neuberg to hiking and
magick. As an *agent provocateur* writing for an English-language German
ganda newspaper in New York, he penned the outrageous and inflammatory
rials that provoked a reluctant United States Congress to enter World War I
ngland's side.[12]

During World War II, at the request of friend and Naval Intelligence officer
Fleming,[13] Crowley provided Winston Churchill with valuable insights into
e superstitions and magical mind-set of the leaders of the Third Reich. He also
ggested to the prime minister, if reports can be believed, that he exploit the enemy's
magical paranoia by being photographed as much as possible giving the two-fingered
"V-for-Victory" gesture. This sign is the manual version of the magical sign of
Apophis-Typhon, a powerful symbol of destruction and annihilationwhich, according to magical tradition, is capable of defeating the solar energies represented by
the swastika.

Astonishingly, Crowley's adventures and achievements—more than any dozen
men of ambition and genius could realistically hope to garner in a lifetime—seem
almost to be distractions when weighed against his monumental exploits of self-
discovery. His visionary writings and his efforts to synthesize and integrate the esoteric spiritual systems of East and West[14] make him one of the most fascinating
cultural and religious figures of the twentieth century.

Even though his highly esoteric (and often ponderous) writings today enjoy a
level of readership and appreciation never approached during his lifetime, the
number of aspirants willing to take up serious study of his Scientific Illuminism
remains relatively small. For those daring and tenacious students, his Thoth Tarot
becomes the cornerstone of their study—a priceless and indispensable treasure. It
is nothing less than a full-color visual textbook of the wisdom of the ages—a living
talisman that distills, in breathtaking pageantry, the essence of the spiritual education and insights of a modern master of the ancient mysteries. Is it any wonder that
such a rare and radiant magical device should cast an irresistible spell upon nearly
everyone with whom it comes in contact? For me, the answer is obvious. However,
I think it is also fair to ask if it is possible for someone to use and enjoy the Thoth
Tarot, even if they have absolutely no interest in Crowley or the Qabalistic, astrological, and magical aspects of the cards.

My answer is an unequivocal "Yes!" The Thoth Tarot happens to be the preferred deck of thousands of tarot collectors, students, and amateur and professional
readers all over the world.[15] Most with whom I have spoken tell me they choose
the deck because of its haunting beauty and its efficacy as a divinatory tool. Those
who know something about Crowley and his work are usually polarized in their
opinions, but even those who consider him a perfectly dreadful individual still main-

tain a healthy admiration for the cards. I was once assailed by a venerable tarot reader who voiced the opinion shared by many professional readers and fans of the Thoth Tarot: "I don't care who Aleister Crowley was, and I don't believe in his *magick*. I just know I like those damned cards and they work!"

While it is undoubtedly true that only a small percentage of owners and users of the Thoth Tarot will ever fully appreciate the esoteric value of the cards, it is also abundantly clear to me that there are a great many people who would sincerely like to know more about them. If you find yourself in this group of seekers, this book is for you.

In recent years, several fine books have been published that use the Thoth Tarot as illustrations. By and large, these books pay respectful attention to the more obvious features of the cards. They are good tarot books in their own right, but they do not, in my opinion, deal satisfactorily with the profound concepts and revelations that make the Thoth Tarot so unique and important. There is, however, one book that does. It is a magnificent work written by the only person truly qualified to comment authoritatively on the cards. The singular shortcoming of this *magnum opus*, however, is not that it doesn't tell us enough—but that it tries to tells us *everything*.

Toward the end of his life, Crowley (writing as The Master Therion) wrote one of his greatest works, *The Book of Thoth—A Short Essay on the Tarot of the Egyptians*.[16] He intended it as an "elementary treatise" on tarot in general and the Thoth Tarot in particular. As anyone who has read it, or attempted to read it, will tell you, it is anything but elementary. In fact, unless one is already extremely knowledgeable in the fields of mythology, philosophy, and religion, unless one is thoroughly steeped in the doctrines of the Hebrew Qabalah, unless one is intimately familiar with the immense body of magical and visionary work that occupied Crowley for nearly fifty years, unless one is fluent in the complex and enigmatic nomenclature these visions spawned, *The Book of Thoth* is most definitely not a user-friendly exposition of the Thoth Tarot.

This is not to say that the uninitiated cannot benefit from reading it. On the contrary, there is much in the text that is immediately comprehensible, indeed, profoundly inspirational. Nevertheless, if it is the reader's desire to gain some practical information about the Thoth Tarot quickly, he or she will most likely not read past the seventh paragraph:

> One important interpretation of Tarot is that it is a Notariqon of the Hebrew Torah, the Law; also of ThROA, the Gate. Now, by the Yetziratic attributions—see table at end—this word may be read The Universe—the new-born Sun—Zero. This is the true Magical Doctrine of Thelema: Zero equals Two. Also, by Gematria, the numerical value of ThROA is 671 = 61 x 11. Now 61 is AIN, Nothing or Zero; and 11 is the number of Magical

Expansion; in this way also, therefore, ThROA announces that same dogma, the only satisfactory philosophical explanation of the Cosmos, its origin, mode, and object.[17]

Please do not think that I am deriding the content of the above statement. It is remarkably lucid and perfectly Crowley. I understand it (to a degree) and, given enough time (with breaks for meals), could explain it to any reasonably intelligent person. However, when I first read it nearly thirty years ago, it made absolutely no sense to me. I knew nothing about Qabalistic world subdivisions, Enochian Aethyrs, or magical societies. I couldn't get through one page of *The Book of Thoth* without encountering references to things I knew nothing about and reference books I did not possess.

Lady Harris was equally overwhelmed, and voiced her frustration in a January 1939 letter to Crowley.

> In reference to your books—I suppose you know that most of them would be easier for a beginner written in Sanscrit and that anyone reading them would go off their heads. Therefore the wise (like myself) take them in snappy bits and only when they are feeling strong.[18]

So it is with much of *The Book of Thoth*. It is a masterpiece without equal, and the perfect companion to the Thoth Tarot. While the latter can be appreciated the moment the cards are taken out of the box, however, the former demands a significant investment of time and study.

It would be many years before I realized that, had I known only just a little bit about the magical life of Aleister Crowley, just a little bit about his revolutionary spiritual world-view and prophetic visions, just a little bit about astrology, just a little bit about the Qabalah, just a little bit about alchemy, just a little bit about the Golden Dawn and the Tree of Life, then *The Book of Thoth* and the Thoth Tarot cards would soon have yielded many of their most important mysteries. What I needed was another book—a book that might have been titled Little Bits of Things You Should Know before Beginning Your Study of Aleister Crowley's Thoth Tarot.

Unfortunately for me, no such book existed at the time. Hopefully, one does now.

CHAPTER TWO

ALEISTER CROWLEY AND THE GOLDEN DAWN

Beyond all other mundane events it was the influence of the Hermetic Order of the Golden Dawn that shaped Aleister Crowley's life. Once exposed to its Qabalistic system of grades and philosophy, its magical practices and ceremonies he was never the same. [19]

Obviously, for us to begin to understand Aleister Crowley's Thoth Tarot, we should first know a little bit about Aleister Crowley. Not forgetting my words in the previous chapter concerning the helpfulness of "little bits" of information, I must confess that, when the subject is Aleister Crowley, a little bit of knowledge can be a very dangerous thing. Those knowing just a little bit about the man vilified him mercilessly during his life and continue to do so to this day. On the other side of the coin, there are those who know just a little bit about Crowley who become instant "true believers." They emulate his every perceived prejudice and vice and zealously worship him as if he were an omniscient and unerring god. Both views are dangerously flawed. Make no mistake about it: a person needs an enormous amount of information in order to arrive at a fair and reasonable understanding of this complex and remarkable character.

Unfortunately, space will not allow us a thorough examination and proper defense of the seventy-two-year adventure that was the colorful life of Aleister Crowley. For those of you who wish to take a more in-depth look, there are four biographies that I do not hesitate to recommend.[20] They are included in the bibliography at the end of this volume.

Understandably, many of you will not care (or be able) to research these texts, nor should this gap in your Crowley education prevent you from using and enjoying the Thoth Tarot. I truly wish I could break every rule of literary decorum and simply say something like: Please trust me on this, folks. I know an awful lot about

Crowley. He wasn't perfect. In fact, he could be perfectly horrible! But despite his outrageous behavior and many shortcomings, his spiritual quest was as sincere, as genuine, and as successful as any ever recorded. In this respect, he was in a very real sense a holy man. Within the mountains of written material he left behind there are priceless treasures waiting to be discovered by anyone willing to dig for them.

Aleister Crowley was born Edward Alexander Crowley on October 12, 1875, at Leamington, Warwickshire, England, to Edward Crowley, a wealthy brewer, and Emily Bertha Bishop. His father was a follower of John Nelson Darby and a lay preacher for the extremely conservative Plymouth Brethren Protestant sect. His mother was an enthusiastic (Crowley wrote "fanatical") member of the same.

Young Alex was a sickly child and endeavored to overcome his health deficiencies by hiking and rock climbing. He was educated by a number of private tutors and private schools, including Malvern College, Tonbridge, Eastbourne College, King's College, London, and finally Trinity College, Cambridge.

At Cambridge, he blossomed into a prolific poet and developed a keen interest in alchemy and all things mysterious and occult. In November of 1898, he offered himself for initiation into the Hermetic Order of the Golden Dawn in London, taking the motto "Perdurabo," meaning "I shall endure to the end." This is an allusion to Matthew 10:22, that is chillingly prophetic of the future that lay before young Crowley: "And ye shall be hated of all men for my name's sake: but he that endureth to the end shall be saved."[21]

Although he would be instrumental in breaking it up just a few years later, the structure and teachings of the Golden Dawn would remain a major influence throughout his life. It would also, quite literally, provide the blueprint for his personal spiritual evolution. As we will soon see, the Golden Dawn's Equinox ceremony (when the Hierophant steps down and a new one is installed) foreshadowed a most profound cosmic event—but more on that later.

In the Golden Dawn's fifth degree (Adeptus Minor), the new initiate is required to paint his or her own deck of tarot cards modeled after one loaned to him or her by the Order. The model deck was almost certainly designed by the Order's master adept, S. L. MacGregor Mathers, and painted by his artist wife, Moina.

For less than a dozen years, this deck had been the most esoteric and secret pack of cards in existence. Candidates were bound by the most solemn and terrible oaths never to reveal the secret correspondences and images. Crowley, as part of his Adeptus Minor duties, most assuredly created his own, and the images of the Thoth Tarot are based solidly upon those of the Golden Dawn model. Later, when I discuss the individual cards, I will make repeated references to these original designs.

The Golden Dawn degree system is based upon the Qabalistic schema called the Tree of Life (see figure 21, chapter 9). This diagram will become very important to us in our study of the Thoth Tarot and the initiatory career of its creator.

The Tree of Life consists of ten sephiroth,[22]—emanations from (or aspects of) the supreme being. These ten sephiroth can be considered levels of consciousness—the lowest (10) being that of the material plane, the highest (1) being the supreme consciousness of deity. In the course of our incarnation adventures, each of us, in one way or another, eventually "climbs" this tree, gaining ever more subtle levels of consciousness, until we finally achieve union with godhead and supreme spiritual liberation.

The tarot is a perfect representation of the Tree of Life. The ace of each suit represents the top sephira (1) and the two, three, four, five, six, seven, eight, nine, and ten of each suit represents its respective sephira on the Tree.

There are also twenty-two paths that connect the ten sephiroth and facilitate the candidate's climb up the tree. These twenty-two paths are represented in tarot by the twenty-two trump cards. We will discuss the Tree of Life in more detail in chapter 9. Here it is only necessary to remember that the ten sephiroth and twenty-two paths of the Tree of Life are the keys to understanding the magical life and career of Aleister Crowley, as well as the key to understanding the Thoth Tarot.

CHAPTER THREE

THE LADY AND THE BEAST

Don't, Aleister, say "like me a little." If I may aspire to such a position, you are my friend and when my friends are rude to me I cannot remember it. They remain the cone, the eye, the node, from which is generated all the pleasure I have in life.[23]
—Harris to Crowley, January 28, 1940.

Was Frieda Harris a Lady? Of course she was, but the first little bit of information we should learn about her concerns her use of the title "Lady." She is almost always referred to in print as "Lady Frieda Harris." This is not technically correct, however. British book antiquarian and Crowley/Harris scholar Clive Harper wrote me the following:

> Percy Harris was made a baronet in 1932 (a baronetcy can be thought of as an inheritable "Sir . . ." title). He was appointed to the Privy Council in 1940 and so became entitled to be called "The Right Honourable . . ." but strictly speaking this is an office, rather than an honour. The wife of a baronet is indeed a "Lady" but as the wife of Sir Percy Harris, she should have been known as "Lady Harris." "Lady Frieda Harris" would only be correct if she was, for example, the daughter of a duke and so entitled to a courtesy title through her father. If she had divorced her husband she would be properly called, "Frieda, Lady Harris." Now it is clear that she herself used "Lady Frieda Harris" and she would certainly have known the protocol for such things. One can but suspect that she was not averse to letting people assume that she came from a noble family, rather than being merely the estranged wife of a baronet.[24]

There is very little information available concerning the personal relationship that existed between Lady Harris and Aleister Crowley. In my mind, it is a story that perhaps could only have been written by E. M. Forrester and filmed by Merchant-Ivory. I can imagine the movie trailer . . . cue the string quartet!

Freethinking London socialite and surrealist painter, Frieda Harris, wife of The Right Honourable Sir Percy Alfred Harris, M. P. (powerful Chief Whip of the Liberal Parliamentary Party) mysteriously falls under the spell of the notorious black magician Aleister Crowley, the most vilified and despised man in England. Ignoring the possible social consequences, she becomes his magical disciple[25] and agrees to focus her immense talent on a strange and monumental task. She would, under his domination, manifest in seventy-eight watercolor paintings his awesome, sometimes terrifying vision of the magical and spiritual forces of nature projected though the ancient archetypal images of the tarot.

True to the art-film milieu, the climax of this melodrama is played out against the chaotic backdrop of wartime London—the troop trains, the rationing, the sirens, the blitz, the blackouts—it really is too romantic for words.

It wasn't exactly like that, however. First, to be fair to the memories of these two brilliant and colorful characters, we must remember that they were both in their sixties. Rumors notwithstanding, Crowley's failing health and Lady Harris's extremely visible social calendar made it highly unlikely their collaboration was one mad and titillating adulterous romp.

Second, it was Harris, not Crowley, who first suggested that he redesign the traditional tarot images and write a book about it, which she would illustrate with seventy-eight paintings. Crowley flatly refused, suggesting simply that they "get hold of the best available old pack and have them re-drawn with occasional corrections and emendations."[26] A project like that, he speculated, would take only six months to complete. Harris was adamant, however. She insisted upon painting entirely new tarot images that would illustrate a comprehensive new book from Crowley. She eventually made Crowley an offer he couldn't refuse. She would pay him a weekly stipend of £2 a week to teach her magick. Crowley was bankrupt. He acquiesced.

Harris was introduced to Crowley by artist friend and London socialite Greta Valentine. They were all mutual friends of Clifford Bax, former coeditor of the literary and art magazine *The Golden Hind.*

Harris was a Co-Mason[27] and no stranger to esoteric subjects and ritual work, but at the beginning of the project, she was a complete magical novice and by no means a tarot expert. Nonetheless, she said she felt impelled by her Holy Guardian Angel[28] to create images that most accurately conveyed the deepest magical and spiritual meaning of each card. She thoroughly acquainted herself with the traditional tarot images and the descriptions found in *The Equinox*.[29] She worked tirelessly from Crowley's sketches and notes, and thought nothing of repainting a single card as many as eight times to satisfy his demands.

Crowley, displaying an uncharacteristic level of gracious candor, readily admitted that Harris's genius forced him to apprehend each card as an individual masterpiece, and that her energy, not his, was the impetus that saw the enormous undertaking through to completion. It was truly a dynamic partnership of two brilliant and intensely motivated artists.

But did Crowley, who fancied himself a good intuitive painter, try to influence Harris's style in executing the cards? The answer is "yes," especially early in the project, when it was obvious that Frieda was bent on a level of expression that might have rendered the Thoth deck unrecognizable as tarot. Crowley's December 19, 1939, note to Harris concerning her work on Adjustment and her fear of painting faces gives us an idea of the direction the Thoth Tarot might have taken had Crowley not put his foot down. He also, with typical Crowley hyperbole, tears into her circle of friends, who were currently influencing her artistic attitudes:

> Your feeling about having no forms and faces is merely symptomatic of
> modern soul-sickness. It is lack of confidence in one's creative powers. It is
> the root of homosexuality as understood in this country and of all these
> crazy movements, the Neo-Thomists, and the Buchmanites and the
> Dadaists and the Surrealists. Picasso took it far enough; he tried to paint a
> chair which could not be any particular chair, and must therefore have no
> colour and no form, but as every chair, in order to be a chair, must have a
> support for the human frame, he did a horizontal line. But this is meta-
> physics and not art; all these half-sexed, half-witted people, sicklied o'er with
> the pale caste of thought, I cannot believe that any of them will ever com-
> mand either the Exeter, the Ajax or the Achilles, and any man who is not
> potentially capable of doing that, is not a man at all; he may be some kind of
> pudding, and I hold no brief against puddings, but all these people who
> resent simplicity resent manhood, they weave their own onanistic web of
> nastiness; these are the shells cast off from the Tree of Life, these are the
> larvae of abomination. It has been your evil fortune to have far too much to
> do with such people without a proper clinical training, such as would have
> enabled you to diagnose their malady; they have small orts of cleverness
> without any breadth of vision or balance, without the sense of space, of
> nature, of fresh air.
>
> . . . I must emphasise that this fear of faces is an appalling symptom of
> cowardice. It is surely a natural instinct to connect expression with moral
> ideas, and it is moral ideas, or more correctly magical ideas, that you are out

to illustrate. It did not matter so much in this particular card because of the tradition of Justice being blind, but on the other hand, the masking of the face suggests deceit which is the absolute opposite of the intention of the card; it was the familiars of the Inquisition, it was the Vehmgericht that administered what they called Justice, hooded. Impartiality is a lovely idea, but it doesn't get you very far; if the impartial person may be impersonated by a demon of malignant darkness.[30]

Why don't you tell us how you really feel, Mr. Crowley!

Lady Harris exhibited the paintings on at least three occasions; first in June 1941 at the Randolph Hotel in Oxford, then again in July 1942 at the Berkeley Galleries on Davis Street, London, and in August 1942 at the Royal Society of Painters in Water Colours on Conduit Street, London. At Harris's insistence, Crowley was not in attendance, nor does his name appear anywhere in the program essays.[31]

In 1944, Crowley published the first edition of *The Book of Thoth*, the textbook the cards were to illuminate. Assisting him financially with this project and several others was a young American soldier, Lieutenant Grady L. McMurtry,[32] a member of Crowley's magical order, Ordo Templi Orientis. In 1969, he would also be instrumental in arranging to have the seventy-eight paintings photographed and published as a deck of tarot cards.[33]

McMurtry was the only person I have ever talked to who actually met Lady Harris. He first met her at Crowley's flat at 93 Jermyn Street, Piccadilly. Shortly afterward, Crowley moved out of the city to Buckinghamshire. McMurtry and Harris would meet once again at her home in London. It was a brief encounter, but his description of the event (which I heard him recount at least a half-dozen times) is such a charming peek at Harris's character and so indicative of the milieu of the times that I cannot resist attempting to retell it here. I hope Crowley biographers will forgive if my recollection of McMurty's oft-told story differs with their understanding of objective history.

It was in late May 1944, less than two weeks before he would be part of the D-Day Normandy invasion. Lieutenant McMurtry visited Crowley at his home at the Bell Inn in Aston Clinton in Buckinghamshire. Because McMurtry had access to a jeep and petrol, Crowley asked him if he could deliver some papers to Lady Harris in London. Excited at the thought of seeing Harris again, he readily agreed.

It was early evening and the city was blacked out by the time he reached the Harris residence at 3 Devonshire Terrace, Marylebone High Street. As he approached the door, he heard piano music and the sweet notes of Debussy's "Claire de Lune" from inside the Harris home. (McMurtry told me he remembered thinking what an awkward contrast he made—a lanky American soldier in jump boots standing at the door of this genteel gathering.) He knocked, and soon a man dressed in eveningwear opened the door. It was obvious there was a party in progress; a pianist was entertaining guests. McMurtry stated his business and was asked to wait out-side the door. In a few moments, Lady Harris opened the door, greeted him politely, and accepted the paperwork with thanks. Then, as she was about to close the door in his face, she turned her head for a moment and gazed upon the bright warmth of her party—the quiet talk, the Debussy. For a moment, McMurtry was sure she was going to invite him in. Then she turned to look at him, in his uniform and boots, and said, "You do understand, of course, I can't invite you in. It would so spoil the mood of the evening."

Contrary to absurd published statements that Crowley grew rich from the sales of the Thoth Tarot while Lady Harris went unrecognized and unpaid, neither Harris nor Crowley would live to profit financially from the project, or even see the paint-ings properly manifested as tarot cards.[34] Crowley died in December of 1947. Harris visited him a few days before he died. He did not recognize her. She became a co-executor of his will and was among the handful of people who attended his funeral. She also hosted a lavish "curry" wake in his honor in her home in London.

After the death of Sir Percy in 1952, Frieda, Lady Harris moved to Srinagar Kashmir to live out her years on a houseboat, her modest income supplemented by the sale of her paintings and writings. Contrary to rumors, the Lady did not die impoverished, nor did she regret her relationship with the Beast. In a 1958 letter to a friend in England, as she describes the virtues and vices of a Kashmiri gentleman friend named Shabau, she fondly contrasts his character with her memories of Crowley.

> But there is Shabau who remains. He is incapable of telling the truth except about God which I can't prove anyhow, but how charming he is, although sometimes I weary of his naïve interpretations & moral narrowness & long for A. C. who was so d—d clever & without limitations."[35]

Frieda Harris died in 1962. Crowley, who was noted for rarely saying anything nice about anyone, paid uncharacteristic tribute to her with adulation in the biog-raphical note from *The Book of Thoth:*

> She devoted her genius to the Work. With incredible rapidity she picked up the rhythm, and with inexhaustible patience submitted to the correction of the fanatical slave-driver that she had invoked, often painting the same card as many as eight times until it measured up to his Vanadium Steel yardstick! May the passionate "love under will" which she has stored in this Treasury of Truth and Beauty flow forth from the Splendour and Strength of her work to enlighten the world; may this Tarot serve as a chart for the bold seamen of the New Aeon, to guide them across the Great Sea of Understanding to the City of the Pyramids![36]

CHAPTER FOUR

THE ART

Why haven't I got living fire which could weave musically these beauties. I can't do it with pigment. I want poetry & music & light, not coloured chalks.[37]

—Harris to Crowley, date uncertain.

When we ask what makes the Thoth Tarot unique, the first and most obvious answer is the artwork. If we appreciate nothing more about these marvelous cards, it is enough for us to invoke the cliché: "I may not know much about art, but I know what I like." Sales figures, year after year, prove that a great many people know that they like these cards.

The cards of the Thoth Tarot display more than just Lady Harris's skillful execution of traditional tarot images, fine-tuned to reflect a more modern understanding of self and the natural universe. Any competent cartoonist following Crowley's instructions could have done that. Harris exceeded Crowley's wildest expectations by actually incorporating within the very fabric of her style the profoundly subtle essence of his spiritual doctrine. It was a supreme wedding of artistic technique and deepest mysticism.

Harris's style is characterized by her graphical conversion of the mathematical concepts of projective geometry.[38] A provocative expansion of Euclidean geometry, projective geometry was, in the mid 1930s, the focus of intense study among the disciples of Rudolf Steiner.[39] Three years before she began painting the Thoth Tarot, Harris studied under two of Steiner's most brilliant students, George Adams and Olive Whicher, and was soon busy transferring theoretical mathematics to canvas.

Projective geometry presumes more than a polarity between a central point and an infinitely distant surface (center and periphery). Because of the fragility (if not the downright nonexistence) of time-space, it allows that a central point and infinite space can occupy the same position. However difficult (or unimportant) it may be for us to grasp the mathematical subtleties of projective geometry, we see it thrillingly manifested in Harris's use of lines, nets, arcs, swirls, twists, and angles stretched and overlaid one upon another, or otherwise combined to visually redefine the fabric of space. Each time we gaze upon one of these cards, we are obliged to transcend the dimensional boundaries of our minds and momentarily place ourselves in an environment where infinite depth can exist simultaneously with infinite projection.

Had Crowley paid Harris anything for her labor, we would have to say that he certainly got his money's worth. Not only did her stylization make the cards hauntingly beautiful, but by incorporating the tools of projected geometry she also paid profoundest homage to the "deities" of his new Aeon cosmology.

"Deities?" "New Aeon cosmology?" You might be thinking that all of this is starting to sound like some new California-crackpot religion. Indeed, it is upon the shoals of terms such as these that many who set sail on the sea of Crowley find themselves shipwrecked and drowned. You can take comfort, however, in the knowledge that Crowley's New Aeon deities are not theological personages, as traditional religions would have us imagine. They are simply convenient terms for natural forces and principles that, because of evolutionary advances in human consciousness, we are able to comprehend more clearly than our spiritual ancestors.

These changes in spiritual consciousness are interpreted into stunning images in the Thoth Tarot and are precisely what differentiate it from the tarot decks of the past. It is, therefore, very important that we know a little bit about New Aeon and the book that Crowley believed to be the fundamental revelation of the age, *The Book of the Law*.

CHAPTER FIVE

THE PROPHET AND THE BOOK OF THE LAW

Oh! thou art overcome: we are upon thee; our delight is all over thee: hail! hail!:
prophet of Nu! prophet of Had! prophet of Ra-Hoor-Khu! Now rejoice! now come in
our splendour & rapture! Come in our passionate peace, & write sweet words for the
Kings![140]

I realize that, for many people, all this talk about New Aeons and shifts of consciousness may seem to have nothing to do with tarot cards. I assure you it has everything to do with the Thoth Tarot. If this book is to live up to the promise of its title, it will be important for you to grasp the key elements that make the Thoth Tarot the Thoth Tarot. Foremost among these are the revolutionary doctrines revealed in a tiny book and the strange assertion that Crowley was a prophet.

I confess that, when I first started to explore the cards, I was very uneasy when I learned that Crowley considered himself some kind of prophet and that the cards might be an illustrated textbook to his weird, and perhaps dangerous, new spiritual movement. I had read some very nasty things about Aleister Crowley and I certainly did not want to waste my time or jeopardize my soul by dabbling with "the dark side."

I soon realized that, if there was any darkness involved, it was the darkness of my own fears, not in *The Book of the Law* or the seventy-eight pieces of printed card stock of the Thoth Tarot. As is often the case when dealing with Mr. Crowley, things aren't always what they appear at first sight—then again, maybe they are. He is like a quirky uncle who makes you pass a test of patience or courage before rewarding you with candy. Only afterward do you discover your real prize was not the candy, but the priceless reward of cultivating the virtues of patience and courage.

On the 8, 9, and 10 of April, 1904 in an apartment in Cairo, Aleister Crowley received (channeled) *Liber AL vel Legis, The Book of the Law.* It is a curious little book consisting of three short chapters of prose poetry. The circumstances leading up to the reception of *The Book of the Law* are extremely interesting and, unfortunately, a subject I will not have much room to discuss in this work. I encourage anyone who wishes to learn more about this fascinating chapter in Crowley's spiritual career to read *The Equinox of the Gods*[41] and any of the excellent recently published Crowley biographies.

Briefly, Crowley and his wife, Rose, were honeymooning in Cairo when Rose fell into a trance in which she claimed to give voice to the gods of ancient Egypt, particularly the god Horus. At first, Crowley dismissed these "messages" as nonsense. After hours of thorough interrogation, however, he became convinced that Rose could not possibly possess enough technical information to be faking it.

He took her to Cairo's Boulak museum (whose collections are now part of the Cairo museum) so she could point out precisely which god was responsible for the messages. Ignoring the more popular images of Horus, Rose excitedly identified a simple wooden stèle from the twenty-third to twenty-fourth dynasties as the source of the communications. It was the funeral stèle of Ankh-af-na-khonsu, a notable political and religious figure of several royal administrations. This Stèle of Revealing (see figure 1 on the inside front cover), as it would later be called, triggered a series of psychic and magical events that culminated with Crowley's reception of *The Book of the Law.*

"Do what thou wilt shall be the whole of the Law." "Love is the law, love under will." These are the two most recognizable watchwords from *The Book of the Law.* The "Law" they refer to is the law of *Thelema* (Greek for "will").

In essence, the book's message is simple. It announces the beginning of a New Aeon in which the spiritual formulae of previous aeons will be amended to better harmonize with humanity's expanded consciousness. The third verse of the first chapter announces that "Every man and every woman is a star"; it describes quite succinctly the fundamental shift in our self-identity that characterizes this new period in human evolution. No longer must we view ourselves as cold, dark satellites helplessly orbiting the "sun" of the family, tribe, race, religion, or nation on whom we depend for light and the fixed trajectory of our lives.

The individual is now to be recognized as the primary and preeminent unit of society. It is now possible for humanity to awaken to the liberating fact that each of us is a star, as unique and self-radiant as our celestial counterparts. Instead of desperately trying to determine the will of God and then clumsily attempting to cooperate with it, each of us must now come to realize that our will, if properly understood and executed, is already in harmony with the divine will. In other words, in this age, the holy quest is to discover one's own way rather than trying to guess what a God wants for you and hope from moment to moment that you are guessing correctly.

Perhaps the most important quality of *The Book of the Law* that sets it apart from all other holy books is the fact that no one is allowed to interpret its meaning to anyone else. No priest, no preacher, no politician, no professor, no philosopher can presume to tell anyone what anything in *The Book of the Law* means. This effectively prevents the formation of the dogma, doctrine, and intolerance that has been the curse of the "great" religions of the past and that continues today to provoke worldwide religious strife.

The three "deities" of *The Book of the Law* are the main figures that appear on the Stèle of Revealing; they express the abstract dynamics of the universe. They are Nuit (sometimes spelled "Nu" or "Nuith"), the goddess of infinite space, the personification of an infinitely expanded universe;[42] Hadit (sometimes spelled "Had" or "Hadith"), the god at the heart of Nuit, the personification of an infinitely contracted point;[43] and their child, Ra-Hoor-Khuit (sometimes spelled "Ra-Hoor-Khu-it," "Ra-Hoor-Khu," "Ra Hoor Khut," "Ra-Hoor-Khut"), who, on the Stèle, is the hawk-headed god enthroned behind an altar of offerings.

These three deities are, in a very real way, the personifications of the key elements of projective geometry: Nuit the periphery, Hadit the center, and Ra-Hoor-Khuit the transcendent "being" that is created when it is recognized that the periphery and center simultaneously occupy the same position. As Nuit is infinite *out*-ness, and Hadit is infinite *in*-ness, they are both equally everywhere and locked in infinite embrace. This is lovemaking on a cosmic scale, and Ra-Hoor-Khuit is the product of this union.

The Book of the Law contains several very interesting references to individual tarot cards, but we'll learn more about that in Part II of this book.

Egyptian deities and projective geometry may seem like pretty weighty subjects for a book about tarot cards. Some of you may even feel uncomfortable when I use the term "god" or "goddess." Please know that when I do, I am not referring to spiritual beings who may or may not be at odds with your religion or spiritual worldview. They are simply convenient terms for natural—indeed mathematical—facts of life that are so fundamental to the fabric of reality that it is appropriate to refer to them as deities.

But what about Aleister Crowley being a prophet? Are we talking about the same Aleister Crowley who caused a sensation in artistic circles by chiseling off the bronze plaque that had been attached (by prudish French authorities) like a fig leaf over the genitals of the stone angel marking Oscar Wilde's grave? The same Aleister Crowley who pranced into the Café Royal wearing the plaque as a codpiece and then presented it to the sculptor, Jacob Epstein? Are we talking about the same Aleister Crowley who joked that he had killed and eaten two of his Himalayan native porters while on a climbing expedition?[44] Are we to believe that this outrageous libertine who seduced scores of women and men could possibly be a prophet?

The Book of the Law declared in no uncertain terms that the "Scribe" (Crowley, or the spiritual entity known to the world as Aleister Crowley) was the prophet chosen by the spiritual forces of human evolution to deliver the good news of the New Aeon to the world. For many of us, the word "prophet" carries with it a great deal of sectarian baggage. Let me assure you that when I refer to Aleister Crowley as a prophet, I am suggesting only that (like shamans of all times and cultures) he was a person who, under certain conditions, was able to observe and then give voice to the great unseen forces and events that shape the spiritual development of humanity.

These forces and events are not the province of any particular religion or cultural movement. Rather they are symbolic expressions of humanity's changing point of view—a point of view that becomes more accurate as our understanding of the universe around us improves; a point of view that changes, sometimes subtly, sometimes radically, step by step, as the inevitable result of our evolving consciousness.

Crowley's revelation (if we choose to call it that) is, in essence, not a revelation at all, but a recognition of certain spiritual facts of life—universal facts that each of us can recognize if we care to, and that each of us could communicate to others if we were skilled enough in the use of language.

I often hear it said by critics of Crowley, and those who, for one reason or another, are afraid of him, that he could not possibly be a prophet because he was so immoral and evil. As each of us have our own ideas concerning what is or is not immoral and evil, it is useless for me to argue that point. Perhaps it is more productive to debate whether being immoral and evil should necessarily prevent one from being considered a prophet.

It is clear to me from reading the Bible that prophets are very human and have their good and their bad days. For example, look at what the Bible tells us happened when the prophet Elisha had a bad day:

> And he [Elisha] went up from thence to Beth-El; and as he was going up along the way, there came forth little boys out of the city and mocked him, saying, "Go up, you bald head, go up, you bald head." And he turned back and saw them and cursed them in the name of the Lord. And there came forth two she-bears out of the forest, and tore forty-two of the boys.[45]

It is true that Crowley could be as petty and cruel as anyone. He took pleasure in doing many things that most of us would not wish to emulate. At no time during his long and infamous life, however, did he commit any felonious crime serious enough even to warrant arrest, let alone so diabolically evil as to use his powers to slaughter forty-two innocent children just because they made fun of his haircut.

While we may concede that all prophets are wild and outrageous characters, it does not necessarily follow that all wild and outrageous characters are prophets. What other qualifications did Crowley possess that might tempt providence to choose him at the turn of the twentieth century to be prophet of the New Aeon?

In my opinion, the character, the personality, yes, even the brash ego of Aleister Crowley combined to make him the perfect candidate for modern prophet-hood.

- He was a passionate and adventurous spiritual seeker, bound from early manhood by severe personal oaths to gain supreme enlightenment;
- He was a master poet, adept in the art of transforming abstract concepts into the imagery of language;
- He was (as much as any man of his day) intimately acquainted with the gods, religions, and mythologies of both the East and West. This familiarity gave him a rich vocabulary of words and images understandable to people of many cultures and religions.

  And most important:
- He was alive at the very moment a great shift of human consciousness was about to dramatically change the world;
- He was sensitive enough to perceive this change and had the language skills to communicate it;
- He was willing to suffer condemnation, ridicule, financial ruin, personal tragedy, and professional vilification to tell the world about it.

You can argue all you want that Aleister Crowley was a flawed and perfectly nasty individual, that he was despised and a dangerous person to know. Despite all his shortcomings, however, it is clear to me that he possessed all the ingredients necessary to make a prophet. A prophet does not need to be perfect. A prophet does not need to be loved. A prophet does not need to be popular. A prophet does not need to be harmless. A prophet need only have a vision of the truth and the courage to give voice to that truth no matter what the consequences.

CHAPTER SIX

THE AEON OF HORUS

Abrogate are all rituals, all ordeals, all words and signs. Ra-Hoor-Khuit hath taken his seat in the East at the Equinox of the Gods.[46]

It is obvious to anyone who is more than casually interested that there are several major features that distinguish the Thoth Tarot from other more traditional decks. First, the four court cards of each suit are titled Knight, Queen, Prince, and Princess, rather than King, Queen, Prince, Princess, (or King, Queen, Knight, Page, or variants found in other decks). Crowley gives us a very interesting explanation for this that I will discuss in detail in chapter 11.

He also makes very significant changes to four of the trumps. Cards that have, in the past, borne the titles Justice, Strength, Temperance, and Judgment (or Last Judgment) are, in the Thoth Tarot, respectively named Adjustment, Lust, Art, and The Aeon. Crowley explains that the new titles more accurately convey the essential meanings of these cards. We will explore why in a moment.

Name changes notwithstanding, the basic images Lady Harris painted for Adjustment, Lust, and Art are more or less consistent with their counterparts in traditional packs. The Aeon, the card that replaces Last Judgment, is a different matter. Instead of displaying a trumpeting angel awaking the dead from their coffins on Judgment day, The Aeon reveals the beautifully stylized figures of the deities from the Stèle of Revealing and *The Book of the Law*: Nuit, the Goddess of infinite space; Hadit, the God of the infinitely contracted point; and Ra-Hoor-Khuit (Horus), the child of their union.[47] This change not only radically differentiates

The Aeon card from the traditional Last Judgment card, it also serves to cast more subtle changes in other cards of the Thoth Tarot.

What is the reason for this dramatic departure from Judgment's traditional image? According to Crowley, the change was necessitated by the fact that the spiritual event depicted in the old versions of the Last Judgment card has already occurred, and The Aeon card has replaced it to illustrate the defining moment when the old aeon gave way to the new.

For many tarot enthusiasts who understand that the tarot is an evolving spiritual organism, the changes manifested in the Thoth Tarot come as logical and welcome improvements. For others, the deck is an affront to their spiritual world-view. The fact that the cards were created by the wicked Aleister Crowley only reinforces their dark suspicions. This attitude, in my opinion, is very unfortunate; in the next few pages, I will do my best assuage the concerns that, for many, may still linger.

The traditional tarot trumps are filled with biblical and classical themes and a cast of characters that seem to have been plucked directly from Mediaeval or Renaissance street theatre. In the Lovers, we find Adam and Eve in the Garden of Eden. The destruction of the tower of Babel is depicted in the Tower card; Fortune displays the wheel of Ezekiel's vision, and his four creatures grace both the Hierophant[48] and the Universe cards. The Goddess Diana is the High Priestess, and Prometheus the Magus. We find an Emperor, his Fool, a Pope (Hierophant), a Hermit, a Hanged Man, Death, and the Devil himself.

There are celestial trumps: the Sun, the Star, the Moon, and the Universe. Looking at the trumps, even a novice astrologer can locate within the twenty-two trumps the seven traditional planets and the twelve signs of the zodiac (see chapter 7). We hold a universe in our hands when we pick up a deck of tarot cards. Heaven and hell, church and state, stars and planets, elements and principals, even ancient gods inhabit the seventy-eight pieces of card stock. Is it any wonder tarot has remained a preeminent tool of divination for centuries?

There is also a dominant theme that runs through the traditional images of the trumps, a theme whose libretto was born in the last and most mysterious book of the New Testament, The Revelation of Saint John the Divine. Here we are first introduced to the trumpet-blowing angel of the Last Judgment card and the Empress, who is obviously "a woman clothed with the sun, and the moon under her feet, and upon her head a crown of twelve stars" (Rev. 12:1). The "woman upon a scarlet colored beast" (Rev. 17:3) graces the Strength (Lust) card, and the angel who sets "his right foot upon the sea, and his left foot on the earth" (Rev. 10:2) is the classic image of Temperance (Art).[49]

Currently, many bible students are reassessing their theories concerning the Book of Revelation—exactly when it was written and what it was originally trying to communicate. There is now a growing consensus among scholars that what John was actually describing (in veiled imagery understandable to his contemporary audience) was not the millennial end of the world, but the all too flesh-and-blood details of the apocalyptic holocaust that ended the second Jewish revolt in A.D. 72.

Be that as it may, it really doesn't matter whether or not John's Revelation is the prophetic vision of "end times" or an elaborately coded inter-office memo. The fact remains that, for over a thousand years, its words and images have been seared into the spiritual consciousness of Western civilization. We may never know the true story behind the book, but the book has become a myth, and myth is truer than history.

No matter what John was originally trying to communicate, his Revelation conveniently provides to both the sincere seeker and the religious extortionist a grotesque vocabulary of terror and hope—the profound terror that comes from contemplating one's human inadequacies when standing before a divine throne of eternal judgment on the day the world is destroyed by fire[50]—and the hope of a future existence free of the fears and injustices of the past. The Revelation of Saint John the Divine certainly has been successful in generating terror. Its singular short-coming, however, is its failure to tell us that the "end of the world" is not really the End of the World!

What, then, does the traditional Last Judgment card represent? Ironically, Crowley tells us that it does indeed represent the destruction of the world by fire, an event that took place on March 20, 1904, in an apartment in Cairo, when Horus, the God of force and fire, took his father's throne at the Equinox of the Gods—an event that signaled the end of the spiritual world of the dying god Osiris, and the birth of the Aeon of Horus.

Crowley taught that, within our racial memory, there have been three aeons. For literary convenience, he labeled them after the three principal gods of Egypt: the Goddess Isis; her husband/brother, Osiris; and their son, Horus.[51] We have just entered the Aeon of Horus, which supplanted the Aeon of Osiris, which supplanted the Aeon of Isis.

Aeons change, not as the result of some war in heaven or astrological event. Rather they are simply the consequence of some improved modification in human consciousness. Obviously, such a mutation needs to be universal and fundamental: something most of us share with our fellows, something as simple as how we perceive our relationship with the Sun.

Yes. It's as simple (and as profound) as that. And the Thoth Tarot, as much as any piece of art or literature, reflects the dynamics of this new evolutionary step. Let's look briefly at the last two aeons to see how our relationship to the Sun has developed and how it affected the spiritual lives of our ancestors. The following is excerpted from my *Angels, Demons, and Gods of the New Millennium*.

THE AEON OF ISIS—The Formula of the Great Goddess
It is impossible for us to pinpoint the dawn of the Aeon of Isis.... Evidence of the worship of the Great Goddess is found as far back as the age of Leo (10,996 B.C. to 8830 B.C.). In this period, when humanity was struggling with the first attempts at social intercourse, the most awesome mystery to excite the imagination was the power of woman. More than any other observable phenomena woman was most godlike. Each month, coinciding with the rhythmic cycles of the moon, she issued blood. Yet miraculously she did not die. When the cycle of bleeding stopped, her body changed; her breasts and belly swelled for nine moons until she burst with water and new life.

Because the earliest Isian-agers were as yet unaware of the cause and effect relationship between sex and birth, it appeared that woman alone was the source of human life. Her life-giving powers were not limited to blood and birth, for from her breasts flowed milk, a rich white blood to nourish and sustain the new life she created. Woman was the human embodiment of the earth itself which appeared to spontaneously bring forth the vegetation and animals needed to sustain the race. It was the most self-evident fact of life ... earth was mother ... mother was life ... god was woman. To be in harmony with the formula of the Great Goddess was profoundly simple, and as long as it was universally perceived that life and nourishment came directly from the earth and from woman, all successful endeavors, magical practices and religious expression did her homage.

So deeply was this perceived reality impressed upon our ancestor's minds that long after they solved the mystery of where babies come from they clung tenaciously to the outward forms of Goddess worship and based all social and religious institutions on her formula. Eventually, however, as our understanding of the universe around us grew, we were confronted with a more complicated world-view and new unsettling mysteries.

THE AEON OF OSIRIS—The Formula of the Dying God
Even though the formula of the dying god became crystallized in the religions and institutions of the astrological age of Pisces (166 B.C. to A.D. 2000), the Aeon of Osiris dawned much earlier.

The advent of agricultural societies necessitated a greater awareness of the cycles of the seasons. Osirian age farmers began to recognize the effects sunlight, or lack of it, had upon vegetation. They observed that at certain times of the year the days grew short and crops did not grow. It eventually became evident that, even though the earth brought forth life, the supreme creative energy that vivified that life came from the sun. Coincidental with this discovery was a universal acknowledgment of the vital role men played in the procreative process. Just as plant life needed the warm penetrating rays of sunlight to flourish, so too woman needed the introduction of the male sperm to avoid being forever barren. The heretofore-unrecognized concept of fatherhood became a dominant theme. The Aeon of Osiris truly began when our forebears raised their eyes to heaven and woke up to the fact that life on earth was a partnership of sun and earth, and the life of the race was a partnership of man and woman. However, the partnership was not perceived as being equal—the male backlash was severe and unmerciful. Deity was now male, a father, and his power was likened to that of the sun.

Even though this shift of consciousness was the result of a more accurate assessment of the facts of life than was realized in the Aeon of Isis, it was not quite accurate enough. A defect in the perception of cosmological facts plunged our Osirian age ancestors into a dark and terrifying insecurity crisis that traumatized the human race so severely that we still suffer its effects. This fundamental flaw in understanding caused us to switch our focus from the mystery of where life comes from to an obsessive preoccupation with death.

The tragic misunderstanding focused on the belief that each day the sun was born at dawn in the east and died in the evening in the west. Speculations abounded about where the dead sun went during the darkness of night and if, indeed, a new one would ever appear again in the east. Perhaps it went to the land of the dead where we temporally visit during our nightly little death of sleep. The terrors and ecstasies of our dreams formed the archetypes of heaven and hell, and, after we die, who better to judge our worthiness for either place than the dead sun itself who created and sustained us during our stay on earth. This is precisely the part the god Osiris would play in Egyptian mythology and Christ's role in Christianity.

To further complicate these fears the sun's yearly escapades caused even greater anxiety. Each year at the zenith of the sun's power in summer, it was observed that each day it rose and set a little south[52] of where it did the day before. Around harvest time the days grew noticeable shorter and the specter of the empty harvested fields accented the leafless trees and browning grasses and painted a melancholy and frightening portrait of nature in articulo mortis. It was unsettling enough to have the sun completely disappear each day, but if it continued to head south until night was perpetual, how long could the world survive in cold darkness before a new sun appears?

In an attempt to calm the shattered nerves caused by such musings a few wise souls took a deep breath and attempted to look at the big picture. Yes, the sun dies each evening in the west, but years of observation and the testimony of the oldest members of society indicated that no one could remember a time when another one did not come up in the east within a relatively short period. Yes, the sun becomes weak and almost dies each year, but the same observations and testimony revealed that it eventually reverses its journey south and the days grow longer again until a new cycle of life returns to the earth. Based on the best information at their disposal they concluded that magical power, an unknown and supernatural force, was responsible for the sun's resurrection. They further surmised that the secret of this magick must be hidden in the very nature of the sun itself, and if they could only harmonize with that nature then perhaps they too could overcome death.

Everywhere they looked in nature, they saw the sun's cycle of birth, life, death and resurrection reenacted. They observed that plants sprouted to the surface in spring and grew tall and strong in the long days and warm sunlight of summer. Then in autumn, at the height of their maturity, they put forth seeds and then died or were cut down at harvest time. Like the earth itself, the seeds lay dead and buried throughout the lifeless winter, only to spring to life when the rains and the lengthening rays of the sun transformed the soil into a moist warm womb.

They also observed accelerated plant growth near the decaying remains of animals or people and wherever large amounts of blood spilled upon the ground. This wonder was the male/solar counterpart of the female/lunar mystery of menstruation. The parallels between sun and phallus, sunlight and semen, the fertilizing power semen had upon woman and that blood had upon the earth did not escape our Osirian ancestor's fertile imaginations. A new "fact of life" (one that conformed to the secret nature of the sun) became the magical formula of the aeon; life comes from death.

In order to harmonize with the new formula it would become necessary to take an active role in the great death/life drama. For the earliest members of the Aeon of Osiris human sacrifice was the supreme pantomime of the sun's daily and yearly sacrifice to the earth. It also illustrated the sacrifice of the potency of the phallus after ejaculation, and the seed's sacrificial death, burial and resurrection. The spilling of human blood in the unsown or newly planted fields resulted in a noticeable increase in the fecundity of the harvest. The most comforting benefit derived from such bloody forms of religious expression was the undeniable fact that as long as they continued the sacrifices the sun always came up in the morning and always stopped its journey south and returned to bring spring and summer. This put a tremendous amount of power in the hands of the priests or priestesses who wielded the sacrificial knife. They positioned themselves between the people and the gods and implied personal responsibility for the rebirth of the sun. With each dawn they became demonstrably more powerful.

At regular intervals all over the world the ceremonial slaughter of the Divine King assured a bountiful harvest and the well-being of the people. Even though the future victim was titular head of state, he was not a ruler in the modern sense. He was the living embodiment of the sun and therefore supreme monarch of the earth. His periodic murder and the coronation of his successor were occasions of great solemnity.

In the waning years of the Aeon of Osiris the character of the sacrifice evolved from human blood to animal blood to bread and wine. Among the more mystically inclined sacrifice became a personal and transcendent experience. Nevertheless, such changes did nothing to disturb the basic magical formula of the Aeon of Osiris. The cycle of birth, life, death, and resurrection remained the dominant theme right up to the time of the magical revival of the late nineteenth century. By this time, however, the old formula was no longer based upon misinformation. It was built upon denial.

THE AEON OF HORUS—
The Formula of the Crowned and Conquering Child

Long after our Isian Age ancestors solved the reproductive mysteries they continued to cling to a magical formula that originated at a time when it was believed that all life came spontaneously from woman and earth. So too, in the Aeon of Osiris, long after it was common knowledge that the earth revolves around the sun, the great religious and political institutions continued to be obsessed with death and resurrection as if they still believed that the sun died every day. . . .

[Today, the scientific "truths" of our] heliocentric solar system [have] become an unquestioned reality for all but the most isolated or mentally disenfranchised inhabitants of our planet. For hundreds of years mothers have assured their little ones at bedtime that the sun is not gone but only shining on the other side of the world. It is this simple reassuring truth that is the key to the formula of the Aeon of Horus. Not a formula of nourishment; not a formula of life, catastrophe, and resurrection; but a formula based upon the magick of continuous growth.

In the Aeon of Isis we identified with the earth. Life came miraculously from earth and woman. All magical pantheons were aspects of the Goddess. Death was a mystery whose depths were impossible to plumb.

In the Aeon of Osiris we identified with the dying/resurrected sun. All magical pantheons were aspects of God the Father. Death could be magically overcome by obedience to formulae, rites and doctrine.

In the Aeon of Horus we identify with the self-radiant, ever-living sun. All magical pantheons have become aspects of ourselves. We, like the sun, do not die. Death, like night, is an illusion. Life is now seen as a process of continual growth and humanity is developing a consciousness of the continuity of existence that will eventually dissolve the sting of death.[53]

It is important for us to remember that the traditional images of the tarot were developed during the Aeon of Osiris, an age when it was universally accepted that the Sun died each night and was reborn magically each morning. The old Last Judgment trump was a perfect example of the death/resurrection theme of the dying god. As we will see, in the Aeon trump of the Thoth Tarot, Crowley has now replaced the images of the old formula (resurrected corpses rising from graves on Judgment Day) with new images (the deities pictured on the Stèle of Revealing), images that reflect the forces at work at the dawn of a new age—the forces that embody the New Aeon formula of continuous life.

This is the "good news" of *The Book of the Law*. This is the "good news" of the Aeon of Horus. The Thoth Tarot is arguably the most brilliant and beautiful attempt to convey in images and color this universal prophetic message. Each card in the deck is set like a stained-glass window in a magnificent cathedral erected as a celebration of evolving human consciousness. Every person who views them is touched in different ways. Some may wish to meditate on the story they tell. Some may feel impelled to dissect each image minutely. Others may simply want to bathe in the light and colors. No one, however, leaves this cathedral of the New Aeon untouched by the experience.

CHAPTER SEVEN

THE VISION
AND THE VOICE

This is the secret of the Holy Graal, that is the sacred vessel of our Lady, the Scarlet Woman, Babalon the Mother of Abominations, the Bride of Chaos, that rideth upon our Lord the Beast.[54]

Now we must briefly address an essential component of the Thoth Tarot that, for many people, demands not only an open mind, but also a great deal of spiritual courage. During his lifetime, this all-important aspect of Crowley's work was understood and appreciated by only a tiny number of his students. Unfortunately, it still remains the source of much controversy and misinterpretation.

It is of particular interest to us because several of the trump cards of the Thoth Tarot are Lady Harris's dramatic renderings of a series of complex and curious visions—visions that communicate, in symbols and words, the shifts of character among the titanic forces that bring an end to one spiritual age and the beginning of another. Some of these visions are intoxicatingly beautiful; some are dark and terrifying; some seem to wallow in blasphemies. All of them, like visions recorded by prophets of old, need a key to unlock their meaning.

When he was a child, Crowley's exasperated mother called him the "Beast 666" whenever she thought he was being naughty. Later in life, he would discover rich Qabalistic significance to this term (and this number) and go on to identify his life and work with his understanding of its esoteric meaning. This is very disturbing to many people.

It is understandable that anyone with a Christian background would recoil in horror when he or she first encounters Crowley's shocking use of words and imagery, such as the Beast 666, Scarlet Woman, All-Father Chaos, Whore of Babylon, or blood of the saints. While these dark "blasphemies" effectively serve to screen out faint-hearted dabblers (and all who choose to remain self-blinded by superstition), they offer a radiant and altogether wholesome spiritual treasure for anyone bold and tenacious enough to do a little research (and a little meditation).

As we discussed in the preceding chapter, Crowley taught that we stand at the threshold of a new aeon—a period of profound intellectual and spiritual growth and self-realization. In order to illustrate the evolutionary forces at work at this pivotal moment, he employed a venerable (but easy to misinterpret) literary device. He proceeded to hijack many recognizable terms, images, visions, and characters of Egyptian, Hindu, Greek, Hebrew, and Christian mythology. He transmuted their character and significance in order to communicate a new message—a message for the ears of modern men and women whose rapidly expanding consciousness has now equipped them to perceive objective and spiritual realities that would be incomprehensible to the seekers of only a few generations ago.

In other words, Crowley took old terrifying concepts such as the Whore of Babylon and the Beast 666 and, in his own way, redeemed them to represent glorious things—as sacred and holy as the concepts of the Madonna and child were in the Aeon of Osiris. He did this, not as a cold-blooded exercise of intellectual gymnastics, but by personally experiencing a series of ceremonially induced visions that communicated these truths to him in a language of scriptural imagery with which he was intimately familiar (and that just happen to be recognizable to much of the Western world).[55]

Foremost among these visions are those he experienced in November 1900 while mountain climbing in Mexico, and between November 23 and December 19, 1909, while walking across the North African Sahara. A record of these thirty visions was first published as *Liber 418: The Vision and The Voice,* in the spring of 1911 as a supplement to *The Equinox.*[56] They are the source and the key to the spiritual doctrines of Thelema, including the almost universally misunderstood theogony of the goddess Babalon and the All-Father Chaos.[57]

Obviously, these visions were intensely personal and, on one level, dealt specifically with Crowley's own initiatory career. On another level (one that should be of particular interest to us), they were also revelations concerning the universal initiation that humanity and the world is undergoing at this pivotal moment in human evolution.

He categorized these initiatory events in the same progressive order as the ten degrees of the Hermetic Order of the Golden Dawn, which represent a spiritual ascent up the Tree of Life. While all the degrees are important and represent levels of human consciousness, the fifth degree and the eighth degree are major landmarks along the spiritual path of return, and Crowley makes frequent references to them in *The Book of Thoth*.

In the fifth degree (Adeptus Minor or Lesser Adept), the aspirant achieves union with the Holy Guardian Angel, a spiritual entity unique to each of us who, once attained, serves as our divine companion, mentor, and guide.[58] I will talk more about the Holy Guardian Angel in chapter 11.

The eighth degree (Magister Templi or Master of the Temple) is most terrible and

> represents the single-most profound moment of our incarnations. It is faced only when the initiate has achieved a level of consciousness so high that in order to proceed farther requires the abandonment of all the old machinery of self-identity and perception. It means quite literally the annihilation[59] of everything that the individual has heretofore believed to be the components of personality and self.[60]

In other words, you can't take anything across the Abyss that isn't the essence of "you."

Now, before you throw up your hands and dismiss all of this as just the complex and ridiculous delusions of a cult of nineteenth-century eccentrics, please pause and keep in mind that terms such as "Holy Guardian Angel" and "Abyss" are simply convenient terms for universal spiritual experiences that, in other times and cultures, are known by other names. Once we grasp the basic concepts, we discover the Angel and the Abyss in the Vedas, the Upanishads, the Chaldean Oracles, the Emerald Tablet of Hermes, in Plato, in Socrates, even in the Old and New Testaments. No matter how these initiations may present themselves, no matter by what name we choose to label them, every human being (indeed every unit of evolving consciousness) will eventually wed the Angel and face the ordeal of the Abyss.

Even so, it is understandable that you would ask why any of us should be concerned with the bizarre visions of one man whose morals we may find repugnant, whose vocabulary of images are an affront to most of the world's great religions, and whose sanity is still a subject of debate? I must confess it took many years before I began to appreciate the archetypal essences of *The Vision and The Voice* and realize how extremely fortunate I was to possess such a document. Once I shed a few superstitions and fears and carefully examined Crowley's symbolic images and words, I found it to be, not only an eloquent and colorful example of one person's initiatory adventures, but also a valuable roadmap to my own spiritual journey.

I wish space allowed me to discuss *The Vision and The Voice* in detail, but that has been done admirably in *The Vision and The Voice with Commentary and Other Papers*[61] It provides an in-depth study of these wondrous visions and brings the spiritual reality of many tarot images to life.

I hope this chapter has assuaged any anxiety you may have harbored concerning the true spiritual nature of the "blasphemies" that seem to spew from Crowley's works, and that you are now prepared to learn more about the Thoth Tarot fearlessly, without "freaking out" at the mention of such things as Babylon, or the Beast, or the Blood of the Saints, or the Scarlet Woman, or Chaos, or the Mother of Abominations.

CHAPTER EIGHT

SECRETS OF THE ROSE CROSS BACK

Is not this Symbol to be found upon the breast of all true Brethren of the Rosie Cross? Hold fast to this Jewel and treasure it as thy Life itself, for many and great are its virtues. . . .[62]

It may seem odd that I dedicate an entire chapter to the design that adorns the back of each of the seventy-eight cards of the Thoth Tarot (see figure 2, inside front cover). I beg your indulgence and assure you (with some confidence) that your patience will be rewarded.

For me, the beautiful Rose Cross that appears on the back of each card is the image that first attracted me to the Thoth Tarot. It is Lady Harris's exquisite interpretation of the Hermetic Rose Cross (see figure 3, inside back cover) and is arguably the most recognizable feature of the deck. As a young tarot enthusiast, I became intimately familiar with every detail of the design by helping a friend reproduce the image as a stained-glass window.

It was clear to me, even as a novice, that the large red, blue, yellow, and green squares that form the extremities of the arms of the cross could represent the four tarot suits of Wands, Cups, Swords, and Disks; and that each of the twenty-two petals of the great rose represented the twenty-two trump cards. One afternoon, after lodge convocation,[63] I was smugly sharing these observations with another neophyte when I was soundly upbraided by an elderly senior member who fixed his gray gaze on me and, in the most solemn tone, informed me, "You have seen but the earliest rays!"

I innocently laughed in his face, not out of disrespect, but because his delivery was so dramatic and corny I was sure he was trying to be funny. He was not amused. "Come with me!" he said. I knew I was in trouble. I felt terrible. I followed him outside the temple, fully expecting to be hurled into the eternal "outer darkness." Instead, we walked about half a block down the street to where his car was parked. I awkwardly started to apologize, but I don't think he heard me. He opened the trunk of his car and lifted a dark purple velvet bag from a leather briefcase. He undid the gold braided tie and lifted out a golden Rose Cross about five inches tall. It hung from a blue ribbon and was proportioned exactly like the Harris cross, but was festooned with many more colorful details. He didn't say a word. He just held it up about a foot before my eyes and let it twirl slowly in the late afternoon sunlight.

It was indescribably beautiful. Every petal of the great rose was brightly enameled and displayed an exquisitely formed Hebrew letter of contrasting color. Upon each arm of the cross was a colored pentagram surrounded by the elemental symbols for fire, water, air, earth, and spirit. The alchemical symbols for salt, mercury, and sulfur were nestled in the triple lobes that decorated the end of each arm. A hexagram surrounded by colorful planetary symbols was centered upon the white square directly beneath the great rose.

The object was obviously made by a skilled craftsman. The only gold visible on the front gleamed from the raised outlines (probably gold wire) that trimmed the edges and each of the twenty-two petals of the rose. Each petal was meticulously filled with a rounded drop of colored enamel that gave the appearance of a precious stone.

The back had no enameling at all, just gold polished to a mirrored finish upon which words were engraved. My street-side psychopomp would not let me read what was written there.[64] After a moment or two of allowing me gawk in wonder, he told me with obvious pleasure: "This is the Rosy Cross. It's all here." He then put it back in the bag and shut the trunk.

I would soon learn that this was the device worn as the personal lamen of initiates of the Golden Dawn who achieved the degree of Adeptus Minor (the same degree in which they are required to paint their own deck of tarot cards). However, the years would reveal to me that it is much more than a colorful decoration or a fraternal order's badge of distinction. Properly understood, it is at once the door, the lock, and the key to the temple of the Western mysteries. It and the Tree of Life (which we will discuss in the next chapter) quite literally are the Table of Contents of the tarot.

THE HOLY QABALAH

As I said earlier, we hold the universe in our hands every time we pick up a deck of tarot cards. The mystery of how the universe was created, how it is sustained, and where you and I fit into it has been the spiritual quest of fools and holy men and women since the dawn of human consciousness. For centuries, students and sages of Hebrew mysticism have developed a unique spiritual science called Qabalah.[65]

Qabalah is not a religion, philosophy, or doctrine. It is a way of thinking, a way of looking at the world, a convenient method by which we dissect, examine, and organize the universe and ourselves. It is a means by which we connect everything in the universe with everything else in the universe. Numbers are the basic working tools of this marvelous discipline, and some of the most important numbers in Qabalistic cosmology are precisely the same numbers upon which the tarot is constructed.

"Oh!" I hear you scream. "Not math again! You said there'd be no more math!" Don't worry. Even though Crowley wrote that the tarot "was designed as a practical instrument for Qabalistic calculations and for divination,"[66] even though he filled forty-eight pages of Part I of *The Book of Thoth* in an attempt to convince us how important the Qabalah is in understanding the tarot, I won't force us to dive too deeply into Qabalistic waters. We will, however, have to get our feet wet, because we won't even begin to understand Aleister Crowley's Thoth Tarot if we don't at least know some very fundamental things about the tarot as it relates to the Qabalah. So put on your yarmulke and make yourself a cup of coffee. It's a wonderful story, and the Rose Cross will help tell it.

Let's start at the very center of all—and I really mean the *center of all*.

THE POINT

FIGURE 4. THE POINT.

In the Harris painting, it is almost impossible to see the minute white point at the heart of the tiny rose at the very center of the design. (If it's not there, it should be!) The white point symbolizes the shining point of pure existence, without size, and (as yet) without position. It is not really a point at all, but a state of infinite potentiality. It is the germ of creation before creation begins. As we will soon see, this point is the inscrutable nail that crucifies the tiny rose to the tiny cross. It also affixes the small rose cross to the large rose cross.

Just where the point came from is a supreme mystery, and Qabalists have soared to dizzying altitudes of speculation and argument in their attempts to understand and explain it. One very popular theory involves three inscrutable qualities of nothingness that, in the dawn of pre-creation, somehow ended up focusing (or contracting) to a point. They called these three veils Ain, Ain Soph, and Ain Soph Aur.

Ain—אין—Nothing that is so nothing that it negates the concept of nothing-as-an-absence-of-something. (In other words, we can't even say,

"It is nothing," because there is no "it" and there is no "is" in this nothing.)

Ain Soph—‏סוף‎—Limitless Nothing. (Nothing defined). There is now an "It" in the statement "It is nothing."

Ain Soph Aur—‏אין סוף אור‎—Limitless Light (Positive emptiness). There is now an "It" and an "is" in the statement "It is nothing."

I won't drag us deeper into these misty musings. I only bring it up because, as we will soon see, there is one tarot card, the Fool, that characterizes this (these) wonderful (non-) state(s) of nothingness. But we'll meet the Fool soon enough. Let's get back to the "point."

Obviously, it is impossible to grasp the true nature of this preexistent point, but it is the essence and identity of absolute deity. It is also the essence and identity of your own secret self—the real you that exists at the very center of all the things you mistakenly think are you. If you truly understand the nature of the point, you understand the nature of yourself and deity.

A graphic artist or photographer would tell us that the massive and complex Hermetic Rose Cross develops outwardly from this central point. A film director trying to illustrate this concept might want to start with a close-up of the point, then slowly move back to show how the various components of the Cross develop. We won't do that.

To really see and understand the essence of this great design, we must go inside the point. We must zoom the camera of our imaginations in, past the circumference past the white nothingness, into the very heart of the germ of creation.

THE CUBIC STONE

FIGURE 5. THE CUBIC STONE.

When the haze of nothingness disappears, we are presented with the image of a cube of what appears to be plain white stone. The ancients symbolized the point as a white cubical stone that contains within itself the potential of all creation. When we take a moment to consider how a cube is constructed, we come face to face with the first great secret of the Qabalah, and the answer to the question: Why does the tarot have twenty-two trump cards?

First, in order to be a cube, a point needs to extend into three dimensions; up-down, right-left, and front-back.

FIGURE 6. CONSTRUCTION OF THE CUBE.

These three dimensions create seven positions (the center and six sides) that create twelve oblique points or edges to the cube (3 + 7 + 12 = 22). Qabalistic tradition[67] tells us this is how deity formed the twenty-two letters of the sacred Hebrew alphabet by which all things in creation are verbally ordered into existence. The Hebrew alphabet is divided into three mother letters (attributed to the three primitive elements), seven double letters (attributed to the seven planets of the ancients), and twelve simple letters (attributed to the twelve signs of the zodiac).

TABLE 1. DIVISION OF THE HEBREW ALPHABET WITH ELEMENTAL, PLANETARY, AND ZODIACAL CORRESPONDENCES

3 Mother letters	7 Double Letters	12 Simple letters
א **Aleph,** *Air*	ב **Beth,** *Mercury*	ה **Hé,** *Aries*
מ **Mem,** *Water*	ג **Gimel,** *Moon*	ו **Vau,** *Taurus*
ש **Shin,** *Fire*	ד **Daleth,** *Venus*	ז **Zain,** *Gemini*
	כ **Kaph,** *Jupiter*	ח **Cheth,** *Cancer*
	פ **Pé,** *Mars*	ט **Teth,** *Leo*
	ר **Resh,** *Sun*	י **Yod,** *Virgo*
	ת **Tau,** *Saturn*	ל **Lamed,** *Libra*
		נ **Nun,** *Scorpio*
		ס **Samekh,** *Sagittarius*
		ע **Ayin,** *Capricorn*
		צ **Tzaddi,** *Aquarius*
		ק **Qoph,** *Pisces*

As long as the cube is sealed, creation is put "on hold," and these twenty-two magick power-letters—these dimensions and positions and concepts—remain suspended in a state of brooding potentiality. They are like the invisible germ in the heart of the acorn that throbs with the potential of an eternity of future oak trees. In order for this sealed cube to initiate creation, it must sacrifice itself upon a cross by bursting open like a kernel of cosmic popcorn.

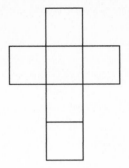

FIGURE 7. UNFOLDED CUBE—THE GOLDEN CROSS.

Creation begins, and we move from potentiality to actuality when, like a living stone, our white cube unfolds as a golden cross of six squares. Once opened, it reveals its secret treasure, a rose of five petals.

FIGURE 8. THE ROSE OF FIVE PETALS.

From time immemorial, the number five has symbolized the microcosm, the little world of humanity (five fingers, five senses, head and extremities, etc.), and the number six has symbolized the macrocosm, the greater world of deity.[68] In the language of images, the rose of five crucified on the cross of six is a statement that tells us that, as human beings, we are inextricably connected to the larger world— the larger reality of deity. As above, so below; the microcosm perfectly reflects the macrocosm; Adam was made in the image of God, and so forth.

You might ask, if we are such perfect images of such perfection, why do things seem so imperfect? Why is there death and suffering? Why are there wars? Why are there fleas and black widow spiders? Why is there bad cholesterol? The answer is simple, but most of us are not yet equipped to accept it.

We are already—right here, right now—the perfect reflection of a perfect deity. The problem is that we do not have a clue who or what we really are. What we recognize as ourselves—the entity that laughs and weeps, that stubs its toes, falls in love, wins and loses, lives and dies—is not a true reflection of ourselves. We are something altogether different and more wonderful than anything we can imagine.

Discovering that the rose of our human fiveness is wedded to the cross of deity's sixness is the first goal of every spiritual seeker. The next (and last) goal is for us to identify completely with our secret self and come to the full realization that we are neither truly five nor six, but a great big beautiful eleven. This endeavor, for lack of a better name, is called the great work.

THE ROSE CROSS OF BEING

This small rose cross is the supreme glyph of the mystery of being and the common denominator between the world of the rose and the world of the cross—between you and me and our huge and all-encompassing counterpart. It is a single shining point of pure existence that radiates from the center of both the rose and the cross.

An unstoppable chain of events is set in motion when the cubical stone of primal existence pops open to create (what I will call) the Rose Cross of Being. Being now needs elbow room to manifest. Position, dimension, time, and space must be the next additions to the creation cycle. Four green barbs radiate in four directions from behind the rose as if to say to being "Now that you are—here's someplace to put yourself."

THE TWENTY-TWO TRUMPS

FIGURE 9. THE ROSE CROSS OF BEING.

The small Rose Cross of Being now gives birth to a larger (graphically speaking) rose. As it does, the heretofore potential qualities of three, seven, and twelve burst forth into actuality, and the twenty-two tarot trumps blossom into existence in three stages as the twenty-two petals of a great Rose of Manifestation.

First to bloom in the primary colors of yellow, blue, and red are the Fool, the Hanged Man, and the Aeon. These three personify the powers and qualities of the three mother letters of the Hebrew alphabet and the primitive elements of air, water, and fire.[69]

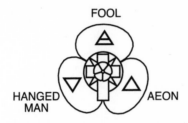

FIGURE 10. THREE PETALS OF THE ELEMENTAL TRUMPS.

Next to flower in the primary and secondary colors of the rainbow (scarlet, orange, yellow, green, blue, indigo, and violet) are the Tower, the Sun, the Magus, the Empress, the High Priestess, the Universe, and Fortune. These seven trumps personify the powers and qualities of the seven double letters of the Hebrew alphabet and the seven planets of the ancients: Mars, Sol, Mercury, Venus, Luna, Saturn, and Jupiter.

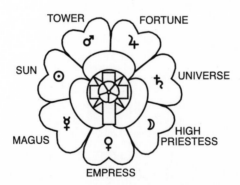

FIGURE 11. SEVEN PETALS OF THE PLANETARY TRUMPS.

Last to burst forth in a riot of primary, secondary, and intermediate colors (scarlet, orange-red, orange, amber, yellowish-green, emerald green, greenish-yellow, green-blue, blue, indigo, violet, and crimson ultraviolet) are the Emperor, the

Hierophant, the Lovers, the Chariot, Lust, the Hermit, Adjustment, Death, Art, the Devil, the Star, and the Moon. These trumps personify the powers and qualities of the twelve simple letters of the Hebrew alphabet and the twelve signs of the zodiac: Aries, Taurus, Gemini, Cancer, Leo, Virgo, Libra, Scorpio, Sagittarius, Capricorn, Aquarius, and Pisces.

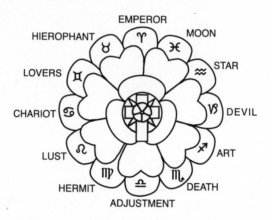

FIGURE 12. TWELVE PETALS OF THE ZODIACAL TRUMPS.

THE ROSE CROSS OF MANIFESTATION

Impelled by the creative dynamics that first formed the small Rose Cross of Being, the great rose crucifies itself on a large unfolded cube. For convenience sake, I will refer to this greater figure as the Rose Cross of Manifestation because it reveals the mysteries of the manifest universe—of principals, energies, forces (represented by the great rose of twenty-two petals and the tarot trumps) crucified upon the cross

FIGURE 13. ROSE CROSS OF MANIFESTATION.

of time and space and matter. These mysteries, we will soon see, abid
cards, and the small cards of the four suits.

YHVH AND THE FOUR SUITS

The Hebrew mystics determined that it was much easier to meditate upon (and deal with) the qualities of the supreme being if they hypothetically divided it (and consequently every-thing else in the universe, including you and me) into four parts. To do this, they created the concept of a single God who exercised its omnipotence in a four-fold manner. They even gave this one God a four-letter name, י ה ו ה (the Hebrew letters Yod Hé Vau Hé, the English letters YHVH, commonly pronounced Jehovah).

In a very real sense, YHVH is the "God" of creation. Creation is, after all, what we on earth, with our limited powers of perception, acknowledge as the reality of the world around us. Most of you reading this book, however, have a pretty good idea that there is more to the ultimate reality than things we can perceive with our senses. That also means that there is a much greater reality beyond, behind, and underlying the powers and forces that make up the God of creation.

The Greeks gave a title to this creator-God who thinks it is God but is too self-centered to realize that it too was created by something greater. They called it Demiourgos, or the demiurge. Zeus was a demiurge. Another name for Zeus is Jove, whose name, spelled in Hebrew, is uncomfortably close to Jehovah י ה ו ה. Because the demiurge is not sure of its origin, it's understandable that it would be a bit insecure. It might even refer to itself as a jealous god and forbid the worship of any other competing deity. Hmm! But I digress.

The formula of YHVH divides the macrocosm into four descending worlds: Atziluth[70] (the archetypal world, the environment of the consciousness of supreme deity), Briah (the creative world, the world of the great archangelic forces), Yetzirah (the formative world, the world of the angelic forces that execute the specific duties of their archangel masters), and Assiah (the material world).

At the same time, the formula of YHVH divides the microcosm (and the human soul) into four descending levels: Chiah (the life force), Neshamah (the divine soul-intuition), Ruach (the intellect), and Nephesh (the animal soul).

Finally, all of these four-part concepts can be expressed metaphorically as the four elements of fire, water, air, and earth, which in the tarot are represented by the four suits, Wands, Cups, Swords, and Disks.

When we speak of the four elements, we are not referring to the chemical elements that are the building blocks of matter. We are simply saying that, for classification purposes, we divide everything in the universe into four very broad categories. If anything is something enough to call it "something," then it is fiery, watery, airy, or earthy in nature, and falls into one of the four categories represented by YHVH and the four tarot suits.

TABLE 2. THE FOUR TAROT SUITS ULTIMATELY REPRESENT THE DIVINE NAME, YOD HÉ VAU HÉ, AND ITS FOURFOLD DIVISION OF CREATION

Great Name	י	ה	ו	ה
Element	Fire	Water	Air	Earth
Qabalistic World	Atziluth Archetypal World	Briah Creative World	Yetzirah Formative World	Assiah Material World
Part of Soul	Chiah Life Force	Neshamah Soul Intuition	Ruach Intellect	Nephesh Animal Soul
Four Tarot Suits	Wands Will	Cups Understanding-Heart	Swords Mind-Intellect	Disks Emotions-Body

SPIRIT

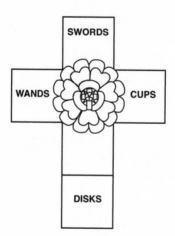

FIGURE 14. THE FOUR SUITS ON THE ROSE CROSS OF MANIFESTATION.

As we face the great cross, we see that the left arm is red to represent the fire suit Wands, the right arm blue for the water suit of Cups, the top yellow for the air suit of Swords, and the lowest extremity green for the earth suit of Disks. The square directly below the great rose is white and represents the fifth element, spirit. No single suit is attributed to spirit, for the influence of spirit pervades the entire deck—indeed, pervades all creation.

In the manifest universe, it is the job of the four elements to combine with each other. Nothing is entirely fire or water or air or earth. Even on the material plane, we see this is so. For example, hot magma from a volcano is fiery because of its heat, watery because it flows, earthy by nature, and exudes gas and steam. A lover's quarrel is fiery and explosive, watery because of the emotions, and airy because it is swift and communicative.

Something is needed to bind the four elements together in infinite proportions and combinations in order to construct the universe. Something is also needed to keep the elements from melding and turning the universe into one big glob of mush. That something is spirit and, in the language of symbols, it is expressed by the pentagram.

FIGURE 15. THE PENTAGRAM—SPIRIT RULERSHIP OF THE FOUR ELEMENTS.

THE ACES AND COURT CARDS

In tarot, the ace of each suit represents spirit in its purist form. Dwelling inside each ace are the four court cards of the suit. It's as though we look at an ace under a microscope and see that it is composed of a fiery component (the Knight), a watery component (the Queen), an airy component (the Prince), and an earthy component (the Princess).

FIGURE 16. THE PENTAGRAM—THE ACE AND THE COURT CARDS.

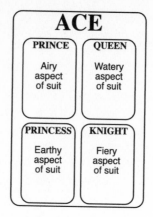

FIGURE 17. THE COURT CARDS ARE ELEMENTAL ASPECTS OF THE ACE.

TABLE 3. ELEMENTAL SUBDIVISIONS OF THE ACES AND COURT CARDS

	ACE *(Spirit aspect of suit)*	KNIGHT *(Fiery aspect of suit)*	QUEEN *(Watery aspect of suit)*	PRINCE *(Airy aspect of suit)*	PRINCESS *(Earthy aspect of suit)*
WANDS (Suit of Fire)	*Spirit of Fire*	*Fire of Fire*	*Water of Fire*	*Air of Fire*	*Earth of Fire*
CUPS (Suit of Water)	*Spirit of Water*	*Fire of Water*	*Water of Water*	*Air of Water*	*Earth of Water*
SWORDS (Suit of Air)	*Spirit of Air*	*Fire of Air*	*Water of Air*	*Air of Air*	*Earth of Air*
DISKS (Suit of Earth)	*Spirit of Earth*	*Fire of Earth*	*Water of Earth*	*Air of Earth*	*Earth of Earth*

Four pentagrams, representing the ace and four court cards of each suit, are placed upon the extremities the Rose Cross of Manifestation.

It is the cosmic duty of the elements to combine and mix with each other in order to facilitate creation. We will see this demonstrated in greater detail later in our discussion of the aces, court cards, and small cards. On the diagram of the Hermetic Rose Cross, this elemental churning process is suggested by the colors of the four pentagrams on the arms of the cross:

- The pentagram representing the ace and court cards of fire (on the left arm) is colored green, (the combination of air-yellow and water-blue);
- The pentagram representing the ace and court cards of water (on the right arm) is colored orange, (the combination of air-yellow and fire-red);

- The pentagram representing the ace and court cards of air (on the top arm) is colored purple, (the combination of fire-red and water-blue).

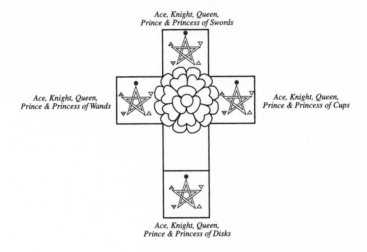

Ace, Knight, Queen,
Prince & Princess of Swords

Ace, Knight, Queen,
Prince & Princess of Wands

Ace, Knight, Queen,
Prince & Princess of Cups

Ace, Knight, Queen,
Prince & Princess of Disks

FIGURE 18. FOUR ACES AND SIXTEEN COURT CARDS.

But what about the pentagram of earth, on the lowermost extremity of the cross?

You will notice, as we continue to study the tarot, that in almost every case, the element of earth is treated differently than the other elements. It is as though earth is the stepchild of the elemental family (no offense to stepchildren). Think about it. We didn't see earth manifest along with fire, water, and air when the Great Rose started to blossom, did we? We will soon discover the Princess (the earthy aspect of her court-card family) doesn't get to rule thirty degrees of the zodiacal year like her father, the Knight; her mother, the Queen; and her brother, the Prince. What gives? Is earth really an element?

The answer is one of the most wonderful mysteries of the tarot, indeed, one of the most important secrets of Western Hermeticsm. Crowley tells us it is "the general doctrine that the climax of the Descent into Matter is the signal for the redintegration by Spirit."[71]

I know that sounds like the kind of snooty Crowleyism that this book is meant to avoid. For years, the above phrase from the *Book of Thoth* didn't make any sense to me at all. I thought the word "redintegration" was a typographical error and that Crowley meant to write "reintegration." "Redintigration" is indeed a word—a very archaic word meaning restoration to a former state. The importance of this word, and the "doctrine" Crowley mentions above will become clearer in chapter 11 (which concerns the Holy Guardian Angel) and when we begin to discuss the individual cards. For now, let's be satisfied to know that element earth is the lowest of the low in the universe. Therefore, it is especially sacred to and especially linked with the highest high.

On the Hermetic Rose Cross, the earth pentagram is pure white, but the entire lower extremity of the cross, upon which it sits, is divided into four sections colored black, citrine (a mixture of blue, red, and yellow but with a predominance of yellow), olive (a mixture of the same colors but with a predominance of blue), and russet (the same but with a predominance of red).

It is as though what began as the pure white light of the minute point at the center of the tiny rose has passed through a prism and separated into all the colors of the spectrum in the Great Rose. Then all the colors have mixed and remixed to form all aspects of creation until, by virtue of their own vibratory weight, they settle to the very bottom of the cross as dark and polluted colors. The pentagram that seals them is pure white, as if to say "This mess may be the lowest of the low, but it has something that no other section of creation has except the highest high— that is, a little bit of absolutely everything!"

THE MACROCOSMIC HEXAGRAM

The white square directly under the great rose contains a hexagram displaying the Sun surrounded by the other six planets of the ancients. Placing this symbol of the macrocosm in the midst of the four pentagrams of the microcosm echoes on a higher octave the symbolic message of the marriage of the human and the divine that was first told by the small rose and cross. Those of you who are familiar with the Lesser Ritual of the Pentagram will recall the words, "For about me flames the Pentagram. And in the column stands the six-rayed Star."[72]

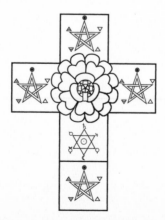

FIGURE 19. ELEMENTAL PENTAGRAMS OF THE MICROCOSM; PLANETARY HEXAGRAM OF THE MACROCOSM; UNION OF 5 AND 6, THE SYMBOL OF THE GREAT WORK ACCOMPLISHED.

FIGURE 20. THE COMPLETED HERMETIC ROSE CROSS.

THE ALCHEMICAL SYMBOLS

Our examination of the Hermetic Rose Cross would be incomplete if we didn't examine the symbols of the three alchemical elements of sulfur, mercury, and salt, whose glyphs are found in the triple lobes at the end of each arm of the Great Cross. Not to be confused with the natural elements of fire, water, air, earth, and spirit, the three alchemical elements represent universal qualities or principals that interact with and are profoundly dependent upon each other. Crowley tells us that

> Sulfur is Activity, Energy, Desire; Mercury is Fluidity, Intelligence, the power of Transmission; Salt is the vehicle of these two forms of energy, but itself possesses qualities which react on them.[73]

Notice that symbols for these three alchemical principals occupy different lobes on each arm of the Cross. Mercury is placed in the central lobe of the top and bottom arm, indicating dominance in air/Swords and earth/Disks. The symbol of salt dominates on the right arm (water/Cups), and the symbol of sulfur dominates the left arm (fire/Wands).

The secondary lobes of each arm are occupied with symbols of the not-so-dominant alchemical principals arranged in a logical and balanced manner. This is very important because, when these three principles are combined and balanced, they create the alchemical substance known as "vitriol," the universal solvent. Vitriol will soon become very import to us as we study the inner mechanics of tarot. It is the initials of the alchemical motto: *Visita interiora terrae rectificando invenies occultum lapidem* (Visit the interior parts of the earth: by rectification thou shalt find

the hidden stone). In his discussion of the trumps, Crowley goes so far as to identify three cards with the alchemical elements: the Magus is mercury, the Empress
is salt, and the Emperor is sulfur.

Other trumps also have alchemical significance. The Art card is identified with
vitriol, and the Lovers, the Hermit, Death, and the Devil all have vital roles to play
in the alchemy of the tarot. There is also one more extremely important alchemical symbol we will see often when we examine the trumps. It is called the Orphic
egg. "This egg represents the essence of all life that comes under the formula of
male and female."[74]

THE THREE GUNAS

Crowley's reference to the rajas of Hindu philosophy necessitates, at this point, a brief
discussion of the gunas. The concept of the three alchemical elements is almost
identical to that of the three gunas of Hindu cosmology. The three gunas are rajas,
sattvas, and tamas (corresponding uncannily to sulfur, mercury, and salt). "All the qualities that can be predicated of anything," Crowley points out, "may be ascribed to
one or more of these Gunas: Tamas is darkness, inertia, sloth, ignorance, death and
the like; Rajas is energy, excitement, fire, brilliance, restlessness; Sattvas is calm,
intelligence, lucidity and balance."[75]

These three qualities are universally present and at work in all manifested
energy (including matter and you and me). They are in constant conflict and, at
any given moment, one of them gains temporary dominance. Cosmic balance, however, dictates that no one principal can remain on top for very long before another
usurps its position to enjoy its moment in the Sun.

The mechanics of this eternal three-way conflict is the driving force that turns
the great wheel of the ever-changing universe. It is illustrated beautifully in the
Thoth Tarot as Atu X, Fortune, where rajas (sulfur) is represented as the figure of
the Sphinx, sattvas (mercury) by Hermanubis, and tamas (salt) by the figure of
Typhon. More about this when we discuss Fortune.

THE BARBED ROSE LEAVES

Radiating like glories from behind the Great Rose are twelve barbed rose leaves—
four large leaves each flanked by two small leaves. The four large leaves contain
the letters I N R I and the astrological symbols for Virgo, Scorpio, Sol, and Virgo
respectively. Three of the smaller leaves contain the letters L V X and three contain the letters I A O. The remaining two smaller leaves contain an additional
letter I and a small Calvary Cross †. To be perfectly frank, I have never learned a
satisfactory explanation for the presence or positioning of these two seemingly
superfluous figures.

The letters INRI are placed on the large leaves in the following order: I—upper left; N—upper right; R—lower left; I—lower right. The letters IAO and an extra I are placed on the smaller leaves to the right of the large leaves in the same order. The letters L V X and a small Calvary Cross are placed on the smaller leaves to the left of the large leaves in the same order. Because the Hermetic Rose Cross is the personal lamen of Adeptus Minor initiates of the Golden Dawn, and because the letters I N R I, L V X, and I A O play a key formulaic role in the mysteries of that degree, it is very appropriate that they appear on the device itself.

I N R I can mean many things, including the venerable alchemical axiom, Igni natura renovatur integra (All of nature is restored by fire), and the powerful spell that I often use to repel obnoxious telemarketers: I'm not really interested! Christian tradition, however, informs us that, at Christ's crucifixion, Pontius Pilate ordered that a sign be posted at the head of the cross declaring in Latin, Greek, and Hebrew, "Jesus of Nazareth, King of the Jews." The real sign must have been pretty large to accommodate the three sets of messages, but future artists would be satisfied to display only the four letters I N R I (the initials of the Latin words "Iesus Nazarenus, Rex Iudaeorum") painted on a wooden board nailed at an angle above the head of a tortured and bleeding Jesus. For at least 1,400 years, the placard displaying the Latin letters I N R I has been an indispensable accessory to every well-dressed crucifix.

Not being satisfied with the officially sanctioned explanations of these letters that appear on holy images and souvenirs, Christian mystics and others toyed with the heretical idea that there just might be something else—some esoteric meanings—to the images of popular religious symbolism. Risking the stake, these spiritual outlaws proceeded to analyze I N R I in such a way that it eventually said something other than Jesus from Nazareth, King of the Jews. That something else was the magical formula (and the signs of that formula) that expressed their highest understanding of the cosmic secrets of life, death, and resurrection. Briefly, here's what they did.

They first took the Latin letters I N R I and translated them into the Hebrew letters ינרי (reading from left to right: Yod, Nun, Resh, Yod). Then they meditated upon the astrological meanings of these Hebrew letters and discovered that they tell (in their own astrological way) the familiar Egyptian solar myth of Isis (Yod/Virgo) who mourns because an evil relative Apophis (Nun/Scorpio) has killed her husband, Osiris (Resh/Sol). Isis eventually raises Osiris from the dead, and the whole cycle starts again every morning and every spring

That is how I N R I becomes I A O (which just happens to be the name of the supreme god of the Gnostics, who embodies the magical formula of life, death, and rebirth). Properly understood, the formula of I N R I / I A O explains the mystery of the annual revolution of the Earth around the Sun and its diurnal rotation upon its own axis. That is the highest mystery our Osirian Age ancestors could understand. It is also the secret mystery knowledge of all agricultural civilizations of the Age of Osiris. Not bad for seven letters (three of which are *I*s).

By tradition, Isis, Apophis, and Osiris, are pictured making certain gestures or signs:

> In the sign of the Mourning of Isis, Isis holds her arms, suggestive of the letter L.

> In the sign of Apophis and Typhon, Apophis thrusts his arms above his head at a ninety-degree angle, suggestive of the letter V.

> In the sign of Osiris Slain, he holds his arms out to his sides as if he were crucified.

> In the sign of Osiris Risen, he crosses his arms over his chest, forming an X on his body.[77]

Taken together, these are the signs of L V X, the Latin word for "light." Here is how the key word I N R I is analyzed in formal ceremony:

I N R I
Yod. Nun. Resh. Yod.
Virgo, Isis, Mighty Mother
Scorpio, Apophis, Destroyer
Sol, Osiris, Slain and Risen
Isis, Apophis, Osiris
I A O
The sign Osiris Slain (give sign)
The sign of the Mourning of Isis (give sign)
The sign of Apophis and Typhon (give sign)
The sign of Osiris Risen (give sign)
(repeat last three signs)
L V X, Lux. The Light of the Cross.

Magical tradition informs us that, on the material plane and in normal waking consciousness, symbols are symbols and living things are living things. On the magical plane and in visionary consciousness, symbols are living things and living things are symbols. In other words, if I have a vision of a lion or a monkey, those images are merely symbols of something far deeper and abstract in my psyche that I need to confront. Conversely, symbols in visions are actually living things in that plane. Let's say I am faced, in a vision, by a terrible fire demon (a symbol of something I need to confront). I need only protect myself with a symbol—perhaps the banishing pentagram of fire, a symbol to me of the mastery of spirit over the elements, but a living thing to the demon who is forced by all the laws of its own existence to submit and obey.

I only bring up this tidbit of magical lore to impress upon you the immeasurable symbolic power stored in the Hermetic Rose Cross. Viewed on the magical plane, the Cross is teeming with magnificent life and energy. The adepts of the Golden Dawn who wear it as their personal lamen are possessed with a most powerful magical tool indeed.

Now, before we look at the cards themselves, let's learn just a little bit about the Tree of Life.

CHAPTER NINE

SECRETS OF THE
TREE OF LIFE

The Tree of Life—This figure must be studied very carefully, for it is the basis of the whole system on which the Tarot is based. It is quite impossible to give a complete explanation of this figure, because (for one thing) it is quite universal. Therefore it cannot mean the same to any one person as to any other.[78]

The Hermetic Rose Cross has certainly yielded many of her secrets concerning the cosmic roots of the twenty-two trumps, the four aces (suits) and the sixteen court cards. However, she does not do a very good job of telling us why there are nine (ten, if you count the Ace) small cards in each suit. To understand the mysteries of the small cards, we are first going to have to learn a little bit about another Qabalistic figure, the Tree of Life (Etz-Ha-Chayim).

The schematic diagram commonly known as the Tree of Life is arguably the most recognizable image of the Qabalah. It was first published in 1652 in Athanasius Kircher's *Oedipus Ægyptiacus*, and quite neatly serves to condense a great deal of Qabalistic wisdom into a very small space. It is particularly illustrative of the opening paragraph of perhaps the most influential Qabalistic texts of all time, the *Sepher Yetzirah (The Book of Creation).*

Yah, the Lord of hosts, the living God, King of the Universe, Omnipotent, All-Kind and Merciful, Supreme and Extolled, who is Eternal, Sublime and Most-Holy, ordained (formed) and created the Universe in thirty-two mysterious paths of wisdom by three Sepharim, namely: 1) S'for; 2) Sippur; and 3) Sapher which are in Him one and the same. They consist of a decade out of nothing and of twenty-two fundamental letters. He divided the twenty-

FIGURE 21. THE TREE OF LIFE.

two consonants into three divisions: 1) three mothers, fundamental letters or first elements; 2) seven double; and 3) twelve simple consonants.[79]

In the previous chapter, we learned that the thirty-two mysterious paths of wisdom are comprised of the twenty-two letters (trumps) and their division by three, seven, and twelve. Now we will learn just a little bit about the "decade out of nothing."

We ten-fingered bipeds have always had a healthy respect for the numbers ten and four. As a matter of fact, it appears that our hands and fingers are the source of much ancient Qabalistic meditation—wisdom that would later help construct the tarot. I won't bore you too much on this subject, but I will pause to point out that:

- The tenth letter of the Hebrew alphabet is Yod, the Hebrew word for "hand";
- Our opposable thumb (working in cooperation with our other four fingers) is one of the most important attributes that separates humans from other animals and is the fundamental key to making us creative beings and the masters of our environment;
- As tradition informs us that we are made in the image of deity, it follows that the creative "hand of God" must be the work of a single deity (spirit/ace) that expresses itself in a fourfold manner (YHVH . . . four Qabalistic worlds, four parts of the soul, four elements, four tarot suits, four court cards);
- Four and ten are inextricably related and mutually definable by simple mathematics ($10 = 1 + 2 + 3 + 4$).

The following is from *Angels, Demons and Gods of the New Millennium* and gives a brief summary of the creation of the "decade out of nothing." Please do not worry if at first you find it difficult to follow the logic of how the Tree of Life is constructed. Believe it or not, once you grasp the basic concept, it is much easier to think about than it is to explain.

The Tree of Life is a linear schematic of ten emanations and twenty-two paths upon which the universal mechanics of energy and consciousness are projected. In one respect it is a very unsatisfactory diagram for it attempts to dimensionalize the transdimensional. It has been called the diagram of the anatomy of God, and if we are indeed created in the image of God then that means that it also reveals the spiritual anatomy of each of us. Students of Kundalini Yoga agree, and point out that the seven chakras or spiritual centers in the human body can be projected quite comfortably upon the Tree of Life.

All ten sephiroth, or emanations, of the Tree are really only aspects or facets of the top (first) sephira, Kether, which represents the totality of existence—the supreme monad. But even the concept of ONE is a blemish upon the sublime perfection of the pre-existent ZERO.[80] If ONE is to exist and become conscious of its oneness it must reflect itself (like a yogi in meditation who reaches to the core of being and exclaims "that's what I am!"). The mere act of reflection creates TWO $\overset{1}{\diagdown}_2$. (ONE is now conscious of itself *and* its reflection.) The knowledge that there is a *difference* between ONE and TWO instantly creates a third condition $_3\overset{\triangle}{\diagdown}_2$. This "trinity" by itself is still an abstraction and exists only in potentiality. Nevertheless, a primal pattern has been established by the process of ONE becoming THREE. This archetypal germ sets into motion a chain-reaction that animates the entire creation scenario—the process of consciousness/light/spirit descending into matter.

The phenomenal universe manifests through a process of degeneration in the next seven sephiroth. The trinity unit FOUR-FIVE-SIX is created by

the reflection of the ONE-TWO-THREE unit $\overset{3\,\overset{\triangle}{\diagdown}\,2}{\underset{6}{5\,\diagdown\,4}}$ and the same process

that created THREE from ONE-TWO creates the third trinity unit of

SEVEN-EIGHT-NINE. $\overset{3\,\overset{\triangle}{\diagdown}\,2}{\underset{8\,\overset{}{\diagdown}\,7}{\underset{9}{5\,\diagdown\,4}}}$ TEN, the world of matter, is rock bottom

and dangles from the Tree of Life like an afterthought of creation: $\overset{3\,\overset{\triangle}{\diagdown}\,2}{\underset{8\,\overset{}{\diagdown}\,7}{\underset{\underset{10}{9}}{5\,\diagdown\,4}}}$ [81]

This is the "decade out of nothing." It is the fundamental pattern of creation. Theoretically, every conceivable idea, quality, principal, aspect, and tendency finds a home in one of the ten pigeon-hole sephiroth of the Tree of Life. But the Hebrew mystics were not satisfied with just one Tree of Life. God is One. True. But the one God has a four-letter name, יהוה YHVH, by which it manifests.

And so, the ancient Qabalists found it easier to meditate upon the qualities of one by considering it in terms of four. Consequently, for practical purposes (and especially for tarot), we find ourselves dealing with four Trees of Life representing the four letters יהוה YHVH, the four Qabalistic worlds, the four parts of the soul, the four elements, and the four tarot suits. The titles of the ten sephiroth are consistent in all four Trees of Life (see page 62).

THE FOUR TREES OF LIFE, THE ACES, AND SMALL CARDS

The ten sephiroth, or emanations, of each of the four Trees of Life are joined together by twenty-two paths that are portrayed in tarot as the twenty-two trump cards and the letters of the Hebrew alphabet. The forty sephiroth of the four trees are perfectly represented in tarot as the four aces and the thirty-six small cards.

1
Kether
The Crown
(Sphere of the Primum Mobile)
The Absolute.
The Supreme Monad.

3
Binah
Understanding
(Sphere of Saturn)
Supreme female concept.
Crowley's Babylon.
Night of Pan/Nuit.

2
Chokmah
Wisdom
(Sphere of the Zodiac)
Supreme male concept.
Crowley's All-Father.
Chaos/Beast/Hadit.

——————————— —— THE ABYSS —— ———————————
&
The false sephira, Daath

5
Geburah
Strength
(Sphere of Mars)
Motion, storm and stress.[82]

4
Chesed
Mercy
(Sphere of Jupiter)
Home of the Demiurge.
Materialization, the rule of Law.[83]

6
Tiphareth
Beauty
(Sphere of Sol)
Energy in complete balanced
manifestation.[84]

8
Hod
Splendor
(Sphere of Mercury)
Illusion, imbalance, weakness.[85]
Effeminate male.

7
Netzach
Victory
(Sphere of Venus)
Illusion, imbalance, weakness.[86]
Masculine female.

9
Yesod
Foundation
(Sphere of Luna)
Seat of the great crystallization
of energy.[87]

10
Malkuth
Kingdom
(Sphere of Earth)
The end of all energy.[88]
The material world.

The area (or non-area) between the supernal triad (sephiroth 1-2-3) and the rest of the Tree is called the Abyss. It is an inscrutable looking glass that separates the ideal (the abstract concepts of 1-2-3) from the actual (the manifest qualities of the phenomenal universe). Consequently, we view the aces, twos, and threes of the four suits a bit differently than we do the other small cards, because they are the supernal triad of their respective Trees of Life. The cards of the supernal triad are one big happy family, a single unit that embodies the essence of the suit. Why are they so happy?

All four aces are happy because they represent the Kethers of their Trees of Life and the root of their elements. All the twos and threes are happy because, along with their aces, they reside comfortably above the Abyss. The twos (Dominion, Love, Peace, and Change) are the first manifestation of their suits as ideas. They are outrageously happy just to exist as the expression of their respective aces. The threes (Virtue, Abundance, Sorrow,[89] and Work) were created automatically at the moment one reflected to become two. The threes exist from necessity to stabilize the twos and form the womb in which all the other small cards can incubate. Pretty abstract, eh?

Please note that, in the above paragraph, I stressed the word "represent." That is because the small cards are not the sephiroth themselves. Even though, for practical purposes, we work with small cards as worthy representatives of the sephiroth, the sephiroth themselves are of a vastly superior order of spiritual reality than could ever be defined by the character and behavior of four sets of ten cards. In fact, the small cards are subelemental in nature—blind forces that are merely sympathetic echoes of the sephiroth that have filtered down into the elemental universe. Nevertheless, even though we are possessed with limited powers of perception, we can learn a great deal about the nature of the sephiroth by listening to these echoes— by observing (in an indirect way) how they color and affect the blind forces of the elements represented by the small cards.

Because Atziluth is the native world of Wands, and Briah is the native world of Cups, and Yetzirah is the native world of Swords, and Assiah is the native world of Disks, one might think that all small-card Wands, Cups, Swords, and Disks would be happy in their respective Tree of Life. It doesn't work that way. Each of the four Trees of Life, because of the uniqueness of the world they represent, has areas of strengths and weaknesses that differ from those of the trees of other worlds. For example, Yesod may be strong in Atziluth (Wands), but weak in Briah (Cups) and Yetzirah (Swords), and so on.

RULES OF THUMB

(I suggest you bookmark this page and refer to it often as you study the characteristics of the of the small cards.)

Unless there are strong astrological mitigating factors (which we will soon discuss), the following is generally true:

- Aces, twos, and threes (cards of the supernal triad) are very strong and together define their suits in principal;
- Fours (being the first manifestation of their suit below the Abyss) define their suits in actuality. As a matter of fact, because they have no idea what life is like above the Abyss, the fours (like the Demiurge) mistakenly believe themselves to be the aces of their suits. They are very strong and, like the Demiurge Zeus, establish their element's "rule of law";
- Fives are active and strong, but unbalanced and troublesome. (Shall we say downright horrible?);
- Sixes are invariably strong and noble representatives of their suits (being the direct reflection and first balanced manifestation of their ace);
- All the sevens (being unbalanced and low on the Tree of Life) are very difficult and for the most part, perfectly awful;
- Eights have much in common with the sevens (unbalanced and low on the tree). However, eights have fallen so low that they are starting to run out of the original energy of the suit, and so their planetary and zodiacal attributes become very important factors. Some are good—some not so good;
- Nines generally are stable and supportive of the suit. The exception is the Nine of Swords;
- Tens generally are a disaster because, with the exception of the Ten of Disks, they are about to completely lose their suit identity and plunge into a lower world. The Ten of Disks is the exception. Being the last small card, it has nowhere to go but back up to the top. That trick, we will ultimately learn, is the secret that sustains the universe.

We can think of the ten sephiroth of the Tree of Life as representing a descent of energy. In that case, we are actually contemplating the creation of the phenomenal universe. We can think of the sephiroth as representing a descent of consciousness. In that case, we are actually contemplating the true meaning of the concept of the fabled "fall of man." We can also think of the sephiroth as the descent of light—and when light descends we have color.

CHAPTER TEN

WORLDS OF COLOR

"... God is light..." (First John: 1:5)

Now that we know a little bit about the Qabalah, the Hermetic Rose Cross, and the Tree of Life, we can discuss one of the most important aspects of the visual magick that is the Thoth Tarot. One of the most striking features of the deck is Lady Harris's curious use of color. Although, in my opinion, all the cards are exotically beautiful, there are a few of them that I have a hard time looking at for any length of time without feeling a bit nauseous. Perhaps this was her intention for cards such as the Seven of Cups (Debauch) or the Nine of Swords (Cruelty), but it is also obvious that her choice of colors was dictated by something other than aesthetics. That something other was the fourfold color scale developed by the adepts of the Golden Dawn.

Imagine, if you will, that the consciousness of the supreme deity is pure light (a venerable universal concept to be sure). Now imagine the divine light passing through a prism and diffusing on the other side into all the colors of the spectrum. This is one way Qabalists (and physicists) visualize the process of creation—pure light (divine consciousness) breaking up and slowing down to become units of energy, mind, and matter.

The magick prism that does all this primal light shattering is none other than יהוה YHVH itself, who, true to its fourfold nature, divides the light into four vibratory frequencies that will eventually manifest as four scales of color. The King scale is the highest, and represents the essence—the invisible foundation of color. With the Queen scale, color actually manifests as the eye beholds it (shades, primary and secondary colors, etc.). The Prince scale combines the colors of the King and

Queen scales, and the Princess scale represents the lowest, most mixed and polluted levels of light.

Now imagine four Trees of Life, one for each of the four Qabalistic worlds. The light of the King scale filters through and paints the ten sephiroth and twenty-two paths of the Tree of Life representing the highest world, Atziluth. The light of the Queen scale filters through and paints the sephiroth and paths of the tree of the next lower world, Briah. The light of the Prince scale filters through and paints the tree of Yetzirah, the next lower world. And finally, the light of the Princess scale filters through and paints the Tree of Life of the lowest world, Assiah.

At the end of the day, we have a total of forty colors representing the aces and small cards and ninety-six colors representing the trumps.[90] Appendix B in *The Book of Thoth* itemizes these colors in four pages of well-organized charts.[91] I refer you to my versions, Tables 4 and 5. For the most part, these charts are arranged according to the *Sepher Yetzirah's* thirty-two paths of wisdom Key scale:[92]

- Key numbers 1 through 10 refer to the ten sephiroth of the Tree of Life (in the tarot, these ten are the ace and the nine small cards of each suit);
- Key numbers 11 through 32 refer to the twenty-two paths of the Tree of Life that connect the sephiroth. The twenty-two Hebrew letters are positioned on these paths. In the tarot, these are, of course, the twenty-two trumps.[93]
- The tarot trumps are numbered 0–21. Do not confuse these numbers with the Key numbers.

Now that we know that the Thoth Tarot is theoretically splashed with one hundred thirty-six colors, we might well ask where these colors came from. The very specific names for many of them were unromantically lifted directly from the labels of tubes of Winsor and Newton water colors (Designers Gouache series), which were popular with Victorian artists and are still available from W&N today.[94] But just who was it who assigned them to their particular Qabalistic pigeonholes? The answer, like most other matters concerning the Thoth Tarot, is complex and open to some speculation.

There is very little debate that the four scales of color issued as part of the Golden Dawn curriculum were ultimately set down by S. L. MacGregor Mathers. It is also clear that he had help from others, including someone who was very knowledgeable in color theory. This was most likely his artist wife, Moina.

The Qabalah, of course, was a major influence in the selection of colors. The mere fact that the degeneration of colors represents a "fall" down the four Trees of Life is proof of that. The King scale appears to be the result of a battle between the red of severity and the white of mercy, as outlined in sections of the *Zohar*. In other scales, we see the elemental, planetary, and zodiacal colors familiar to us from the *Sepher Yetzirah*. But Qabalah is not the only tradition Mathers and company drew

TABLE 4. COLORS ATTRIBUTED TO THE TRUMPS

Key Scale	Card #	Trump Title & Attribute	Knight Scale	Queen Scale	Prince Scale	Princess Scale
11	0	The Fool (Air)	Bright Pale yellow	Sky Blue	Blue Emerald green	Emerald, flecked Gold
12	1	The Magus (Mercury)	Yellow	Purple	Grey	Indigo, rayed Violet
13	2	The HighPriestess (Moon)	Blue	Silver	Cold Pale Blue	Silver, rayed Sky Blue
14	3	The Empress (Venus)	Emerald Green	Sky Blue	Early Spring Green	Bt.Rose or cerise, rayed pale green
28	4	The Emperor (Aries)	Scarlet	Red	Brilliant Flame	Glowing Red
16	5	The Hierophant (Taurus)	Red Orange	Deep Indigo	Deep warm Olive	Rich Brown
17	6	The Lovers (Gemini)	Orange	Pale Mauve	New Yellow leather	Reddish Grey, inclined to muave
18	7	The Chariot (Cancer)	Amber	Maroon	Rich bright Russet	Dark greenish Brown
22	8	Adjustment (Libra)	Emerald Green	Blue	Deep Blue-Green	Pale Green
20	9	Hermit (Virgo)	Green (yellowish)	Slate Grey	Green Grey	Plum colour
21	10	Wheel of Fortune (Jupiter)	Violet	Blue	Rich Purple	Bright Blue, rayed yellow
19	11	Lust (Leo)	Yellow (greenish)	Deep Purple	Grey	Reddish Amber
23	12	The Hanged Man (Water)	Deep Blue	Sea-green	Deep Olive-Green	White, flecked Purple
24	13	Death (Scorpio)	Green Blue	Dull Brown	Very dark Brown	Livid indigo Brown
25	14	Art (Sagittarius)	Blue	Yellow	Green	Dark vivid Blue
26	15	The Devil (Capricorn)	Indigo	Black	Blue-black	Cold dark Grey nearing black
27	16	The Tower (Mars)	Scarlet	Red	Venetian Red	Bright Red, rayed azure or emerald
15	17	The Star (Aquarius)	Violet	Sky Blue	Bluish Muave	White, tinged Purple
29	18	The Moon (Pisces)	Crimson (ultra Violet)	Buff, flecked silver White	Lt. Translucent pinkish Brown	Stone colour
30	19	The Sun (Sun)	Orange	Gold Yellow	Rich Amber	Amber, rayed Red
31	20	The Aeon (Fire)	Glowing Orange Scarlet	Vermillion	Scarlet,flecked Gold	Vermillion, flecked crimson and Emerald
32	21	The Universe (Saturn)	Indigo	Black	Blue-black	Black, rayed Blue
32bis	21	The Universe (Earth)	Citrine,Olive, Russet&Black	Amber	Dark Brown	Black, flecked Yellow
31bis	20	The Aeon (Spirit)	White merging into Grey	Deep Purple nearly Black	7 prismatic colours (violet outside)	White, Red, Yellow, Blue, Black (this outside)

TABLE 5. COLORS ATTRIBUTED TO THE SMALL CARDS

Key Scale	Card #	Sephira	Knight Scale WANDS	Queen Scale CUPS	Prince Scale SWORDS	Princess Scale DISKS
1	Ace	Kether	Brilliance	White Brilliance	White Brilliance	White, flecked Gold
2	Two	Chockmah	Pure soft Blue	Grey	Blue pearl Grey, like mother of pearl	White, flecked Red, Blue and Yellow
3	Three	Binah	Crimson	Black	Dark Brown	Grey, flecked Pink
4	Four	Chesed	Deep Violet	Blue	Deep Purple	Deep azure, flecked Yelow
5	Five	Geburah	Orange	Scarlet Red	Bright Scarlet	Red, flecked Black
6	Six	Tiphareth	Clear Pink Rose	Yellow (gold)	Rich Salmon	Gold Amber
7	Seven	Netzach	Amber	Emerald	Bright Yellow-Green	Olive, flecked Gold
8	Eight	Hod	Violet	Orange	Red Russet	Yellowish-Brown, flecked White
9	Nine	Yesod	Indigo	Violet	Very dark Purple	Citrine, flecked azure
10	Ten	Malkuth	Yellow	Citrine (N) Olive (E) Russet (W) & Black (S) Saltire	As Queen Scale but Gold, flecked Black	Black, rayed Yellow

Citrine combines blue, red, and yellow with a predominance of yellow; olive, with a predominance of blue; russet, with a predominance of red; and these represent respectively the airy, watery, and fiery subelements. Black is the earthy part of earth.

upon for inspiration. Astrology and alchemy are also rich in color symbolism and traditions that surely influenced many of the color selections. Perhaps most intriguing is the likelihood that some colors were selected as the result of magically induced visions. Skrying in the spirit vision and aura experiments were part and parcel of the Golden Dawn curriculum. The various rays and flecks found in the suit of Disks are especially characteristic of such astral visions.

I would love to be able to tell you that Lady Harris simply chose the dominant colors for the individual cards directly from the appropriate box in the four scale charts. But, if we spend just a few minutes with the cards and the charts, we see that this is not the case. If we look deeper, however, we discover that Harris does most certainly use the scale charts and with the greatest skill and innovative genius. Let's take the Six of Wands as an example:

If we look to the column representing Wands (Knight scale) in table 5 and refer to the Key scale #6, we find that the color for the Six of Wands should be clear pink rose. There is no (or very little) clear pink rose in the Six of Wands, however. As a matter of fact, the background is violet and purple, and the wands themselves are greenish yellow, outlined with reddish amber. Two of the wands on the card are surmounted by winged solar disks with bright blue feathers and blue uraeus serpents outlined in yellow. Where did these colors come from?

In chapter 14, I will discuss how each of the thirty-six small cards represents one decan (period of ten degrees) of the zodiac.[95] Each is also assigned a planet. The Six of Wands represents the planet Jupiter in the second decan of Leo. If we look at Key scale #19 (Leo) on table 4, we find the colors yellow (greenish), deep purple, grey, and reddish amber. If we look at Key scale #21 (Jupiter), we find the colors violet, blue, rich purple, and bright blue rayed with yellow. A perfect match.

Not all the cards are so easily analyzed. Instead of using the colors separately, as she does in the Six of Disks, Harris often blends two or more colors that represent contending or inharmonious astrological or elemental aspects. This is more apparent in the higher-numbered cards, which represent lower sephiroth on the Tree of Life and therefore characterize more imbalanced and polluted forces.

No matter how difficult it may be to work out the method of the color madness of every card in the Thoth Tarot, we can be relatively confident that Lady Harris was not careless or arbitrary in her selections.[96] Her painstaking efforts to express in colors the complex and wonderful forces of the universe resulted in the creation of a unique and powerful meditative tool. Each time we work with the cards—each time we lay them out and allow our eyes to drink in their interwoven and interconnected colors—we silently activate those same connective webs of universal influences within ourselves.

CHAPTER ELEVEN

THE HOLY GUARDIAN ANGEL

Here at the remotest outpost of the divine empire lies a buried treasure. Because the inferior agrees with the superior, *the genetic code of Kether and the entire involving/ evolving universe sleeps like a dormant seed inside each of us. It takes a gardener to awaken and germinate this seed, and that gardener is the Vau ι of the ineffable name, our Holy Guardian Angel."*[97]

In *Magick,* Crowley wrote,

> The Single Supreme Ritual is the attainment of the Knowledge and Conversation of the Holy Guardian Angel. It is the raising of the complete man in a vertical straight line. Any deviation from this line tends to become black magic. Any other operation is black magic.[98]

"Oh my goodness!" I hear many of you gasping. "Guardian Angels! Black magic! I knew this DuQuette fellow was up to no good! I just wanted to understand a little more about the Thoth Tarot. Now we're talking about angels and black magic! What am I getting into? Where's it going to stop—human sacrifice?"

Having come this far with me, I hope you are not harboring any such fears. It would be foolish indeed, because the subject of the Holy Guardian Angel is just that—holy. It is directly related to the spiritual evolution of each and every one of us, no matter what our religion or philosophy. It also has everything to do with the structure and behavior of tarot, especially the unique and mysterious status of the Princess court cards and the small cards, aces, and tens.

Hang on to your hats. I'll try to make this short. But please, don't skip over this part. It is the last and most important of the little bits of things you should know before beginning your study of Aleister Crowley's Thoth Tarot.

In 1888, S. L. MacGregor Mathers translated an unusual text, *The Book of the Sacred Magic of Abra-Melin the Mage as Delivered by Abraham the Jew unto His Son Lamech, a Grimoire of the Fifteenth Century.*[99] The original manuscript was first written down in Hebrew by the famous Qabalist and magician, Abraham the Jew, in 1458. It was housed in the Bibliotheque de l'Arsenal in Paris and translated into French in the late seventeenth century. It is a fascinating book of technical magic. The following is excerpted from my *Angels, Demons, and Gods of the New Millennium.*

Abra-Melin reveals that each of us is linked to a spiritual being whom he calls the Holy Guardian Angel. Until we have become spiritually wedded to this being, we are not fully equipped as human beings to rule the denizens of our lower nature or advance spiritually. The primary focus of the Abra-Melin operation is union (Knowledge and Conversation) with one's Holy Guardian Angel. Until this is accomplished, it is useless to even attempt to manipulate the circumstances of life because we are as yet spiritually unprepared to adequately comprehend the nature of our true will, and so incompetent to exercise that will upon the cosmos. After Knowledge and Conversation is achieved the Angel becomes the magician's counselor and directs from a position of supreme wisdom all subsequent magical activities.

While the term "Holy Guardian Angel" used in this capacity appears to have originated with the *Sacred Magic of Abra-Melin the Mage*, the concept of a personal divine entity is unquestionably much older. Zoroaster[100] writes of the Agathosdaimon, a personal guardian spirit who must be contacted before any theurgic ceremony is initiated. . . . The Platonic philosophers taught that between humanity and the gods there exists an intermediate class of spiritual beings called Daemonos. Each individual is assigned a personal daemon and it is the daemon, not the gods, who directly hears and answers the prayers of our race. Socrates called his daemon "genius."

Spirit guides, who from prehistoric times have shepherded the shamanic visions of every culture on earth, serve to demonstrate that Knowledge and Conversation of the Holy Guardian Angel is a fundamental and universal spiritual experience. Jesus said, ". . . no man cometh unto the Father but by me." Krishna told Arjuna, "Only by single-minded devotion I may in this form be known and seen in reality, and also entered into." Everywhere we look within the sacred writings and spiritual practices of the world's religions we find the basic theme of a personal relationship with a spiritual being who is the representative of, or the conduit to, a supreme (and perhaps impersonal) deity. So ingrained is this basic truth upon the collective unconscious of the race that we find it embedded deeply in our myths and fairy tales. It takes no stretch of the imagination to see the H.G.A. as the prince who awakens with a kiss (Knowledge and Conversation) the sleeping beauty (the unenlightened soul), and takes her to the palace of his father the king (God), where the new couple will eventually become king and queen themselves (supreme enlightenment and re-absorption into god-head)....

The Holy Guardian Angel is more than the projected image of our per-fected self, or the voice of our conscience; it is more than the innocent, inherent knowledge between right and wrong; it is more than the divine ear that hears us when we look to heaven and pray . . . "Oh God . . . if you just get me out of this, I'll never do anything so stupid again!" But what that "more than" is is difficult to discuss.[101]

Difficult indeed, but we must try to discuss it if we are going to understand how this relates to tarot. Let's expand the fairytale analogy and look at the charac-ters as if they were the letters הוהי YHVH and see where they might live on the Tree of Life. Please remember that every time I talk about the Tree of Life, I am talk-ing about more than just great cosmological abstractions. I'm talking about you and me. Each of us is an individual living, breathing Tree of Life. Every Tree of the four Qabalistic worlds, every path, every sephira has its counterpart in our own bodies, our own minds, our own spirits, our own souls.

Ultimately, all the characters in our fairytale are already living in the first sephira, Kether (the ace of each suit). Of course, they will only realize this in the timeless moment of ecstasy when they and all the units of consciousness in the cosmos finally wake up and realize we are one big consciousness. For practical purposes of dis-cussion, however, we can safely say that:

- The ace is Kether, the Monad—the environment of supreme deity—above all concepts of duality, above the separation of male/female/King/Queen.
- Our fairytale King is the Yod of YHVH, and lives in the second sephira, Chokmah. (His head, however, like the pointy little tip of the Hebrew letter Yod, really pokes up into Kether. But, as long as the King identifies himself as King, he is unaware of his more exalted identity and has convinced himself that he lives in Chokmah.)
- The Queen is the first Hé in YHVH, and lives in the third sephira, Binah.
- It is only fitting that this royal couple lives above the Abyss in the supernal triad. They unite and become one, as good couples should, and for a moment enjoy the ecstasy of being one (Kether). Then, after a cosmic cigarette, the King rolls over and goes to sleep. As the King snores away in Chokmah, the Queen becomes aware that, in this brief moment of ecstasy, she has become

pregnant with twins. She eventually delivers. The two babies (a Prince and a Princess) plop out below the Abyss. The Prince doesn't fall too far from the supernal triad palace, but the Princess slides all the way to the bottom, Malkuth.

- The young Prince is the Vau in YHVH. He's a bright boy and organizes a neatly ordered principality in sephiroth four through nine. These six sephiroth are often referred to in Qabalistic literature as the macrocosm, the greater world. Even though his principality is all six sephiroth of the macrocosm, our fairytale Prince's headquarters and main corporate office is in the sixth sephira, Tiphareth. (By the way, in our personal Tree of Life, the Prince is our own Holy Guardian Angel. Can you see where this is heading?)

- The Princess is the final Hé in YHVH, and is literally trapped in the tenth sephira, Malkuth. In Qabalistic literature, Malkuth is often referred to as the microcosm, the lesser world. If the Princess were not sleeping most of the time, we would see that she is a very complicated and confused character. She, of course, is the daughter of the King and Queen, but, mysteriously, she belongs to an even younger generation than that of her brother, the Prince. As a matter of fact, even though she is closely related to the King, Queen, and Prince, her magical genes are so polluted and far enough removed from those of the rest of the family that, should she marry her brother, the Prince, it would not even be considered incest in a court of cosmic family law.

You've probably guessed that you and I are the fairytale Princess. We are almost completely asleep to the larger spiritual reality and are restlessly thrashing around in the bed of the material plane, trying to understand everything with our laughably inadequate senses, and explain it with our laughably inadequate language. It's kind of depressing, isn't it?

Nevertheless, we quite literally have an ace up our sleeves, because, low as the Princess is on the Tree of Life—banished as she is from the supernal triad, separated as she is from her brother/lover the Prince in his macrocosmic principality, trapped as she in a microcosmic tomb of matter—the Princess is the most important character in our mystic fairytale.

Her importance lies in the fact that she is the lowest of the low, and is the key to the "general doctrine that the climax of the Descent into Matter is the signal for the redintegration by Spirit"[102] that I mentioned briefly in chapter 8. No other character in our fairytale (except the inscrutable singularity that is Kether/ace) has what the Princess has, that is, a little bit of everything from the highest-high to the lowest-low. As Proclus wrote, "The heaven is in the earth, but after an earthly manner; . . . and the earth is in the heaven, but after a heavenly manner."[103]

The Holy Guardian Angel/Prince doesn't have any lowest of the low. He's stuck in cosmic middle management and passionately needs a bit of the Princess' divine DNA if he is ever going to clone himself back to being a King. One kiss from the Princess is all it will take. He will then wake up and realize he is King, which will cause the Princess to wake up more and realize she is his bride, the Queen. These two newlyweds will then unite in a cosmic orgasm that explodes and melts away all sense of separateness. In the truest sense, the King (Chokmah) and Queen (Binah) are again annihilated in the one eternal moment they realize that they are not two, but one (Kether).

From an alchemical point of view, the King and Queen's ecstatic dissolution was caused by the universal solvent, vitriol (see page 135). The Princess was the hidden stone and she certainly was buried in the interior parts of the earth, and she certainly got herself rectified by marrying the Prince and becoming Queen, and so on ad infinitum.

And does everyone live happily ever after? Well, after a fashion.

Unfortunately, the cycle immediately repeats itself because, when the ecstatic afterglow of the realization of oneness wears off, the Queen once again finds herself pregnant. The King again falls asleep and awaits the Queen's loving nudge. Of course, she will only be in the mood to give the old man the nudge when she is comforted by the fact that the royal children are once again safely home.

This dynamic and somewhat incestuous love story is the secret of YHVH. It is the electricity of creation—a divine alternating current coursing eternally in two directions at the same time—from ace to Princess, from Princess to ace.

I hope my little fairytale has helped you more clearly understand the dynamics of this universal formula. Many of you may even think that I was being overly childish in my narrative. Crowley's version is decidedly more adult and ultimately far more informative. As we learned in chapter 7, he delighted in using wild and blasphemous words and imagery to communicate perfectly wholesome spiritual concepts.

- Crowley's Queen is the "Whore of Babalon, Mother of Abominations";
- Crowley's King is the "Beast, the All-father, Chaos";
- When Crowley's King and Queen unite, it is "Babalon Riding the Beast";
- Crowley's returning new-wedded Prince and Princess are (is) the "Blood of the Saints";
- Crowley's Queen does not just rejoice at the homecoming of the royal children, she throws a cosmic party and becomes "drunk of the Blood of the Saints";
- Instead of a Queen who politely nudges her King awake to make love, we have Babalon the Great in her whoredom, awakening the "poison of the Eld" of the All-Father, and then once again "mounting the Beast."

I again remind you that, when we talk about these characters, we are talking about aspects of ourselves and levels of consciousness most of us have yet to experience. If we could wake up and see the big picture, we would realize that we are at once the ace, King, Queen, Prince, and Princess of this cosmic fairytale. But we are not awake. As Rabbi Ben Clifford says,

> The you that you think is you is not you. It is a dream you. In fact, the you that you think is you is a dreamer inside a dreamer inside a dreamer inside a dreamer. You are the King of the universe who has fallen asleep and is dreaming he is the Queen who has fallen asleep and is dreaming she is the Prince who has fallen asleep and is dreaming he is a sleeping Princess.[104]

In a most personal and intimate way, each of us is the sleeping Princess. Each of us waits as a bride-to-be for the kiss of our Prince (our Holy Guardian Angel) and the return to our spiritual estate. Recall Crowley's quote at the beginning of this chapter.

> The Single Supreme Ritual is the attainment of the Knowledge and Conversation of the Holy Guardian Angel. It is the raising of the complete man in a vertical straight line. Any deviation from this line tends to become black magic. Any other operation is black magic.

The vertical straight line is the raising of our consciousness from Malkuth—10 (the sephira of the microcosm) to Tiphareth—6 (the central sephira of the macrocosm). Until this is accomplished, until each of us has united our microcosm with the macrocosm of the Holy Guardian Angel, we not playing with a full deck. We are not balanced enough to know good from evil, and all our actions tend to become "black magic."

Crowley devised a magical word to illustrate knowledge of and conversation with the Holy Guardian Angel. He mentions it several times in *The Book of Thoth* and Lady Harris incorporates it graphically in the trump card the Chariot. It is a word that symbolizes the union of the numbers five and six—five representing the microcosm (the little world centered in Malkuth, you and me, the Princess); six representing the macrocosm, (the big world centered in Tiphareth, the Holy Guardian Angel). The magical word is ABRAHADABRA. It is composed of five *A*s amid six other letters.

KING OR KNIGHT? QABALISTIC ROMANCE

Before we get too far away from our fairytale, I need to bring up something very important. The four royal characters in the above story are called King, Queen,

Prince, and Princess. The court cards of the original Golden Dawn deck were titled exactly the same. Each suit had a King on a horse, a Queen on a throne, a Prince in a chariot, and a standing Princess. With only one exception, the court cards of the Thoth Tarot are titled and positioned the same way. The exception is, Crowley uses the title Knight instead of King. His reason for doing so is "Qabalistic Romance." Simply put, a knight is sexier than a king.

In the imagery of cosmic chivalry, the knight on horseback wins his queen, the old king's daughter, and replaces the old king on the throne. If we were to project this dynamic upon our fairytale, the Knight would be the character who wins and makes love to the Queen, and a King is the guy who afterward turns around and falls asleep. Crowley considered the more active, virile concept of the Knight to be the most appropriate title and character for the court card that represents the Yod in YHVH.

While I'm on the subject of sexy tarot cards, I would surely be remiss in my pledge to introduce all the little bits of things you should know before beginning your study of the Thoth Tarot if I didn't spend a little time on an important subject that dominated a great deal of Crowley's magical life and influenced profoundly the nature of the Thoth Tarot—sex magick.

SEX MAGICK, TAROT, AND THE HOLY GUARDIAN ANGEL

The Magick of Thelema tells us that

> All Magick is sexual. Indeed, all life is sexual. It is either overt or implied, invoked or directed, stored or released. The Mass of the Roman Catholic Church is every bit as much a pantomime of the sex act as the "Great Rite" of the witches. The real question is "what is sex symbolic of?"[105]

What do you think of when you hear the words "sex magick"? Maybe you picture wild orgies where people dress up in bizarre costumes and intone spooky chants while they perform unspeakable sexual acts upon each other and an assortment of other creatures and inanimate objects? Perhaps you imagine people being abused by a diabolical magician and his minions in order to evoke evil spirits. You might even think that you can join a sex magick cult where (even if you do not possess even a minimum level of intelligence, attractiveness, social skills, or charm) you will be rewarded with eager and willing sexual partners. Dream on!

For nearly thirty years, I have been an active member and officer of one Crowley's own magical societies, Ordo Templi Orientis. The O.T.O. is the largest Thelemic order in the world. It is a fraternal and religious organization that provides degree initiations and engages in various social and publishing endeavors. Magically, however, the Order exists primarily to protect and perpetuate a particular magical secret of great potential efficacy. The degree structure of the Order is designed to prepare its most serious and tenacious initiates and provide them with the tools to discover this secret and use it safely and effectively. This supreme secret is a particular technique of sexual magick. It is held sacred and secret by members of the Sovereign Sanctuary of the Gnosis (the Order's Ninth Degree), whose duty it is to use the secret for the benefit of his or her spiritual evolution.

I know it will be a painful revelation for some of you to learn that none of the fanciful scenes of erotic excess that I've described above even remotely resemble anything that takes place at any O.T.O. degree initiation or any other official ceremony or activity, public or private. The Order does not read its members' diaries, monitor their magical or sexual lives, or violate their bodies. In other words, you may learn the principles of sex magick in the O.T.O., but you'll have to practice on your own.

Now you may be asking, if the world's largest sex magick organization isn't an orgy cult, then what is sex magick about? My good friend Donald Michael Kraig gives one very excellent definition: "A variety of techniques which harness the energies raised during sexual activity and direct them to fulfill the desires of the people practicing sex magick."[106]

The key word in Don's definition is "desires." What the magician desires is technically called "the object of the operation." Desire spells the difference between an ill-conceived attempt to bewitch your neighbor's cow and the attainment of perfect spiritual liberation. I bring all this up in this chapter because nothing should be more ardently desired than the Holy Guardian Angel. It should not surprise anyone that the experience of knowledge of and conversation with one's H.G.A. is often described as being exquisitely sexual.

Most everyone knows the ecstasy of orgasm. In that golden moment, our self is annihilated just like the consciousness of the King and Queen in our fairytale. In that timeless moment, there is no difference between you and everything else in the universe—including (potentially) the object of the operation (your heart's desire). Can't you see how, by working like a disciplined yogi with the forces and energies that lead up to that timeless moment, a person can literally become one with the object of their desire and then gestate and eventually give birth to it? This is technical magick of the highest order and should not be identified in any way with the prurient shenanigans of sex cults or clubs.

Human sexuality is only one very narrow expression of this sexual alchemy. The formula is truly universal and its mechanics are at work at all levels of existence. It is the magick that turns energy into matter, sunlight into gold, you and me into God.

And so ends Part I of this book. I now would like to pause and congratulate you for enduring all these little bits of things I thought you should know before beginning your study of Aleister Crowley's Thoth Tarot. I realize that, for many, it has been an ordeal. I have done my best to make things as clear as I would have wanted them presented at the beginning of my studies, but I'm sure there are those who may still feel hopelessly confused. I hope you will persevere and refer often to the material in Part I and the definitions in the glossary in chapter 21 as you study the next section, which deals with the individual cards.

PART II

The Cards

CHAPTER TWELVE

INTRODUCTION
TO THE CARDS

*I know enough about the works of Aleister Crowley to know that it would be unwise
for me to presume to interpret him. There is more than enough Crowley material
available to allow Crowley to explain Crowley. Finding that material when you need
it, however, can be a problem.[1]*

Now that we are familiar with many of the little bits of things you should know
before beginning your study of Aleister Crowley's Thoth Tarot, I think we are about
ready to examine the cards themselves without the distraction of having to digress
repeatedly into fundamental discussions of Qabalah, Thelema, alchemy, or Enochiana.
Knowing the place whereon I standest is holy ground, it is with no small measure
of trepidation that I begin my comments on the individual cards. I have tried to
the best of my ability to put off the sandals of presumption and keep my personal
speculations and theories to an absolute minimum.

If I should state, for instance, that the goddess of the Adjustment card is the
Fool's girlfriend, or that the Devil is God as misunderstood by the wicked, or that
the Magus is cursed so that all his words are distorted and misunderstood, it will be
because, somewhere in his voluminous writings, Crowley has said so. I make no
apologies for quoting Crowley liberally, and quoting him often, from a number of
texts including *The Book of Thoth, The Heart of the Master,[2] Magick, Book IV, The
Equinox, Konx Om Pax, Orpheus,* and letters between Crowley and Harris. I have
taken great pains to identify and reference all such quotes. That being said, I must
remind the reader that not every aspect of the Thoth Tarot is new or revolutionary.
Spending too much time and energy searching for secret Crowleyisms hidden in every
curious brushstroke or printing flaw is more often a symptom of mental instability than spiritual revelation.

The fact is that the format and fundamental images of most of the individual cards of the Thoth Tarot are not the invention of Aleister Crowley. As a member of the Golden Dawn, Crowley was encouraged to paint his own personal deck using specific images and colors outlined in Order documents. Lady Harris possessed the written descriptions and was also familiar with the published deck painted by Pamela Coleman Smith under the direction of Arthur Edward Waite. In discussing each card, I will describe the original Golden Dawn design and, as much as possible, point out similarities and differences.

THE MAJOR AND MINOR ARCANAS

When we break the seal and open a new deck of tarot cards we usually discover that they are neatly organized and ordered. The first twenty-two cards are numbered with roman numerals 0–XXI and are called the Major (or Greater) Arcana. The remaining fifty-six cards are called the Minor (or Lesser) Arcana and are divided into four suits. The suits are usually ordered Wands, Cups, Swords, and Disks. Each suit contains fourteen cards consisting of four court cards (Knight, Queen, Prince, and Princess)[3] and ten small cards (ace through 10).

That is how most decks of tarot cards are arranged when they first come from the manufacturer. However, the true hierarchy of the tarot would have them arranged as I show below. (The logic behind these divisions will soon become clear.)

- The twenty-two trumps ordered 0–XXI;
- The four aces ordered Wands, Cups, Swords, and Disks;
- The sixteen court cards ordered by suit (Wands, Cups, Swords, and Disks) and by title (Knight, Queen, Prince, and Princess);
- The thirty-six small cards ordered by suit (Wands, Cups, Swords, and Disks) and by number (2–10).

From a Qabalistic point of view, the relationship between the two Arcanas is complex, if not downright inscrutable. I could digress at this point into hundreds of pages of debate over which Qabalistic world plays host to which Arcana,[4] but I intend to spare us that detour. Crowley said, "the Tarot will lose all its vitality for one who allows himself to be side-tracked by its pedantry."[5] I couldn't agree more, so let's try to make it easy on ourselves.

A simple (if not altogether accurate) way of looking at the two Arcanas is by projecting them upon the pentagram.

In figure 22, the Major Arcana (the twenty-two trumps or atus) represents spirit and is placed on the top point of the pentagram. Each trump is, in essence, a divine personage "possessing its own private, personal and particular Universe."[6] Each presents an aspect—a facet of supreme reality. Like the element spirit, the

FIGURE 22. THE PENTAGRAM OF THE MAJOR AND MINOR ARCANAS. THE MAJOR ARCANA RULES THE MINOR ARCANA IN THE SAME WAY THAT SPIRIT RULES THE FOUR ELEMENTS.

influence of the trumps pervades all levels of consciousness and creation—attracting, repelling, connecting, and separating the infinite elemental combinations.

The Minor Arcana represents the four elemental arms of the pentagram that spirit (the Major Arcana) simultaneously unites and separates. The cards of the Minor Arcana are not divine personages, but "primarily sub-Elements, parts of the 'Blind Forces' under the Demiourgos, Tetragrammaton."[7]

I know this is a lot to absorb, especially for those of you who are not particularly interested in the details of Qabalistic thought. Perhaps all this will be easier to understand if we look at it this way:

- Each trump is a world all its own—one one-twenty-second facet of the totality of consciousness—the ultimate spiritual and cosmological reality;
- Each of the trumps can be thought of as having an entire set of fifty-six Minor Arcana cards that it rules and with which it executes its particular aspect of influence.

We could argue quite correctly that there are really 1,232 (22 × 56) tarot cards in a complete deck; fifty-six cards of the Minor Arcana dutifully playing out their elemental roles in twenty-two different, but intimately connected, drama/comedies written and directed by each of the twenty-two trumps. In *The Book of Thoth*, Crowley uses the Three of Disks, Work, as an example of how this plays out:

> The *Three of Disks* belonging to the *High Priestess* or the *Lovers* might represent the establishment of an oracle like that of Delphi. The *Hierophant's Three of Disks* might point to the construction of a cathedral. The *Tower's Three of Disks* perhaps indicating the massing of a standing army. The ideas that such pairings evoke can be an infinite source of meditation, and an invaluable exercise for anyone wishing to use the cards for divination.[8]

In the pages that follow, I briefly discuss each of the seventy-eight cards of the Thoth Tarot. I will focus primarily upon the magical and spiritual traditions that gave birth to it as a tarot entity, and upon demonstrating how the various astrological and Qabalistic components blend to create each card's unique character. (For divinatory meanings and Crowley's method of divination, see chapter 20.) Wherever possible, I also include excerpts of letters between Harris and Crowley concerning the card. I find these particularly interesting.

Now on to the seventy-eight cards of the Thoth Tarot. We will start with the Major Arcana.

CHAPTER THIRTEEN

INTRODUCTION
TO THE MAJOR ARCANA

All these old letters of my Book are aright but ⅄ *is not the Star. This is also secret: my prophet shall reveal it to the wise.*[9]

Nobody really knows where tarot cards originated. Obviously, they could not have existed as cards before the invention of paper. As a matter of fact, we cannot with any degree of certainty trace them any further back than northern Italy in the first half of the fifteenth century, where they were called *carte da trionfi* (cards of the triumph) and used to play a game similar to modern bridge. Later, in the 1530s, the cards became known as *tarocchi* (singular form *tarocco*, meaning "tarot").

Early examples displayed imagery that inspired the imaginations of the Renaissance elite—ancient gods, heroes, virtues, vices, and principals enthroned in chariots and "trumping" one another by order of importance as part of a great triumphal procession. These were later supplemented with other figures, including mystical images from the prophetic books of the Old and New Testaments. Still later, Masonic concepts like the four public and private virtues of Temperance, Fortitude (Strength), Justice, and Prudence (Lovers?) all make their appearance in tarot decks.

THE ORDERING OF THE TRUMPS

For the most part, the individual trump cards of the Thoth Tarot should be immediately recognizable to anyone who is familiar with the traditional images of tarot. The Aeon is the most striking exception.

In the Thoth Tarot, the twenty-two trumps are formally referred to as "Atus of Tahuti." According to Crowley, "Atu" was Ancient Egyptian for "house" or "key"; Tahuti is the God Thoth (the Egyptian Hermes, or Mercury). He also informs us that the word "atout" is short for the French phrase, *bon á tout*, meaning "good for anything," or what card players call a "wild card."

The earliest decks did not have titles printed on the trumps themselves, and the number of trumps and their ordering differed. As early as the 1490s, however, a basic collection of twenty-two characters and images, ordered more or less as we find them in modern decks, appeared as the standard model throughout Europe.

There is no real evidence that this standardization was the result of anything more occult or mysterious than the natural congealing of the conventions of a popular game. Nevertheless, that phenomenon in itself may have profound implications concerning how the human mind is hardwired to respond to archetypal images.

In a time when artificial images were limited to rare paintings, statuary, and architecture, the introduction of a portable pack of colorful images that could be viewed and enjoyed at one's leisure for hours on end must have had as much impact upon the psyche of fifteenth-century Europe as photography and motion pictures had upon that of the nineteenth and twentieth centuries.

With one exception, the Atus, or trumps, of the Thoth Tarot conform to the Tarot de Marseilles sequence, which is the same as that originally established by the deck of Catelin Geoffroy in 1557.[10] The Thoth Tarot also follows, with one exception, the Golden Dawn's secret scheme of attributing certain Hebrew letters and their corresponding elemental, planetary, or zodiacal attributions. That one exception has been, and continues to be, the source of much discussion and argument among students of modern occultism. In the next few pages, I will do my best to explain why the Thoth Tarot attributes the Hebrew letter Tzaddi (צ) to the fourth trump, the Emperor, and the Hebrew letter Hé (ה) to the seventeenth trump, the Star instead of the other way around. It is all because of one sentence of one verse of *The Book of the Law:* "All these old letters of my Book are aright; but צ is not the Star."[11]

Don't feel badly if, at first, you find what follows difficult to understand. Lady Harris was quite frank with Crowley about her confusion.

> Also I don't feel you have made it clear about Tzaddi—The Emperor. Can't you have a diagram? I have been reading your book to Ann Christie in the evenings & altho she is very interested she could not understand your book and I am not sure I did in the end. It will be a point about which there will be the most argument. Is there any reason for the 2 loops except secrecy? Sure! & if not why not undo the loop & is the Emperor to be numbered 17 or IV or 4 or 17 ditto Star also Strength XI and Justice VIII. I expect I have still got it all wrong but if I have, you must be clearer because I am only just below sub-normal intelligence. A bientot.[12]

I wish we had Crowley's response to the above letter. It might have been something like his commentary on this verse later published in *The Law Is for All:*

I see no harm in revealing the mystery of Tzaddi to "the wise"; others will hardly understand my explanations. Tzaddi is the letter of the Emperor, the Trump IV, and Hé is the Star, the Trump XVII. Aquarius and Aries are therefore counterchanged, revolving on the pivot of Pisces, just as in the Trumps VIII and XI, Leo and Libra, do about Virgo. This last revelation makes our Tarot attributions sublimely, perfectly, flawlessly symmetrical.[13]

Without illustrations, this explanation is rather hard to picture. *The Book of Thoth* contains diagrams and tables that do not always agree with each other. What follows is my best attempt to sort things out.

The adepts of the Golden Dawn, (working from existing and or innovated esoteric doctrine) assigned Hebrew letters to each of the trumps. Among many other things, these twenty-two Hebrew letters also represent the three primitive elements, seven planets, and twelve signs of the zodiac.

TABLE 6. THE TRADITIONAL SEQUENCE USING THE TITLES OF THE THOTH
TAROT AND GOLDEN DAWN ATTRIBUTES

Traditional Trump#	Trump Title (Thoth Tarot)	Hebrew Letter Sequence	The 22 Hebrew Letters
0	FOOL	1	Aleph (Air)
1	MAGUS	2	Beth (Mercury)
2	HIGH PRIESTESS	3	Gimel (Moon)
3	EMPRESS	4	Daleth (Venus)
4	EMPEROR	5	Hé (Aries)
5	HIEROPHANT	6	Vau (Taurus)
6	LOVERS	7	Zain (Gemini)
7	CHARIOT	8	Cheth (Cancer)
8	ADJUSTMENT*	→ 12	Lamed (Libra)* ← (Teth-Leo belongs here in sequence)
9	HERMIT	10	Yod (Virgo)
10	FORTUNE	11	Kaph (Jupiter)
11	LUST*	→ 9	Teth (Leo) ← (Lamed-Libra belongs here in sequence)
12	HANGED MAN	13	Mem (Water)
13	DEATH	14	Nun (Scorpio)
14	ART	15	Samekh (Sagittarius)
15	DEVIL	16	Ayin (Capricorn)
16	TOWER	17	Pé (Mars)
17	STAR	18	Tzaddi (Aquarius)
18	MOON	19	Qoph (Pisces)
19	SUN	20	Resh (Sun)
20	AEON	21	Shin (Fire & Spirit)
21	UNIVERSE	22	Tau (Saturn & Earth)

With only two exceptions (as indicated in table 6 by the double arrows), the order of the twenty-two trumps neatly follows the sequential order of the twenty-two letters of the Hebrew alphabet. The exceptions to this otherwise tidy arrangement relate to the traditional positioning of two trumps, 8 (Adjustment, Justice in older decks) and 11 (Lust, Strength in older decks). If we were to follow the natural order of the Hebrew alphabet, Adjustment would be assigned the ninth letter, Teth (which represents the zodiacal sign of Leo), and Lust would be assigned the twelfth Hebrew letter, Lamed (which represents the zodiacal sign of Libra). This is not the case, and the adepts of the Golden Dawn made the correction.

This is easier to see in table 7, which shows only the zodiacal trumps. Notice how, by making Strength (Lust) trump number 8 and assigning it the Hebrew letter Teth, and by making Justice (Adjustment) trump number 11 and assigning it the Hebrew letter Lamed, the Golden Dawn arrangement restores the natural order to the signs of the zodiac and to the Hebrew alphabet.

As tidy and logical as this switch is, it nevertheless disturbs the traditional sequence of trumps, and this bothered many Golden Dawn members, including Crowley. The Thoth Tarot follows the Golden Dawn model in that it assigns Teth/Leo to the Lust card and Lamed/Libra to the Adjustment card, but it retains the traditional sequence of Lust as the eleventh and Adjustment as the eighth trump.

TABLE 7. GOLDEN DAWN ARRANGEMENT:
THE NATURAL SEQUENCE OF THE SIGNS OF THE ZODIAC AND THE
HEBREW ALPHABET RESTORED

Trump #	Trump Title (Thoth Tarot)	Zodiac Sign	12 Hebrew Letters Representing Zodiac Signs
4	EMPEROR	Aries	Hé
5	HIEROPHANT	Taurus	Vau
6	LOVERS	Gemini	Zain
7	CHARIOT	Cancer	Cheth
8	LUST*	Leo	Teth*
9	HERMIT	Virgo	Yod
11	ADJUSTMENT*	Libra	Lamed*
13	DEATH	Scorpio	Nun
14	ART	Sagittarius	Samekh
15	DEVIL	Capricorn	Ayin
17	STAR	Aquarius	Tzaddi
18	MOON	Pisces	Qoph

If we were to project this change upon the belt of the zodiac, it would be as if a twist or loop is formed around the sign of Virgo, changing the natural order of signs from Leo-Virgo-Libra to Libra-Virgo-Leo.

Figure 23 shows the natural order of the signs of the zodiac; figure 24 shows the Leo/Libra twist.

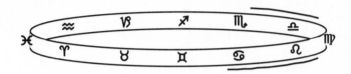

FIGURE 23. NATURAL ORDER OF THE ZODIACAL BELT.

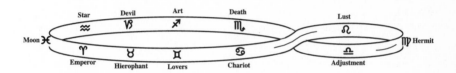

FIGURE 24. ZODIACAL BELT WITH A TWIST. TETH (LEO) AND LAMED (LIBRA) ARE SWITCHED. NOTE THAT VIRGO RETAINS ITS POSITION.

This arrangement leaves us with a curious and somewhat imbalanced diagram of the zodiacal belt, but it didn't seem to bother Crowley, at least not until shortly after twelve noon on April 8, 1904. He was in the middle of receiving the first chapter of *The Book of the Law* in his hotel room in Cairo. Aiwass, speaking for the Goddess Nuit, had just dictated the words, "Invoke me under my stars! Love is the law, love under will. Nor let the fools mistake love; for there are love and love. There is the dove, and there is the serpent. Choose ye well. He, my prophet, hath chosen, knowing the law of the fortress, and the great mystery of the House of God."[14]

When Crowley "heard" the reference to "the fortress" and "the House of God" (alternate titles to trump XVI, the Tower), a question arose in his mind concerning the general correctness of the ordering of the tarot trumps. Instantly, his question was answered, when Aiwass dictated the next line: "All these old letters of my Book are aright but is **צ** not the Star. This is also secret: my prophet shall reveal it to the wise."[15]

This comment puzzled Crowley. If Tzaddi was not the Star, then what card was? And what Hebrew letter should be attributed to the Star card? The answer was some time in coming, but when it did come, there was no doubt in Crowley's mind that he had figured it out. Tzaddi was the Emperor.

> This card is attributed to the letter Tzaddi, and it refers to the sign of Aries in the Zodiac. This sign is ruled by Mars, and therein the Sun is exalted. The sign is thus a combination of energy in its most material form with the idea of authority. The sign TZ or TS implies this in the original, ono-matopoetic form of language. It is derived from Sanskrit roots meaning Head and Age, and is found to-day in words like Cæsar, Tsar, Sirdar, Senate, Senior, Signor, Señor, Seigneur.[16]

The Emperor's old letter was Hé. It would now be attributed to the Star. Hé is the letter for both female components of YHVH (the Supernal Mother Hé of Binah, and unredeemed Daughter Hé of Malkuth) and a perfect representation of the Star Goddess depicted on Atu XVII. Why hadn't someone thought of this before?

Of course, Crowley was not satisfied with just knowing what the switch was; he had to find a more esoteric and technical reason why Tzaddi was not the Star.

As we see in table 8 and figure 25, switching the trumps that represent the Hebrew Letters Hé and Tzaddi upsets the natural order of the signs of the zodiac on the opposite side of the zodiac, as if another loop had formed on the belt of the zodiac that twisted around the sign of Pisces and changed the natural order from

TABLE 8. CROWLEY ARRANGEMENT: THE NATURAL SEQUENCE OF SIGNS
ARRANGED TO ACCOMMODATE THE NEW ORDER

Trump #	Trump Title (Thoth Tarot)	Zodiac Sign	12 Hebrew Letters Representing Zodiac Signs
4	EMPEROR	Aries	Tzaddi ←
5	HIEROPHANT	Taurus	Vau
6	LOVERS	Gemini	Zain
7	CHARIOT	Cancer	Cheth
8	ADJUSTMENT	Libra	Lamed*
9	HERMIT	Virgo	Yod
11	LUST	Leo	Teth*
13	DEATH	Scorpio	Nun
14	ART	Sagittarius	Samekh
15	DEVIL	Capricorn	Ayin
17	STAR	Aquarius	Hé ←
18	MOON	Pisces	Qoph

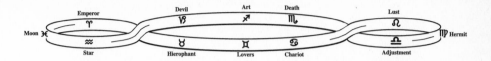

FIGURE 25. ZODIACAL BELT WITH TWO TWISTS. TETH (LEO) AND LAMED (LIBRA) ARE
SWITCHED BY THE GOLDEN DAWN; EMPEROR (TZADDI) AND STAR (HÉ) ARE SWITCHED
BY CROWLEY.

Aquarius-Pisces-Aries to Aries-Pisces-Aquarius.

It is likely that there will always be confusion and controversy over this matter.
It doesn't help that Crowley offers us conflicting diagrams and statements in *The
Book of Thoth*. The most vexing are:

- Table XX, which assigns Aquarius to the Emperor and Aries to the Star;
- The last paragraph of his comments on the Emperor (page 78), where he
  talks of the path of the Emperor as if it held its old position on the Tree of
  Life, joining sephira 2, Chokmah, with sephira 6, Tiphareth.

Whether this is because of inevitable typographical errors or because of Crowley's
reticence to form a strict doctrine around any particular verse of *The Book of the
Law*, will probably remain a mystery, but here's a quick reference that I would loved
to have had at the beginning of my study of the Thoth Tarot. It may not conform
to every statement and diagram in *The Book of Thoth*, but it is the most consistent summary I could create.

Trump 4 is the Emperor

- The zodiac sign assigned to the Emperor is Aries;
- The Hebrew letter for the Emperor is צ Tzaddi (and everything צ Tzaddi
  represents);
- On the Tree of Life, the Emperor is found on path 28, which joins the
  seventh sephira, Netzach, to the ninth sephira, Yesod.

Trump 8 is Adjustment

- The zodiac sign assigned to Adjustment is Libra;
- The Hebrew letter for Adjustment is ל Lamed (and everything Lamed
  represents);
- On the Tree of Life, Adjustment is found on path 22, which joins the fifth
  sephira, Geburah, to the sixth sephira, Tiphareth.

Trump 11 is Lust

- The zodiac sign assigned to Lust is Leo;
- The Hebrew letter for Lust is ט Teth (and everything Teth represents);
- On the Tree of Life, Lust is found on path 19, which joins the fourth sephira, Chesed, to the fifth sephira, Geburah.

Trump 17 is the Star

- The zodiac sign assigned to the Star is Aquarius;
- The Hebrew letter for The Star is ה Hé (and everything Hé represents);
- On the Tree of Life, Hé is found on path 15, which joins the second sephira, Chokmah to the sixth sephira, Tiphareth.

THE DIVISION OF THE TRUMPS

There are near infinite ways the twenty-two trumps can be divided and combined for meditative and instructive purposes. The most obvious, of course, are the divisions by three elemental, seven planetary, and twelve zodiacal cards. Another very popular method of division places the Fool at the top of three rows of seven cards, ordered consecutively. Each of the three rows can represent some aspect or quality of character or consciousness. The cards are then considered as seven columns of three cards, each relating in some way to each other. For example, the first column would have the Magus at the top, Adjustment in the middle and the Devil on the bottom, perhaps suggestive of some cosmic truth relating to the manifest nature of the Magus, or some such spiritual lesson. Personally, I believe that any way we organize or combine the cards is a legitimate meditative exercise. After all, the trumps are a universal alphabet of images and, no matter how we throw them together, they are bound to spell something.

Buried in *The Book of Thoth,* as the last paragraph of his comments on the High Priestess, Crowley reveals a most remarkable secret concerning the fundamental nature of the twenty-two trumps:

> It is especially to be observed that the three consecutive letters, Gimel, Daleth, Hé (Atu II, III, XVII) show the Feminine Symbol (Yin) in three forms composing a Triune Goddess. This Trinity is immediately followed by the three corresponding and complementary Fathers, Vau, Tzaddi, Yod (Atu IV, V, IX). The Trumps 0 and I are hermaphrodite. The remaining fourteen Trumps represent these Primordial Quintessences of Being in conjunction, function, or manifestation.[17]

If the above leaves you somewhat unexcited let me get out my Crowlese-English dictionary and attempt to translate.

Eight trumps (the Fool, the Magus, the High Priestess, the Empress, the Emperor, the Hierophant, the Hermit, and the Star) are a special class of trump. They are primordial quintessences of being. (Just for fun, let's call these eight first-class trumps.)

These first-class trumps are divided by gender into three categories:

1. The Fool and the Magus are hermaphrodite;
2. The High Priestess, the Empress, and the Star show the feminine symbol in three forms;
3. The Emperor, the Hierophant, and the Hermit show the masculine symbol in three forms. These three correspond and are complementary to the High Priestess, the Empress, and the Star (though Crowley is not clear how they are paired).

Each of the remaining fourteen trumps (let's call them second-class trumps) represents one or more of the first-class trumps, and they do so in one of three ways:

1. As an expression of the character and behavior of the first-class trump when it is combined with one or more of its seven fellows;
2. As an expression of how the first-class trump functions;
3. As an expression of how the first-class trump manifests.

Crowley doesn't give us any examples and leaves us to our own devices as to how to apply this doctrine, but just a few minutes with the cards can provide much food for thought. For example (and the most obvious), the second-class trump the Lovers can be studied as the expression of the character and behavior of first-class trump the Empress when combined with first-class trump the Emperor (or for that matter with the High Priestess and the Hermit).

This exercise, and many more you are likely to discover in your tarot career, will naturally become more effective (and more fun) as you become more familiar with the cards. In my opinion, the most important thing to keep in mind is that none of the trumps (indeed, no single tarot card) stands alone. They are all intimately interconnected. The Major Arcana is one master play with twenty-two modular acts that can be performed in an infinite numbers of ways.

That being said, I think it's time we bring up the curtain and take a look at our cast of characters. Before we do, however, I would like to remind you that the tarot tells a story, and like a play or a movie, it is best to see it first from beginning to end to appreciate its message. Once you are familiar with the actors and plot, you can skip around to examine your favorite scenes and characters more closely. I therefore strongly suggest that the first time you read the following sections concerning the individual cards, you do so straight through and in the order they are presented.

The tarot's story is your story. Savor it. When you are finished reading it—you will be someone else.

CHAPTER FOURTEEN

ATU OF TAHUTI—
THE MAJOR ARCANA TRUMPS

All these symbols of the Trumps ultimately exist in a region beyond reason and above it. The study of these cards has for its most important aim the training of the mind to think clearly and coherently in this exalted manner. This has always been characteristic of the methods of Initiation as understood by the hierophants.[18]

ATU 0
THE FOOL

The Spirit of the Æther

Elemental Trump of Air

Original Design: A bearded ancient seen in profile. He laughs, bearing a sphere containing Illusion in his left hand, but over his right shoulder, a staff 463 lines long in his right. A lion and a dragon are at his feet, but he seems unaware of their attacks or caresses.[19]

Hebrew Letter: Aleph (ox).

Tree of Life: Path 11, joining ❶ Kether—Crown to ❷ Chokmah—Wisdom.

Colors: Bright Pale Yellow; Sky Blue; Blue Emerald Green; Emerald, flecked Gold.

Know Naught!

All ways are lawful to innocence.

Pure folly is the Key to Initiation.

Silence breaks into Rapture.

Be neither man nor woman, but both in one.
Be silent, Babe in the Egg of Blue, that thou mayest grow to bear the Lance and Graal!

Wander alone, and sing! In the King's palace his daughter awaits thee.[20]

I will struggle with the Fool. He does writhe about. I can't see him. Has he got any children with him & is not his bag a jester's balloon? That innocent gaiety asks for the brush of a saint & my lines come out like treacle. I wish I could paint in crystals.[21]

—Harris to Crowley date uncertain.

This may seem odd to you, but I am going to open my remarks about the first tarot trump, the Fool, by quoting what Crowley wrote about the last trump, the Universe:

In the card itself there is consequently a glyph of the completion of the Great Work in its highest sense, exactly as the Atu of the Fool symbolizes its beginning. The Fool is the negative issuing into manifestation; the Universe is that manifestation, its purpose accomplished, ready to return. The twenty cards that lie between these two exhibit the Great Work and its agents in various stages.[22]

In essence, there are not really twenty-two trumps, there is only one—the Fool. All the other trumps live inside (and issue from) the Fool. Of all seventy-eight tarot cards, none is more revered and misunderstood. In *The Book of Thoth* Crowley devotes over twenty-four pages to this card alone and, in doing so, gives us a whirlwind tour of the greatest hits of Greek, Roman, Hindu, Hebrew, pagan, and Christian mythology.

The most familiar image of the Fool is that of a young vagabond, his head wreathed with laurel or ivy. He holds a white rose and wears a motley coat. Over his shoulder rests a staff, at the end of which is tied a bag or satchel. A dog or a crocodile sometimes nips at his feet. He strolls mindlessly toward the edge of a high mountain cliff, his eyes cast irresponsibly skyward. He still has one foot upon the earth, the other poised to take the fateful step into the abyss. Lady Harris's Fool is different. This Fool has both feet planted unfirmly in air!

Why is the Fool such a mysterious and awesome character? Isn't he just another mediaeval cast member jesting to the Emperor, Empress, and Hierophant? Perhaps. That picture certainly fits many of the traditional images of this card. From a mystical point of view, however, the Fool is much more (actually, much, much less). The Fool propounds the ultimate riddle. Creation and the meaning of life are an incomprehensible joke. The Fool is more than God. The Fool is the "nothing" we refer to when we say, "Nothing created God. Nothing is beyond God. Nothing is greater than God." The Fool is perfectly empty-headed, for if there were anything inside, his innocence would be destroyed.

As the first trump it is only logical that the Fool be considered Key number 1. He is not, however, Key number 1. He is Key number 0. This is the Fool's first and greatest trick—creating the one (and consequently everything else) out of nothing.

"That's crazy!" your rational mind says; and your rational mind is correct—up to a point. It doesn't make sense that something can come out of nothing. If we wanted to personify the irrational concept of something coming from nothing, however, what better mascot could we choose than that of an idiot who makes no sense—a fool?

I have seen several early drafts that Crowley rejected. To my absolute delight, I discovered that two of them bore the unmistakable image of Harpo Marx. How perfect! In Marx Brothers' films, Harpo was the archetypal fool. Even his name betrayed his identity. Not only was he the girl-chasing clown who made fools of all the straightlaced and uptight characters, he did it all without saying a word. He was silent like the very mythological characters from whom the Fool is constructed; silent like Harpocrates, the Greek god of innocence; silent like Dionysus when he was asked by king Pentheus "What is Truth?"; silent like Christ standing before Pilate when he was asked the exact same question.

The Fool of the Thoth Tarot retains the familiar elements of traditional decks, but boldly asserts that the character we are dealing with is none other than the inscrutable supreme deity of every age and culture. He is the pagan Green Man of spring; Parsifal, the pure fool who wins the Holy Grail; Hoor-Pa-Kraat, the innocent Egyptian lord of silence, who treads upon the crocodile god Sebek, the Devourer. His wild eyes, horns, tiger, pine cones, grapes, and ivy show him to be the secret essence of the cosmos worshipped for centuries as Dionysus. Dionysus Zagreus, the horned son of Zeus, and Bacchus Diphues, the drunken and mad omni-sexual god of divine ecstasy.

Lady Harris's Fool is a cornucopia of sacred images, many of which reveal themselves only after long meditation (and the aid of a magnifying glass). He bursts into midair of existence from behind three swirling rings that issue from and return to his heart. These are the three veils of negativity (Ain, Ain Soph, and Ain Soph Aur)[23] that Qabalists teach gave birth to the singularity of creation. His satchel is filled with the entire universe in the form of planetary and zodiacal coins.

The Fool is the Holy Spirit itself. The dove, symbol of the Holy Spirit; the butterfly, symbol of transformation; winged globe, symbol of Mercurial air; and the Egyptian vulture-goddess Maut[24] pour from the Holy Grail in the Fool's right hand. Like the Virgin Mary, Maut became impregnated by the spirit (breath) of the wind. "The whole picture," Crowley tells us, "is a glyph of the creative light."[25]

With that in mind, I would finally like to draw the reader's attention to the image of the Sun covering the groin area of the Fool, and the almost invisible image of the Moon directly above the head of the crocodile. Between these two primary symbols of male and female are what Crowley describes as "twin infants embracing on the middle spiral. Above them hangs the benediction of three flowers in one."[26]

We can only speculate on the meanings of these symbols. In my opinion, it is highly likely that they allude, at least in part, to certain aspects of sexual alchemy that Crowley was not inclined to dwell upon in detail in published material. Certainly, the powers and unlimited potential of the generative processes might fall appropriately into the category of "the creative light." Other speculations aside, here at the very beginning of our study of the other cards I ask that you not lose sight of the obvious fact that the Fool's genitals are hidden by the Sun.

ATU I
THE MAGUS

The Magus of Power

Planetary Trump of Mercury

Original Design: A fair youth with winged helmet and heels, equipped as a Magician, displays his art. His attitude suggests the shape of the Swastika or thunderbolt, the message of God.[27]

Hebrew Letter: Beth (house).

Tree of Life: Path 12, joining ❶ Kether—Crown to ❸ Binah—Understanding.

Colors: Yellow; Purple; Grey; and Indigo, rayed Violet.

The True Self is the meaning of the True Will: know Thyself through Thy Way!

Calculate well the Formula of Thy Way!

Create freely; absorb joyously; divide intently; consolidate completely.

Work thou, Omnipotent, Omniscient, Omnipresent, in and for Eternity.[28]

I have had a wrapper for the catalogue made by the Sun Engraving Co. This will be beautifully printed with the Magician reproduced perfectly as a card, the right size & engraved on it."[29]

—Harris to Crowley May 11, 1941.

Before I discuss the symbolism of the Magus card, I have to set to rest the absurd rumor that Crowley intended there to be three Magus cards in the Thoth Tarot. By no stretch of imagination did Crowley intend to create twenty-four trumps or an eighty-card tarot deck. Any theory or suggestion to the contrary would have him spinning in his grave (if he had one) and displays a profound ignorance of Crowley and *The Book of Thoth*. Crowley approved only one Magus card for inclusion in the Thoth Tarot. It is the image reproduced in *The Book of Thoth* and is the only Magus in the deck currently included in decks published by U.S. Games Systems, Inc.

The mystery of the three magi of the Thoth Tarot, is no mystery at all. The seventy-eight cards of a standard tarot deck are printed on four sheets of twenty cards per sheet. This provides room for eighty card-size images per print run. Most publishers fill the extra spaces by printing two instructional or promotional cards. Rather than doing that, the Swiss publishers, A. G. Mueller, decided to treat Crowley/Harris aficionados to a little bonus by filling the extra spaces with two earlier versions of the Magus that Harris completed but Crowley rejected. The two extra magi are nothing more esoteric than a thoughtful bonus from a generous publisher. So please, no more talk of the Three Wise Men!

The Magus is not only the title of the Mercurial trump that, in older decks, bears the title Magician or Juggler; it is also a title of the second highest level of spiritual illumination a human soul can attain. Toward the end of his life, Crowley calculated he reached this initiatory degree on his fortieth birthday, October 12, 1915 E.V. Six years previously, on December 17, 1909, in the North African Sahara near Biskra, Algeria, he recorded his ceremonially induced vision of the third Enochian Aethyr[30] that is the source of much of the imagery found in the Magus card. He describes it as follows:

> Mercury is pre-eminently the bearer of the Wand: Energy sent forth. This card therefore represents the Wisdom, the Will, the Word, the Logos by whom the worlds were created. . . . It represents the Will. In brief, he is the Son, the manifestation in act of the idea of the Father. He is the male correlative of the High Priestess.[31]

The Magus is also the first of the alchemical trumps, and represents the alchemical element and principal of Mercury. "Mercury," Crowleys explains, "represents action in all forms and phases. His is the fluidic basis of all transmission of activity; and, on the dynamic theory of the Universe, he is himself the substance thereof."[32]

The figure of the Magus actually forms the alchemical glyph of Mercury. The two snakes at his head are the horns and the huge stylized wings at his feet make the arrowhead. He is projected upon the caduceus of Mercury. Behind the left wing at his feet, barely visible, is a golden sunburst affirming Mercury's role as herald of the Sun. Behind the right wing is the Cynolcephalus, the Ape of Thoth. This creature, who seems to be groping its way up from the lower right-hand corner of the card, is the personification of an ironic curse that afflicts Thoth-Mercury and all who attain the grade of Magus. Because falsehood and misunderstanding are inherent in all speech and writing, it is the cosmic duty of the Ape of Thoth to constantly mock the work of the Magus and distort his words. As Crowley points out, "Manifestation implies illusion."[33]

The traditional weapons of the Magus are the wand, cup, sword, and disk. "With the Wand," Crowley observes, "createth He. With the Cup preserveth He. With the Dagger destroyth He. With the Coin redeemeth He."[34] These are the weapons the Magus joyfully juggles in midair along with four additional symbols: the style, papyrus, torch, and winged egg. The wand is the phoenix wand that symbolizes resurrection through the natural generative process; the cup is of Grecian style with two handles; the sword appears to be a stiletto, the weapon of stealth, deceit, and vengeance; the disk displays the eightfold star of Mercury; the style and papyrus are tools and instruments of the scribe.

The winged egg is an especially important factor in the evolving symbolism of the Thoth Tarot. In this card, it aptly represents the preexistent zero, which, like the Magus himself, is the source of all positive manifestation, but it will soon reappear in Atu VI, the Lovers, and other trumps as the symbol known as the Orphic egg. As the trumps develop, this egg will undergo a most wonderful alchemical adventure, one that is that is told only in the Thoth Tarot.

Other elements of the card are at first difficult to see. If we look carefully, we see that the caduceus is much larger than it first appears. Its rod reaches below the feet of the Magus to the very bottom of the card, where, by virtue of its upward thrust, it appears to have stretched and finally penetrated the membrane of space.[35] The wings of the caduceus span the entire width of the top of the card and reach down behind the neck of the Magus. What appears to be a downward-pointing arrow in the disk of the caduceus is actually the symbol of the descending dove.

ATU II
THE HIGH PRIESTESS

The Priestess of the Silver Star

Planetary Trump of the Moon

Original Design: A crowned priestess sits before the veil of Isis between the pillars of Seth. She is reading intently in an open book.[36]

Hebrew Letter: Gimel (camel).

Tree of Life: Path 13, joining ❶ Kether—Crown to ❻ Tiphareth—Beauty.

Colors: Blue; Silver; Cold Pale Blue; and Silver, rayed Sky Blue.

Purity is to live only to the Highest; and the Highest is All: be thou as Artemis to Pan!

Read thou in The Book of the Law, and break through the veil of the Virgin![37]

The Moon, partaking as she does of the highest and the lowest and filling all the space between, is the most universal of the Planets.[38]

It may seem curious that the Priestess represents the Moon, but Atu XVIII, the Moon, represents the zodiac sign of Pisces. We will see what Crowley has to say about that when we discuss the Moon. Here, let's be satisfied to know that the Priestess represents the Moon in her higher aspect—the aspect that joins the human to the divine. The Moon in Atu XVIII is—well—something else.

As the only middle-pillar path that spans the Abyss, the position of the High Priestess on the Tree of Life is unique. She links the ultimate Father of Kether to the Son of Tiphareth and, in doing so, joins the supernal triad to the rest of the Tree. "In this card," Crowley points out, "is the one link between the archetypal and formative worlds."[39] The Abyss she traverses is, quite literally, the desert of the soul, and like the desert camel, she is the only vehicle capable of crossing that terrible wasteland.

The principal deities connected with this card are those who, by tradition, represent the lunar goddess, virgin priestess, huntress, and, most importantly, the powers and mysteries of woman as the initiatrix. If you look carefully, you will see that her bow is actually a three-stringed harp "for she is a huntress, and hunts by enchantment."[40]

This card is a textbook display of the graphic principles of synthetic projective geometry.[41] The arms of the Priestess sweep upward, pulling and distorting the webbed network of space and light, forming the crescent bowl of a magnificent Moon-colored cup.[42] The pillars on either side of her are obscured by the diagonal webbing and somewhat difficult to see, but it is important to be conscious of their presence when meditating on the composition of the card. Harris has brilliantly executed Crowley's description as

> the most spiritual form of Isis the Eternal Virgin; the Artemis of the Greeks. She is clothed only in the luminous veil of light. It is important for high initiation to regard Light not as the perfect manifestation of the Eternal Spirit, but rather as the veil which hides that Spirit. It does so all the more effectively because of its incomparably dazzling brilliance. Thus she is light and the body of light. She is the truth behind the Veil of Light. She is the soul of light.[43]

The High Priestess is the initiatrix. Initiation means "beginning." The objects that appear at the bottom of the card are not lunar symbols per se. The camel is, of course, indicative of the Hebrew letter Gimel (the Hebrew letter attributed to the High Priestess), but the other objects, the crystals and seeds, are suggestive of the hidden and mysterious secrets of the beginning of life.

ATU III
THE EMPRESS

The Daughter of the Mighty Ones

Planetary Trump of Venus

Original Design: Crowned with stars, a winged goddess stands upon the moon. She bears a scepter and a shield, whereon is figured a dove as symbol of the male and female forces.[44]

Hebrew Letter: Daleth (door).

Tree of Life: Path 14, joining ❷ Chokmah—Wisdom to ❸ Binah—Understanding.

Colors: Emerald Green; Sky Blue; Early Spring Green; Bright Rose or cerise, rayed pale green.

This is the Harmony of the Universe, that Love unites the Will to create with the Understanding of that Creation: understand thou thine own Will!

Love and let love. Rejoice in every shape of love, and get thy rapture and thy nourishment thereof.[45]

It is impossible to summarize the meanings of the symbol of the Woman, for this very reason, that she continually recurs in infinitely varied form. "Many-throned, many-minded, many-wiled, daughter of Zeus."[46]

Thank you very much Mr. Crowley!

At least we can say this—Daleth means door, and woman is the door of heaven when we are conceived, and the door of life and when we are born. The Empress is the trump of Venus and, in mythology, Venus, or Aphrodite, certainly had (or seemed to cause) her share of trouble. Most of the time, however, she was less the guileful instigator of mischief and more the tragic victim of circumstances. In either case, almost everybody was in love with her, and she certainly added a bit of spice to the Olympian soap opera.

Speaking of spice, the Empress is the second of the alchemical trumps and represents the element and principal of salt. Like Venus reclining on her love-couch awaiting the arrival of her next lover, Crowley describes her as "the inactive principle of Nature; Salt is matter which must be energized by Sulfur to maintain the whirling equilibrium of the Universe."[47]

Sulfur, as we will see in the next trump, is represented by the Emperor—who represents the zodiacal sign of Aries—which is ruled by Mars—who was the lover of Venus. (It gets scary when this stuff starts to make sense, doesn't it?)

This card is more than just the full-color foldout of the Scarlet O'Hara of the gods, however. The path of Daleth is one of only three paths on the Tree of Life that lies entirely above the Abyss. It connects the second sephira, Chokmah (the Supernal Father) to the third sephira, Binah (the Supernal Mother). This is the hallway down which the queen of our Qabalistic fairytale tiptoes to get to the bedroom of the king. This is the path of the exchange of unimaginable love.

Harris's Empress is perhaps the most tasteful and soothing card in the pack. The cool colors immediately lower my blood pressure. At first glance, she appears to be the goddess of vegetation, which is exactly what she is. Her presence cuts a doorway through towering plants and grasses. The supports of her throne are formed from twisted blades of grass, and upon their tops are perched the sparrow and dove, birds sacred to Venus. Her green skirt is topped with a blouse of passionate red, ornamented with bees and what appear to be dominos surrounded by spiral rings. Around her waist is the golden belt of the zodiac.

Her arms suggest the glyph of salt. She bears the lotus scepter in her left hand, and her right hand and arm curve delicately as if she were holding an invisible baby to her breast. This is the magical gesture called Mater Triumphans (Isis suckling the infant Horus). Perhaps this is just a rehearsal for what is to come. The Empress, if you haven't noticed, is pregnant (her baby floating blissfully in a salty sea of amniotic fluid).

In keeping with the motherhood theme, we find, at the lower left of the card, a white pelican feeding its young from the blood of her own breast. On the lower right is a shield displaying a white double-headed eagle holding the Moon in its beaks. This represents the alchemical white tincture whose nature is of the Moon and silver. There is also a red tincture, and we'll discover it in the next trump, the Emperor.

All of these symbols sit upon a carpet adorned with fleurs-de-lis and tiny fish that Crowley suggests "seem to be adoring the Secret Rose which is indicated at the base of the throne."[48] The secret rose of the Empress is certainly worthy of adoration. Her credentials are impeccable:

> I am Nature and God: I reign, I am, alone.
>   None other may abide apart: they perish,
> Drawn into me, into my being grown.
>   None other bosom is, to bear, to nourish,
> To be: the heart of all beneath my zone
>   Of blue and gold is scarlet-bright to cherish
> My own's life being, that is, and is not other;
> For I am God and Nature and thy Mother."[49]

ATU IV
THE EMPEROR

Sun of the Morning, chief among the Mighty

Zodiacal Trump of Aries

Mars Rules—Sol Exalted

Original Design: A flame-clad god bearing equivalent symbols. His attitude suggests the symbol of alchemical sulfur, and he is seated upon the cubical stone, whose sides show the green lion and white eagle.[50]

Hebrew Letter: Tzaddi (fish hook).

Tree of Life: Path 28, joining ❼ Netzach—Victory to ❾ Yesod—Foundation.

Colors: Scarlet; Red; Brilliant Flame; Glowing Red.

Use all thine energy to rule thy thought: burn up thy thought as the Phoenix.[51]

I have only just got your letters returned today after travelling from 11 A.M. to 7.30 P.M. Sitting in stations & huddling with savage soldiers & children in stuffy railway carriages.[52]

—Harris to Crowley, May 21, 1941.

In chapter 13, I mentioned a paragraph in *The Book of Thoth* where Crowley throws us a real curve regarding the whole "Tzaddi is not the Star" matter. It is one of several instances in the book where he seems to contradict himself on this subject. Before I go on about the Emperor, I will try to overcome my complete exasperation and calmly address this most frustrating issue. The trouble, it seems, stems from the direction the light comes from in this card. Let's start by reviewing what Crowley tells us in no uncertain terms (and in multiple places) is the situation:

1. Atu IV is the Emperor.
2. The zodiac sign assigned to the Emperor is Aries.
3. The Hebrew letter for the Emperor is צ Tzaddi (and everything צ Tzaddi represents).

4. On the Tree of Life, the Emperor is found on path 28, which joins the seventh sephira, Netzach, to the ninth sephira, Yesod.

Fine! I'm happy with that. It agrees with Crowley's detailed explanations for the Tzaddi/Hé switch. It agrees with his charts and diagrams of the Tree of Life. What it doesn't agree with is the last paragraph of his comments on the Emperor on page 78 of *The Book of Thoth*, where he tells us:

> It is finally to be observed that the white light which descends upon him indicates the position of this card in the Tree of Life. His authority is derived from Chokmah, the creative Wisdom, the Word, and is exerted upon Tiphareth, the organized man.[53]

The "white light" in the card issues from the upper right corner and shines diagonally toward the center of the card. In other words, Crowley is talking as if the Emperor is positioned on the Tree of Life on the path that runs from the second sephira, Chokmah, to the sixth sephira, Tiphareth—the path that he tells us in nearly every other reference should be occupied by the Star. Arghhhh!

Personally, I think that, in this case, Harris, was operating from the traditional understanding of the trumps and their placement on the tree, and Crowley's words carelessly neglected to make that point. Still, I am sure that students of tarot and Crowley will debate this subject forever. As for me, the only thing I know for sure is that the author of *The Book of the Law* himself tells us, "All these old letters of my Book are aright but צ is not the Star."[54] Now, let's move on—please!

Atu IV, the Emperor, represents the sign of Aries, where Mars rules and Sol is exalted. "The sign," Crowley points out, "is thus a combination of energy in its most material form with the idea of authority."[55] Referring to this card, Crowley even goes so far as to actually give us a somewhat cynical lesson in civics:

> He is seated upon the throne whose capitals are the heads of the Himalayan wild ram, since Aries means a Ram. At his feet, couchant, is the Lamb and Flag, to confirm this attribution on the lower plane; for the ram, by nature, is a wild and courageous animal, lonely in lonely places, whereas when tamed and made to lie down in green pastures, nothing is left but the docile, cowardly, gregarious and succulent beast. This is the theory of government.[56]

The Emperor is the third of the alchemical trumps and represents sulfur. His arms form the triangle and his legs form the cross of the glyph of sulfur, which Crowley tells us is "the male fiery energy of the Universe, the Rajas of Hindu philosophy. This is the swift creative energy, the initiative of all Being."[57]

Upon his shield is the red eagle that identifies him with what the alchemists call the red tincture. The red tincture is symbolic of the fiery action and nature of the Sun and gold, just as the white eagle on the Empress's shield identifies her with the white tincture, symbolic of the action and nature of the Moon and silver. The great alchemical recipe dictates that we must first find the white tincture, then the red tincture, then unite them to accomplish the great work. This, of course, suggests that the Empress and the Emperor enjoy a much more intimate relationship than what we expect of governmental officials. We will see them get very cozy in Atu XIV, Art.

ATU V
THE HIEROPHANT

The Magus of the Eternal

Zodiacal Trump of Taurus

Venus Rules—Luna Exalted

Original Design: Between the pillars sits an ancient. He is crowned, sceptered, and blessing all in a threefold manner. Four living creatures adore him, the whole suggesting a pentagram by its shape.[58]

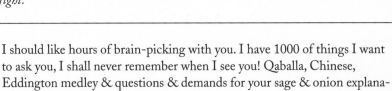

Hebrew Letter: Vau (nail).

Tree of Life: Path 16, joining ❷ Chokmah—Wisdom to ❹ Chesed—Mercy.

Colors: Red; Orange; Deep Indigo; Deep warm Olive; Rich Brown.

Offer thyself Virgin to the Knowledge and
Conversation of thine Holy Guardian Angel!
All else is a snare.

Be thou athlete with the eight limbs of Yoga;
for without these thou are not disciplined for
any fight.[59]

I should like hours of brain-picking with you. I have 1000 of things I want to ask you, I shall never remember when I see you! Qaballa, Chinese, Eddington medley & questions & demands for your sage & onion explanations pierce the ether all round me.[60]
> —Harris to Crowley, January 28, 1940.

This card is so rich in traditional and Thelemic symbolism that it is difficult to know where to begin. One thing is immediately obvious—this is not your Aeon-of-Osiris Pope. The whole card is presented as the shrine of the Hierophant of the Aeon of Horus, and this guy has some sex appeal.

Instead of the pale, humorless features of a delicate prelate officiating at some demure worship service, we are thrilled by the bold, confident image of a Babylonian priest-king—an initiator in every sense of the word. He's not humbly served by docile acolytes like the Osirian Hierophant; instead he is actively supported in his work by his sword-bearing Scarlet Woman, the embodiment of heavenly Venus who rules Taurus. "Let the woman be girt with a sword before me," *The Book of the Law* commands.[61] "This woman," Crowley states, "represents Venus as she now is in this new aeon; no longer the mere vehicle of her male counterpart, but armed and militant."[62]

She carries the Moon, which is exalted in the sign of Taurus. Moreover, we see evidence of this new initiatory love relationship dramatically highlighted in the ornate window that illuminates the shrine, which Crowley describes thus:

> This symbolism is further carried out in the oriel where, behind the phallic headdress, the rose of five petals is in blossom. The symbolism of the snake and dove refers to this verse of *The Book of the Law*—chap. I, verse 57; "there are love and love. There is the dove, and there is the serpent."[63]

The window is held in place by nine nails, the number nine being symbolic of the ninth sephira, Yesod, the sphere of the Moon. The Hierophant's shrine is guarded (as every good shrine should be) by the four Kerubic beasts. And here I think we should address what appears at first glance to be a mistake Lady Harris has made as to the positioning of the four Kerubic beasts.

The four Kerubic beasts represent the four fixed signs of the zodiac: Leo (the fixed sign of fire, symbolized by the Lion), Scorpio (the fixed sign of water, symbolized by the eagle), Aquarius (the fixed sign of air, symbolized by a man or angel), and Taurus (the fixed sign of earth, symbolized by the bull). Tarot decks, reaching back to the earliest packs, have traditionally displayed the Kerubic beasts in the corners of various trumps (most often the Wheel of Fortune and the World). The placement of the four beasts on these old decks is almost universally consistent—the lion of Leo is in the lower right corner; the eagle of Scorpio is in the upper right; the man or angel of Aquarius is in the upper left; and the bull of Taurus is in the lower left. This is the natural order of the fixed signs as they appear on the zodiacal belt, and the logical place to put them.

In the Thoth Tarot, however, Harris appears to break with this tradition in her placement of the Kerubic beasts in the Hierophant and the Universe trumps. The bull and the lion dutifully occupy the traditional corners, but the angel and the eagle have switched positions. Could it be that she was ignorant of the order of the signs of the zodiac and that Crowley let her get away with it in two important cards? Could it be that, in the Aeon of Horus, the signs of the zodiac have been rearranged? The answer to both of these questions is "no." In the New Aeon, it's not the position of the zodiac signs, but the symbols of the Kerubs, that have changed.

In Crowley's vision of the twenty-third Enochian Æthyr, it is revealed that the emblem for fixed-air Aquarius is now the eagle, and the emblem for fixed-water Scorpio is now the angel:

The Beast and the Scarlet Woman are attributed to Leo and Scorpio. They are the two-in-one Chief Officers of the Temple of the New Æon of Heru-Ra-Ha. (Note the Eagle Kerub in the 23 Aire is Aquarius. Scorpio is the Woman-Serpent. This is important, for the old attribution is of the Eagle to Scorpio[64]

The Hierophant's throne is flanked by elephants. He is seated upon the bull of Taurus itself. He holds in his right hand a wand surmounted by three rings symbolizing the ascendancy of the Aeon of Horus from the preceding Aeons of Isis and Osiris. His left hand is open in benediction.

All this New Aeon imagery is wonderful, but what we should keep foremost in our minds is the fact that the Hierophant, is the ו Vau of הוהי YHVH. He is the six of the divine macrocosmic consciousness to whom we must "nail" the five of our earthly microcosmic consciousness. He is the Prince Charming in the cosmic fairytale—our Holy Guardian Angel. The initiatory level characterized by the knowledge and conversation with the H.G.A is illustrated on this card by the union of the pentagram and hexagram. Our microcosmic self is the dancing child in the pentagram upon the Hierophant's macrocosmic breast. The hexagram can be seen enclosing the whole body of the Hierophant.

ATU VI
THE LOVERS

The Children of the Voice

The Oracle of the Mighty Gods

Zodiacal Trump of Gemini

Mercury Rules—Dragon's Head Exalted

Original Design: A prophet, young, and in the sign of Osiris Risen. He is inspired by Apollo to prophesy concerning things sacred and profane: represented by a boy with his bow and two women, a priestess and an harlot.[65]

Hebrew Letter: Zain (sword).

Tree of Life: Path 17, joining ❸ Binah—Understanding to ❻ Tiphareth—Beauty.

Colors: Orange; Pale Mauve; New Yellow leather; Reddish Grey, inclined to mauve.

The Oracle of the Gods is the Child-Voice of
Love in thine own Soul! hear thou it!

Heed not the Siren-Voice of Sense, or the
Phantom-Voice of Reason: rest in Simplicity,
and listen to the Silence.[66]

Dear Aleister, I have been struggling with a bad cold & the Lovers—the latter begins to cheer up. I haven't decided whether I'll come back & brood on the Fool or stay here.[67]

—Harris to Crowley, date uncertain.

Atu VI, the Lovers, is the fourth of the alchemical trumps. A familiar alchemical maxim reads *solve et coagula*, "solution and coagulation." The process of *solve* is represented in tarot by the Lovers; the process of *coagula* in the Art card. This makes sense astrologically because, in the zodiac, Gemini (the Lovers) is opposite Sagittarius (Art). Between these two trumps are other trumps that represent developmental phases between *solve et coagula*.

Solve et coagula is a story of a marriage and pregnancy. The main character in this alchemical love story is not the bride nor the groom, but the child of their union. In the

Thoth Tarot, the child is symbolized as the Orphic egg that, as Crowley reminds us, "represents the essence of all life that comes under the formula of male and female."[68]

Like the events surrounding the birth of any child, our alchemical scenario develops in stages. Atu VI, the Lovers, is the wedding ceremony; Atu XIV, Art, is the honeymoon; in Atu IX, the Hermit fertilizes the egg; and Atu XIII, Death, keeps it nice and warm in the last stage before hatching.

This card is a scene from one of the most famous alchemical texts of all time, *The Chymical Marriage of Christian Rosenkreutz*, which Crowley describes as "a masterpiece too lengthy and diffuse to quote in this place. But the essence of the analysis is the continuous see-saw of contradictory ideas. It is a glyph of duality."[69] Let's look how Lady Harris uses this card to set the scene for the first phase of this great romance.

Starting at the bottom of the card, we find the Orphic egg. It has wings as if it just flew in from the Magus card. In this beginning phase of the operation, it is just the latent seed of life. It sits between a white eagle and a red lion symbolic of the female and male components of our formula—the white and red tinctures of the Empress and the Emperor. Later, in the Art card, we will see the advanced stage of the operation—the red lion will turn white and the white eagle will turn red.

The children attending the bride and groom are none other than Cain and Abel. Their presence, together with Lilith and Eve in the upper corners, springs from Crowley's vision of the Second Aethyr of *The Vision and The Voice*. The bride is white and wears a silver crown. She holds a golden cup that bears the image of the descending dove of the Holy Spirit. Her robe is ornamented with bees like the ones we saw on the blouse of the Empress and the Emperor. The groom is black and wears a golden crown. He holds the sacred lance, the complementary weapon to the bride's cup. His robe is ornamented with snakes like those found on the blouse of the Emperor.

The officiating priest is none other than the Hermit of Atu IX. He makes the magical sign of the Enterer by thrusting his hands forward over the couple. Around his arms a scroll of the word (the cosmic marriage certificate) is twisted to form the eternal mobius strip.

Above all their heads, the blindfolded figure of Cupid or Eros aims his arrow threateningly in a direction that appears to threaten no one. This is the downward arrow[70] spoken of by the angel of the fifth Aethyr of *The Vision and The Voice*. The downward arrow is said to be shot by "the topmost point"[71] of the Yod of YHVH. As we learned in chapter 9, the Yod has its topmost point in Kether, but it resides mostly in Chokmah. As we see in the Lovers, Cupid is pointing his arrow directly from Kether to Chokmah.

The entire ceremony takes place beneath an arch of steel swords (Zain, the Hebrew letter attributed to the Lovers, means "Sword."). We will see how all this symbolism reverses and blends when we discuss Atu XIV, Art. But first, we have other trumps to discuss, including those that represent the alchemical phases between *solve et coagula*.

ATU VII
THE CHARIOT

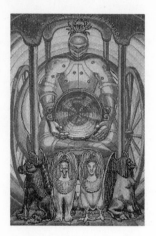

The Child of the Powers of the Waters

The Lord of the Triumph of Light

Zodiacal Trump of Cancer

Luna Rules—Jupiter Exalted

Original Design: A young and holy king under the starry canopy. He drives furiously a chariot drawn by two sphinxes. As Levi drew it.[72]

Hebrew Letter: Cheth (fence).

Tree of Life: Path 18, joining ❸ Binah—Understanding to ❺ Geburah—Severity.

Colors: Amber; Maroon; Rich bright Russet; Dark greenish Brown.

The Issue of the Vulture, Two-in-One,
conveyed; this is the Chariot of Power.

TRINC: the last oracle![73]

> The alteration of Abracadabra (Charioteer) & the Taurus Disk card are complete. Please forgive this brief statement, it is because I know your are so lucid and logical that I can write & tell you I have taken such arbitrary action without consulting you as you will realize this was a moment to say "Snap!"[74]
> —Harris to Crowley, May 11, 1941.

I hope the reader will forgive me for not spending a great deal of time discussing the superficial features of this card. They are much like those found in traditional versions of this trump. The Chariot is drawn by sphinxes representing the elemental blending of the Kerubic beasts. The starry canopy of the chariot represents the night sky. The charioteer is in full armor, much like the crab of the zodiac sign of Cancer, which this card represents. He bears the Holy Grail, in this case a magnificent carved amethyst (sacred to Jupiter, which is exalted in Cancer). The whole is a rendering of Crowley's vision of the 12th Aethyr in *The Vision and The Voice*.[75]

What I would like to focus upon is a secret of sexual alchemy that Crowley seemed anxious to convey in his comments on the Chariot in *The Book of Thoth*.

Let's start by reviewing the above quote from Crowley's "General Characters of the Trumps as They Appear in Use":

The Issue of the Vulture, Two-in-One,
conveyed; this is the Chariot of Power.

TRINC: the last oracle![76]

This is perhaps the most obscure of all the verses of that work. It talks about "Two-in-One, conveyed"; The Chariot, of course, conveys the charioteer, who conveys the Holy Grail. Therefore, the Holy Grail must represent (or contain) the Two-in-One. But what is the Holy Grail and what is the Two-in-One?

Grail mythology tells us that the Holy Grail is the cup from which Christ drank at the Last Supper, and the same one that Joseph of Aramathea used to catch the blood and water that spilled from the liplike spear wound in the side of the crucified Christ. Joseph later conveyed the Grail and the spear to a magically constructed castle, where their mysterious powers complicated the lives of many generations of noble knights. In one very real way, the Chariot is the Chapel of the Holy Grail on wheels.

Am I trying to tell you that the precious bodily fluids of Christ are really ingredients of the Two-in-One cocktail of the Holy Grail? In a way, yes. But let's look at it another way—let's look at it as "The Issue of the Vulture."

In Egyptian mythology, the vulture was sacred to Maat, the goddess of justice and supreme balance. The vulture was said to conceive without mating. Its child immaculately conceived in a mysterious internal process that, for other creatures, requires contributions of from both male and female. The Issue of the Vulture is therefore the product (or child) of an internal marriage of two perfectly balanced things, or Two-in-One.

That's all fine and good, but in real life, vultures mate like every other bird, and even if they didn't, how would we humans go about emulating that magical process. For us, neither the male nor the female is a complete human unit capable of reproduction. What is absent in the male is present in the female, and vice versa. Our creation of the Two-in-One that results in the issue of a human baby is the most natural and (and usually the most pleasant) of all cooperative endeavors. How are the principles that effect the very human sexual act reflected on a cosmic scale, however? What would we do with the real Two-in-One even if we knew how to create it?

The answer is "TRINC," an oracular word that comes from the story of Gargantua and Pantagruel, a mystical satire by François Rabelais (1494–1553). In the story, one of the main characters, Panurge, seeks the answer to the question, "Should I marry?" He and his companions eventually decide to seek the Oracle of the Bottle for the answer. After many adventures, they finally reach the Temple of the Bottle." They pass through the door upon which is written *En Oino Aletheia* (In wine lies truth), where Bacbuc, the Priestess of the temple, takes them into the presence of the Holy Bottle. Panurge poses his question, and the Holy Bottle answers by making a sharp sound like that of cracking glass: "Trinc!" (Drink!). Panurge interprets this as an affirmative answer and an admonition to drink deep from the wellspring of life and knowledge.

As you have probably guessed, Panurge's question "Should I marry?" has deeper magical implications than simply questioning the wisdom or folly of matrimony. It should be of particular interest to us because we see so much "marrying" going on in the trumps of the Thoth Tarot. Recall that our Qabalistic fairytale in chapter 10 is all about marriage; the marriage of the Prince and Princess (the Holy Guardian Angel and his client), and the marriage of the supernal King and Queen. Two things becoming one seems to be a formula of supreme spiritual importance in the tarot. But Trinc (drink) is a curious answer to the question, "Should I marry?" Drink what?

The Hebrew letter associated with the Chariot is Cheth, which, when spelled in full, enumerates to 418, the same number as ABRAHADABRA, the magical word that expresses the formula of the marriage of the microcosm with the macrocosm (or the aspirant to his or her Holy Guardian Angel). This word (with a slight Lady Harris typo) can be seen embroidered in the canopy of the Chariot. ABRAHADABRA is also indicative of the uniting of male and female that we see expressed in other trumps as alchemical images such as the red/white lion and white/red eagle.

The Chariot represents the zodiac sign of Cancer, whose symbol is a not-too-subtle glyph for a particular technique of tantric yoga in which male and female energies and essences are perfectly prepared, balanced, and exchanged to create the Two-in-One elixir of life. The elixir is then conveyed in a particular manner to serve as a eucharistic talisman of unlimited creative potential.

In the language of Thelemic imagery, the elixir is brewed in the Holy Grail by Babalon/Nuit in Binah (the Queen of our Qabalistic fairytale), who then offers it to the Beast/Hadit in Chokmah (the King of our Qabalistic fairytale) and they both drink (TRINC) and become ecstatically drunken. In doing so, they annihilate all sense of separateness, and so on. (See chapter 10 if you need to review the whole story.)

The path of the Chariot crosses the Abyss and joins the fifth sephira, Geburah, to the third sephira, Binah. Being so high on the Tree of Life, its mysteries deal with the most sublime and profound aspects of nature and consciousness. Please keep this in mind when you are tempted to view this card (and my comments) as simply an expression of sexual alchemy. As effective as this operation can be, it is only a reflection of the magick of the gods, a faint echo of the titanic forces, energy, and love that creates, sustains, and destroys the universe.

ATU VIII
ADJUSTMENT

The Daughter of the Lords of Truth

The Ruler of the Balance

Zodiacal Trump of Libra

Venus Rules—Saturn Exalted

Original Design: A conventional figure of Justice with scales and balances.[77]

Hebrew Letter: Lamed (ox goad).

Tree of Life: Path 22, joining ❺ Geburah—Severity to ❻ Tiphareth—Beauty.

Colors: Emerald Green; Blue; Deep Blue-Green; Pale Green.

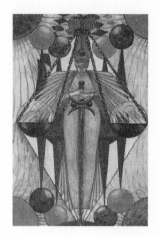

Balance against each thought its exact
Opposite! For the Marriage of these is the
Annihilation of Illusion.[78]

The Woman Satisfied. From the cloak of the vivid wantonness of her dancing wings issue her hands; they hold the hilt of the Phallic sword of the magician. She holds the blade between her thighs.[79]
   —Harris to Crowley, between November 3 and December 19, 1939.

I will do a new Justice, damn her. Do you think there was ever "a woman satisfied"? With what a smirk she would greet the dawn.[80]
   —Harris to Crowley, December 19, 1939.

My experience of satisfied women is that they do greet the dawn with a smirk; if not the dawn, any time up to five o'clock in the afternoon, and only when it wears off does one have to start all over again. . . .
  These notes on Justice, or as we have preferred to call her "Adjustment.". . . I suppose I was in a very bad temper when I made my criticism, but I do feel strongly that the plumes of Maat are too insignificant, and the Dove and Raven look simply stuck on; nor do I think that the tessellated pavement is quite right. The general criticism is that the card is a little too cold; Libra is the sign of autumn, season of mists and mellow fruit-

fulness, close-bosomed friend of the maturing sun. In your card you have got the idea of balance static, whereas it ought to be dynamic. Nature is not the grocer weighing out a pound of sugar; it is the compensation of complicated rhythms. I should like you to feel that every adjustment was a grande passion; compensation should be a festival, not a clerk smugly pleased that his accounts are correct. It seems to me that this doctrine is very important as a commentary on the text "Existence is pure joy", and I feel sure that the connection of Venus and Saturn with the sign is significant in this respect. The compensation is surely the awakening of the Eld of the All-Father, the constant reproduction of the original purity from the last stage of illusion. (Compare what I said above about the number Ten). . .

To return to "Adjustment"; those birds bother me very much. I don't think they belong. I think they come from Noah's Ark. It would be better to simplify this card by leaving them out altogether. I feel sure that when you get the Venus and Saturn dancing motive firmly in your mind, you will produce a lady whom you will like better.[81]

—Crowley to Harris, December 19, 1939

The Adjustment is being queer with me. She has, after all, insisted on being Beardsley![82] Also Harlequin comes in & out of it so I must have to submit. But why Harlequin? Is there any connection? Also she won't sit down but stands on her toes just balanced. The design-result is good. That blue is cobalt I take it. The instruction says Blue-Blue Green. Pale green Emerald. That Emerald is a vile pigment in poster paints.[83]

—Harris to Crowley, July 12, 1940.

Judging from what is written in the above excerpts from the Crowley-Harris correspondence, it is clear that the early drafts of Adjustment bore little resemblance to the finished product. Crowley obviously had a clear idea what was needed, and the fact that he wrote so passionately on the matter underscores the importance he ascribed to this trump. His words are aimed, however, not only at Frieda Harris, the artist, but at Soror Tzaba, the magical student. He not only wanted the Adjustment card to turn out the way he wanted, he wanted Harris to appreciate its spiritual importance and achieve an epiphany of understanding. It appears to me that they both were successful.

The goddess of Adjustment is in perfect balance, left to right and top to bottom. Amid spheres of light and darkness, she stands on tiptoe at the very point of her sword. An enormous set of balances suspends from the perfect point of her crown (the ostrich plumes of Maat, the Egyptian goddess of justice). The left scale pan holds the alpha, and the right the omega. The lines from her toes to the scale pans to the tip of her crown create a lozenge, a type of vesica[84] (by which students of mystic geometry measure the immeasurable), which stretches the fabric of space to reveal the goddess. Crowley calls Adjustment "the feminine complement of the Fool."[85]

The combined Hebrew letters these cards represent, Aleph and Lamed, spell AL and enumerate to 31. AL is the root of the Hebrew word for "God"; LA is the Hebrew word for "not." In the Western Zen of Thelema, "God-Not-God" is a very important concept.

ATU IX
THE HERMIT

The Prophet of the Eternal

The Magus of the Voice of Power

Zodiacal Trump of Virgo

Mercury Rules—Mercury Exalted

Original Design: Wrapped in a cloak and cowl, an ancient walketh, bearing a lamp and staff. Before him goeth upright the Royal Uræus Serpent.[86]

Hebrew Letter: Yod (hand).

Tree of Life: Path 20, joining ❹ Chesed—Mercy to ❻ Tiphareth—Beauty.

Colors: Green (yellowish); Slate Grey; Green Grey; Plum color.

Wander alone; bearing the Light and thy Staff! And be the Light so bright that no man seeth thee!

Be not moved by aught without or within: keep Silence in all ways![87]

> Why don't you like my egg question? Is it because you don't know the answer?[88]
>
> —Harris to Crowley, November 30, 1939.

By now, you are probably tired of hearing me talk about the special virtues inherent in the element earth. You probably think you've heard enough about how humble earth is uniquely connected to spirit, and how it helps regenerate the highest high because of the simple fact that it is the lowest low (see chapter 11).

Well, get ready to hear some more, because we are not through yet. As a matter of fact, in the pages that follow, you are going to get some pretty big doses of this doctrinal medicine that Crowley calls the "climax of the Descent into Matter."[89] Why is it so important for you to keep taking this medicine? First of all, because it will help you understand the living nature of tarot. More important, however, because *you* are the grand climax of the descent into matter.

I have tried to organize the material of this book so that by the time you read about the last card of the tarot, the Ten of Disks, you will be armed with enough occult knowledge to comprehend the great magick that takes place there. It is a process that Crowley calls, "the mode of fulfillment of the Great Work."[90]

I'm sure you wouldn't do this, but if you were to turn to the back of the book and read what I have written about the Ten of Disks, you would learn (albeit prematurely) that the three key cosmic players that are responsible for creating that "mode of fulfillment of the Great Work" are Earth, Mercury, and the Sun. That shouldn't surprise you really. After all, Earth is that special lowest-of-the-low element you're getting so tired of hearing about; tarot is the province of Thoth/Mercury; and the Sun is the secret seed of universal life that we knew was going be so important since we first saw it radiating from in front of the Fool's groin. Earth, Mercury, and the Sun have their first important strategy meeting in Atu IX, the Hermit.

Just look at how Earth, Mercury, and the Sun come together in the Hermit. He represents the zodiac sign of Virgo. Virgo is the mutable sign of Earth. Virgo is ruled by Mercury, and Mercury is exalted in Virgo. The Hermit carries the lamp of the Sun, with which he gives his light to the world. It's a simple as that.

We've met the Hermit once before as the hooded figure that officiates at the royal wedding in Atu VI, the Lovers, and, while he is sexually ambivalent, he is indeed a "he" and an important expression of male creative energy. The Hebrew letter sacred to Virgo and the Hermit is ' Yod, the tenth letter, and the first and supreme letter in הוהי YHVH. In a very real way, the tiny flame of Yod is the fundamental Hebrew letter. All the other letters are created from this basic form. As the hidden seed of the Hebrew alphabet, Yod also symbolizes the mystery of sperm, the hidden seed, and a central secret of fertilization. (See how the Hermit stares at the Orphic egg? If I were that egg, I'd be nervous!) Crowley writes, "In this Trump is shewn the entire mystery of Life in its most secret workings."[91]

While, in my opinion, this remains true, we have to remember that Crowley died before the discovery of DNA, and so his understanding of biology was naturally incomplete and based upon obsolete doctrines and theories. There is, however, an abundance of images in this card to handily accommodate more recent scientific discoveries, and it doesn't take a rocket scientist to tell us this card is loaded. Let's see how Harris graphically handles all of this.

First of all, the figure of the Hermit himself is one big stylized Yod. He sports the ibis head of Thoth/Mercury. The only other visible part is his hand. (Yod in Hebrew) He stands in the fertile field of wheat. The heavy-headed shafts suggestive of sperm. He carries the lamp of the Sun. He is dogged by Cerberus, the three-headed guardian of the gates of the underworld, whom Hermes/Mercury tamed with honey cakes during his mission to rescue Persephone from Hades.

Perhaps the most intriguing image on the card is what appears to be a wriggling sperm cell in the lower left corner. Actually, it is the Homunculus image, first drawn in 1694 by Nicholas Hartsoecker, a noted advocate of the long-discredited theory of reproduction called the principal of spermist preformation.[92] If you look closely at the head of the Homunculus, you will see a large-headed baby curled in the fetal position. While this concept is based upon biologically inaccurate science, it expresses the more universal and magically correct doctrine of correspondence: As above, so below.

You may find it rewarding to study the Hermit trump in conjunction with Atu XV, the Devil.

ATU X
FORTUNE

The Lord of the Forces of Life

Planetary Trump of Jupiter

Original Design: A wheel of six shafts, whereon revolve the Triad of Hermanubis, Sphinx, and Typhon (☿ ♃ ⊖ alchemical mercury, sulfur, and salt, or the three gunas sattva, rajas, and tamas).[93]

Hebrew Letter: Kaph (palm of hand).

Tree of Life: Path 21, joining ❹ Chesed—Mercy to ❼ Netzach—Victory.

Colors: Violet; Blue; Rich Purple; Bright Blue, rayed yellow.

Follow thy Fortune, careless where it lead thee!
The axle moveth not: attain thou that![94]

If you are expecting the Tarot to be a means of getting money, or my position as useful for pushing it—I am sorry I am not the right vehicle for such an enterprise as I intend to remain anonymous when the cards are shown as I dislike notoriety. Your books are wonderful but you must not expect the reading or money making world to buy them as they don't want to think.[95]
—Harris to Crowley, May 10, 1939.

For centuries, the Wheel of Fortune has been interpreted as the card of good luck. That is only partially true. It is also the card of bad luck; and the card of luck getting better; and the card of luck getting worse. Whatever kind of luck we are talking about, one thing's a sure bet. It's going to change. "This card," Crowley insists, "thus represents the Universe in its aspect as a continual change of state."[96]

Change is stability, and with stability comes order, and the god that brings order to so-called creation is the Demiurge,[97] the highest god below the Abyss—the "creator" god who thinks it is the supreme deity, because it is unaware of the circumstances of its own creation. Allow me to put this concept in terms of Roman mythology.

Saturn and his wife, Cybele, were Titans, aspects of the old chaotic forces that preceded the so-called "ordered universe." Saturn was warned in prophesy that one of his own offspring would one day dethrone him, so each time Cybele gave birth,

Saturn swallowed the child. As long as he kept doing this, the universe remained in pure potentiality, and "creation" (as we know it) was put on hold. Cybele eventually got tired of all this baby eating and, when she gave birth to her sixth child, Jupiter, she tricked Saturn by giving him a stone to swallow. She then secretly removed the child from Saturn's presence and brought him to Earth to be raised. Saturn eventually got indigestion and threw up the rock and the five other divine children. As prophesied, Jupiter dethroned Saturn, organized his brothers and sisters, brought order to the cosmos, and, from our mortal point of view, created the universe.

Why am I telling you this story here? Because, in Qabalistic terms, when Cybele removed baby Jupiter from Saturn's presence, she disturbed the status quo of pre-creation chaos and, in doing so, created the three landmark environments of the Tree of Life: the supernal triad (the pre-creational state), the Abyss (that separates the supernal triad from creation), and the seven sephiroth below the Abyss.

Above the Abyss, all opposites are reconciled. There is no concept of change or luck or anything else we can comprehend. It is only below the Abyss that the lumbering apparatus of forces and principals that appear to drive the universe is set in motion. The fundamental flywheel that keeps this great machine churning out everything we interpret as existence is a very efficient little perpetual-motion device located in the highest sephira below the Abyss, Chesed—the sphere of Jupiter, where the three gunas revolve. The blueprint for this three-stroke engine is Atu X, Fortune.

If you look very carefully at Lady Harris's interpretation, you will see a large triangle, its apex pointing upward, just behind the wheel. The base of the triangle is somewhat obscured by several of the ten plumes of energy that spray from the ends of each spoke of the wheel like the fiery sparks that propel a fireworks pinwheel. The hub of the wheel is positioned within the triangle. This two-part symbol is called *Centrum In Centri Trigono*[98] and is the symbolic key to the secret of Jupiter. It is also the key to transcending the secret of Jupiter.

Every year, various O.T.O. bodies throughout the world present public performances of Crowley's seven planetary rituals, *The Rites of Eleusis*. If you ever get a chance to attend these lively audience-participation plays, I strongly urge that you do so. At the beginning of the Rite of Jupiter, the stage is set to represent Atu X, Fortune. Dominating the scene is a large wheel. At the hub of the wheel sits *Centrum In Centri Trigono*. Three actors portraying Hermanubis, Typhon, and the Sphinx are positioned upon the rim of the wheel. They spend the better half of Act I bickering with each other while they circle the rim of the wheel in a fruitless attempt to reach the motionless center.

Although Hermanubis, Typhon, and the Sphinx are not openly identified as the alchemical elements (mercury, salt, and sulfur), or as the tarot trumps (the Magus, the Empress, and the Emperor), or as the gunas (sattvas, tamas, and rajas), that is exactly what they are, and they are locked in a perpetual game of one-ups-manship

C.I.C.T. addresses Typhon as "Feeling," Hermanubus as "Thought," and the Sphinx as "Ecstasy." In a moment of fatherly magnanimity, he shares with them the Zen-like secret of Jupiter:

Feeling, and thought, and ecstasy
Are but the cerements of Me.
Thrown off like planets from the Sun
Ye are but satellites of the One.
But should your revolution stop
Ye would inevitably drop
Headlong within the central Soul,
And all the parts become the Whole.
Sloth and activity and peace,
When will ye learn that ye must cease?[99]

ATU XI
LUST

The Daughter of the Flaming Sword

Zodiacal Trump of Leo

Sol Rules—Uranus Exalted

Original Design: A smiling woman holds the open jaws of a fierce and powerful lion.[100]

Hebrew Letter: Teth (serpent).

Tree of Life: Path 19, joining ❹ Chesed—Mercy to ❺ Geburah—Severity.

Colors: Yellow (greenish); Deep Purple; Grey; Reddish Amber.

Mitigate Energy with Love; but let Love devour
all things.
Worship the name _____,
foursquare, mystic, wonderful, and the name of
His House 418.[101]

(Crowley note): This Name to be communicated to those worthy of that Initiation.

> Well you must understand the feeling of it. Now how do you feel if you see nice chocolates & there, you get them & how good they taste. That is a picture of how you feel about those chocolates.[102]
> —Harris to Crowley, March 25, 1942.

That is how at an exhibition of her paintings Lady Harris explained the Lust card to an inquisitive child. The principal deities connected with this card are those who, by tradition, are associated with the power of the female to arouse, harness, and direct the animal nature: Demeter and Astarte borne by lions; Venus repressing the Volcanic fire; Babylon the Great and the Beast of The Book of the Revelation.

Lust is perhaps the most beautiful and provocative of the entire deck and one of the trumps that exemplifies Crowley's visionary and initiatory experiences chronicled in *The Vision and The Voice,* particularly his vision of the 12th Aethyr.

While very tame by modern standards, the naked image of the Babylon,[103] the Scarlet Woman, elevating the Holy Grail and straddling a fantastic and terrible seven-headed[104] Beast is still too daring for many twenty-first-century sensitivities. In state and federal prisons throughout the United States, the Thoth Tarot (because of the Lust card) is considered pornographic contraband and its possession by inmates is forbidden. Even seasoned taroists who should know better, point to the Lust card as another example of Crowley polluting the tarot with his dirty mind.

Nothing could be further from the truth. The imagery is illustrative of the most sublime and universal spiritual arcanum—that of the ecstatic dissolution of all we are (referred to in Thelemic texts as the "blood of the Saints") into the universal self of godhead (symbolized as a great "whore" and the Holy Grail she embodies). This is not—I repeat—this is not a statement concerning morality or immorality! It is perhaps the most perfect example of Crowley's use of an old Aeon "blaspheme" to illustrate a more accurate view of new Aeon spiritual perception.

For two thousand years, the symbol of the virgin has been the symbol of the pure vessel and the supreme female spiritual ideal in Western civilization. It's a wonderful symbol, as far as it goes, that deals with the great mystery of the descent of divine spirit into matter. The mystery of Babylon concerns an entirely different concept—that of the reabsorption of all evolving life and consciousness into Binah, the great supernal female. In this mystery, the symbol of the whore (who is indiscriminately receptive to all) becomes the supreme and holy image. Listen to how Crowley's angel of the 12th Aethyr describes her:

> This is the Mystery of Babylon, the Mother of abominations, and this is the mystery of her adulteries, for she hath yielded up herself to everything that liveth, and hath become a partaker in its mystery. And because she hath made herself the servant of each, therefore she is become the mistress of all.[105]

The supreme spiritual message of this card may be summed up something like this: Eventually each of us will come to a level of consciousness so profoundly high that the only level higher is the universal consciousness of deity itself. Our dissolution into the infinite is the ultimate sacrifice, the ultimate marriage. Deity lusts for that moment when all her children will return to her. Someday, each one of us will also lust for that moment.

ATU XII
THE HANGED MAN

The Spirit of the Mighty Waters

Elemental Trump of Water

Original Design: The figure of a hanged or crucified man. From a gallows shaped like the letter ד
(Daleth) hangs by one foot a young fair man. His
other leg forms a cross with the suspending one.
His arms, clasped behind his head, form and
upright triangle, and this radiates light. His mouth
is resolutely closed.[106]

Hebrew Letter: Mem (water).

Tree of Life: Path 23, joining ❺ Geburah—Severity
to ❽ Hod—Splendor.

Colors: Deep Blue; Sea-green; Deep Olive Green; White, flecked Purple.

Let not the water whereon thou journeyest wet
thee! And, being come to shore, plant thou the
Vine and rejoice without shame.[107]

We will finish like Alice through the Looking Glass by having the whole
pack on our heads. Goodnight.[108]

—Harris to Crowley, Fall, 1939.

I have long foreseen the "Alice in Wonderland" conclusion of our labours,
but that if you remember was the signal for the awakening to the beauty of
life.[109]

—Crowley to Harris, December 19, 1939.

To paraphrase what I said concerning the Hierophant, Atu XII is not your Aeon of Osiris
Hanged Man. Neither is it the Hanged Man of the Aeon of Isis. Crowley makes a
tremendous attempt to explain why this is so in *The Book of Thoth*. Please don't mis-
understand me. I mean no disrespect when I use the words "attempt to explain," and
I am certainly not suggesting that I could explain these things any better. It is just very
clear to me that, before Crowley sat down to write his commentary on this card, he
must have swallowed a handful of I-think-I-will-try-to-explain-the-innermost-secret-
of-life-and-all-the-mysteries-of-High-Magick-and-the-Universe-in-general pills.

He gives it a pretty good try. He even offers us several very revealing paragraphs concerning the most profound secrets of sexual alchemy and magick that, for those who are interested in those subjects, will certainly be worth further study and meditation (see chapter 11). Perhaps the reason he apparently goes so far afield in his comments is that he believed that the Hanged Man, as historically and traditionally understood, is now obsolete in a New Aeon tarot deck. In fact, he tells us to regard it as an evil legacy from the old Aeon and goes on to compare it rather unflatteringly with the appendix in the human body:

> This card is beautiful in a strange, immemorial, moribund manner. It is the card of the Dying God; its importance in the present pack is merely that of the Cenotaph.[110]

A cenotaph is a tomb or a monument erected to honor a person whose actual body is buried somewhere else. Be that as it may, he goes on to give us a very good Aeon-of-Horus interpretation of the Hanged Man, the highlights of which (even though I don't have any ITIWTTETISOLAATMOHMATUIG pills) I will try to summarize.

First, observe that the arms and legs of our crucified hero make the figure of a cross surmounting a triangle. Crowley tells us that this symbolizes "the descent of the light into the darkness in order to redeem it."[111] It is nothing less than the cosmic sacrifice that creates, sustains, and destroys the universe. Our perception of how we are part of this grand sacrifice has evolved over the aeons. The sacrifice meant one thing to our ancestors in the Aeon of Isis, another thing in the Aeon of Osiris, and now, as we shall see, means something altogether different in the present Aeon of Horus. (If, for some reason, you have not read chapter 6, I suggest that you do so before reading on.)

Crowley identifies the Aeon of Isis with the element water. This was an age when it was universally perceived that human life came from woman alone. The sacrifice was made by the woman on the altar of her own body, and the Hanged Man was the unborn baby who floated upside down in the water of the womb just prior to birth.

The Aeon of Osiris is identified with the element air, which is sympathetic to both water and fire. Therefore, in the Aeon of Osiris, the sacrifice was one of compromise. This was the age of the dying god, when a guy just couldn't be a real savior unless he first came out of the water (baptized, etc.) and then compromised his own body by allowing himself to be tortured, murdered, then hung or nailed to a tree to redeem the lives of his people. A couple of thousand years ago, this selfless gesture was a big step forward in spiritual politeness. As a matter of fact, for the Aeon of Osiris, it became the supreme formula of adeptship expressed by I N R I / I A O (see chapter 8).

The Aeon of Horus is identified with the element fire (represented by the Hebrew mother letter ש Shin and the Aeon trump). In the Aeon of Horus, the water of the Hanged Man and the fire of the Aeon don't get along at all. In this Aeon, Crowley warns, "The whole idea of sacrifice is a misconception of nature . . ."[112] The gesture of sacrificial suicide is not only obsolete, it is downright counterproductive:

> But now, under a Fiery lord of the Aeon, the watery element, so far as water is below the Abyss, is definitely hostile, unless the opposition is the right opposition implied in marriage.[113]

The marriage he is talking about is the "annihilation of the self in the Beloved."[114] This is symbolized in the card by the ankh (the union of the Rose and Cross, of male and female.) It is the devotional ecstasy that dissolves all sense of separateness that I wrote about in chapter 11. This "marriage," as mystics and saints of every age and culture have tried to tell us, is the supreme sacrifice.

The Hanged Man of the Thoth Tarot still symbolizes the descent of the light into the darkness in order to redeem it, but the word "redeem" no longer implies an existing debt that needs to be paid. Instead, redemption in the Aeon of Horus is the noble duty of the enlightened to bring enlightenment to the unenlightened.

Please note how Lady Harris ingeniously uses projective geometry to link this card with other water-related cards. Try placing the Hanged Man top-to-top with the High Priestess and the Queen of Cups. Other items of interest include her stylized Enochian tablets in the background, and her use of the color green to inject a Venusian influence.

ATU XIII
DEATH

The Child of the Great Transformers

The Lord of the Gate of Death

Zodiacal Trump of Scorpio

Mars Rules—Pluto Exalted

Original Design: A skeleton with a scythe mowing men. The scythe handle is a Tau.[115]

Hebrew Letter: Nun (fish).

Tree of Life: Path 24, joining ➏ Tiphareth—Beauty to ➐ Netzach—Victory.

Colors: Green Blue; Dull Brown; Very dark Brown; Livid Indigo Brown.

The Universe is Change; every Change is the effect of an Act of Love; all Acts of Love contain Pure Joy. Die daily!

Death is the apex of one curve of the snake Life: behold all opposites as necessary complements, and rejoice.[116]

I will try out what you suggest. "More work for the undertaker" says I.[117]
—Harris to Crowley, Fall, 1939.

In Hamlet, Marcellus tells Horatio, "Something is rotten in the state of Denmark." He might just as easily have said, "Something smells fishy." Both statements are uncannily appropriate when the subject is the Death card. The Hebrew letter assigned to Death is Nun, which means "fish." The fish is one of the most revered symbols of tenacious life and resurrection in the traditions of Western civilization. Dead fish decay quickly and smell terrible (in Denmark and everywhere else!), but the secret of life is in that stinky stuff.

It is very difficult to discuss the Death card without also discussing the next trump, Art. From an alchemical point of view, Death really should come after Art for the not-so-simple reason that Art foreshadows the final stage of the great work. Death is the final stage itself. Even though it is not pictured in the Death card, our snake-wrapped Orphic egg—the latent seed of life that we first saw in the Magus card, whose elements were married in the Lovers, and which then was fertilized by the Hermit—is now entering the last stage of development before hatching into new life.

In a way, the Art card actually incorporates the Death card in its imagery. If you turn forward a few pages and look at the illustration of the Art card, you will see an androgyne figure pouring fire and water upon the heads of a lion and an eagle and then into a great cauldron. If you look closely at the cauldron, you will see the image of a raven perched upon a human skull. Lady Harris may as well have painted a sign on the cauldron that reads, "This is cauldron is the Death card."

The emblem of the raven and skull is called the *caput mortuum*, and indicates the alchemical process that takes place inside the cauldron. That process is putrefaction, and putrefaction is what the Death card is all about:

> In alchemy, this card explains the idea of putrefaction, the technical name given by its adepts to the series of chemical changes which develops the final form of life from the original latent seed in the Orphic egg.[118]

Things may be rotten in Denmark, but in the alchemy of tarot, the stink of putrefaction is the sweet smell of impending success. It is a threefold process that gently warms the Orphic egg during its last most sensitive phase before birth. If we were to look into the cauldron, we would see that process bubbling away as a scorpion, a serpent, and an eagle, the three images and aspects of Scorpio.

The scorpion is found in the lower right corner of the Death card, and symbolizes, according to Crowley, the lowest aspect of Scorpio.

> The lowest is symbolized by the Scorpion, which was supposed by early observers of Nature to commit suicide when finding itself ringed with fire, or otherwise in a desperate situation. This represents putrefaction in its lowest form. The strain of environment has become intolerable, and the attacked element willingly subjects itself to change.[119]

The middle aspect of Scorpio, Crowley explains, is represented as a serpent, which can be seen in the lower left corner:

> The serpent is sacred, Lord of Life and Death, and its method of progression suggests the rhythmical undulation of those twin phases of life which we call respectively life and death.[120]

The third symbol of Scorpio is the eagle that we see in the upper left corner of the card. The eagle, as described by Crowley, is a real gas!

The highest aspect of the card is the Eagle, which represents exaltation above solid matter. It was understood by the early chemists that, in certain experiments, the purest (i.e., most tenuous) elements present were given off as gas or vapour.[121]

If all three of these aspects of putrefaction are in turn allowed to unfold perfectly, they generate the gentle heat necessary to incubate the Orphic egg in its final stage of development.

The Death card of the Thoth Tarot is the antithesis of those found in traditional packs. This is no stiff grim reaper standing on the Earth, indiscriminately mowing down people, young and old, humble and highborn. This Death is vivacious and flexible. He wears the crown of Osiris and dances madly on the bottom of the sea. Instead of mowing down the living, he uses his scythe to stir up bubbles of new lives from the out of the seemingly dead and decaying sediment. "So also," Crowley observes, "the formula of continued life is death, or putrefaction."[122] Death is, thus, in truth, "the original secret male creative God."[123]

ATU XIV
ART

The Daughter of the Reconcilers, the Bringer forth of Life

Zodiacal Trump of Sagittarius

Jupiter Rules—Dragon's Tale Exalted

Original Design: The figure of Diana huntress. A winged and crowned goddess, with flashing golden belt, stands, and pours from her right hand the flame of a torch upon an eagle, while from her left hand she pours water from an urn upon a lion. Between her feet a Moon-shaped cauldron of silver smokes with perfume.[124]

Hebrew Letter: Samekh (serpent).

Tree of Life: Path 25, joining ❻ Tiphareth—Beauty to ❾ Yesod—Foundation.

Colors: Blue; Black; Blue-black; Cold dark Grey nearing black.

Pour thine all freely from the Vase in thy right hand, and lose no drop! Hath not thy left hand a vase?

Transmute all wholly into the Image of thy Will, bringing each to its token of Perfection!

Dissolve the Pearl in the Wine-cup: drink, and make manifest the Virtue of that Pearl![125]

Temperance is a kettle of fish.[126]

—Harris to Crowley, date uncertain, 1939.

Sagittarius means "the archer"; the traditional image of this card is that of Diana the Huntress. We see echoes of this original theme in the two bows near the top of the card and the tiny upward-pointing arrow rising in the rainbow fumes of the cauldron. The celebrated Diana of Ephesus is portrayed in statuary as having many breasts. The deeply plunging neckline on the dress of the Art card's main figure reveals three columns of neatly stacked breasts reminiscent of the famous Ephesian statue of Diana.

With these exceptions, the Sagittarian imagery is almost completely smothered in alchemical symbolism. After all, as Crowley points out, "This card represents the Consummation of the Royal Marriage which took place in Atu VI"[127] and Art is the "*coagula*" to the Lovers "*solve*." Also, in this card, the white tincture of the Empress is united with the red tincture of the Emperor.

We've already learned, in chapter 8, that the Magus, the Empress, and the Emperor represent the alchemical elements of mercury, salt, and sulfur. We also learned that these three principals, when combined and perfectly balanced, create the universal solvent, vitriol. What we haven't as yet learned is what to do with our vitriol. Just what are we supposed to dissolve with it? I guess the simplest answer would be to say that vitriol dissolves old life in order to create new life. Let's look at the Art card and see where that new life is going to come from.

First of all, notice that the figures in the forefront of the card are positioned before a huge golden egg. This is, of course, the Orphic egg, and everything we see happening in front of the egg is actually the secret work that is being done inside. Shimmering around the egg, as if to advertise the radiant life within, is a golden aura displaying in beautiful penmanship the alchemical motto: *VISITA INTERIORA TERRAE RECTIFICANDO INVENIES OCCULTUM LAPIDEM*—"Visit the interior parts of the earth: by rectification thou shalt find the hidden stone."

Cooking up the potion that is making that visit possible is a strange and wonderful being whom we first met as two characters, the bride and groom, in Atu VI, the Lovers. The black King and white Queen have now merged and become a single character with two heads. The white bride now has black hair and wears the golden crown; the black groom now has golden hair and wears the silver crown. Her/his arms are exposed to reveal that the body is also countercharged.

His/her dress is decorated with both bees and serpents, and she/he stands behind a cauldron into which he/she pours water from a silver chalice from his/her left hand, and fire from her/his right hand. Flanking the cauldron (as they flanked the Orphic egg in the Lovers) stand the lion and the eagle. They have also made a dramatic change. The lion has turned white and the eagle is now red, having transmuted to their opposite characteristic by the dual baptism of fire and water (the union of the white and red tinctures).

At the very bottom of the card, the fire and the water exist together in harmony. Crowley writes,

> But this is only crude symbol of the spiritual idea, which is the satisfaction of the desire of the incomplete element of one kind to satisfy its formula by assimilation of its equal and opposite.[128]

I understand that, for many readers of this book, these forays into the strange and abstruse world of alchemy may seem like unwelcome detours from the subject of tarot. They are, however, Crowley's forays, and they are an important aspect of the Thoth Tarot that set it apart from the more traditional decks. The alchemical aspects of the Thoth Tarot are implicit in the fundamental structure of the tarot itself. Indeed, until I became familiar with the alchemical processes Crowley introduces in *The Book of Thoth*, I really had no idea why the original title of the Temperance/Art card was "The Daughter of the Reconcilers, the Bringer forth of Life."

ATU XV
THE DEVIL

The Lord of the Gates of Matter

The Child of the Forces of Time

Zodiacal Trump of Capricorn

Saturn Rules—Mars Exalted

Original Design: The figure of Pan or Priapus. Levi's Baphomet is sound commentary on this Mystery, but should not be found in the text.[129]

Hebrew Letter: Ayin (eye).

Tree of Life: Path 26, joining ❻ Tiphareth—Beauty to ❽ Hod—Splendor.

Colors: Indigo; Black; Blue-black; Cold dark Grey, nearing black.

With thy right Eye create all for thyself, and
With the left accept all that be created
Otherwise![138]

> The Devil does not exist. It is a false name invented by the Black Brothers to imply a Unity in their ignorant muddle of dispersions. A devil who had unity would be a god.[131]

The Devil may not exist, but there is most definitely a Devil card in the tarot, and, in my opinion, he is the most universally misunderstood character in the entire deck. (But then, you probably guessed I would say that.)

This is the trump of Capricorn, the sign of the goat. Indeed, for the purpose of fortune telling, the Devil has truly been the scapegoat for all the perceived evils that could befall us, and the sinful temptations that are constantly luring us toward self-destruction. How convenient!

But if the Devil is supposed to be the card that represents evil, which card should we pick to represent good? All the other trumps have the potential of representing the qualities of both good and evil. Why do we need one card just for evil?

Can't the Fool be thoughtless enough; the Magus larcenous enough, the High Priestess seductive enough, the Empress wicked enough, the Emperor tyrannical enough, the Hierophant bigoted enough, the Lovers unfaithful enough, the Chariot pretentious enough, Lust lascivious enough, the Hermit self-abusive enough, Fortune ill-fated enough, Adjustment unfair enough, the Hanged Man tormented enough, Death murderous enough, Art chaotic enough, the Tower catastrophic enough, the Star despondent enough, the Moon deceitful enough, the Sun narcissistic enough, the Aeon destructive enough, or the Universe cold and cruel enough to handle all the evil in the world?

It should be obvious that the Devil is something other than the ultimate evil. That something other is just what his full title proclaims. He is Lord of the Gates of Matter. That, in itself, can be pretty scary, especially if you've been convinced that earthly life is somehow an estrangement from God, and that all things on the material plane, including you and me, are inherently evil. Grow up!

Whatever the supreme being is, it would not be the supreme being if it weren't everything, including you and me—and the Devil. It seems pretty obvious that the Devil is just God as misunderstood by the ignorant and wicked. Crowley explains it like this:

> This card represents creative energy in its most material form; in the Zodiac, Capricornus occupies the Zenith. It is the most exalted of the signs; it is the goat leaping with lust upon the summits of earth. . . . In this sign, Mars is exalted, showing in its best form the fiery, material energy of creation. The card represents Pan Pangenetor, the All-Begetter.[132]

Crowley tells us elsewhere, that the Fool, the Hermit, and the Devil, "offer a threefold explanation of the male creative energy; but this card (The Devil) especially represents the masculine energy at its most masculine."[133] Masculine energy at its most masculine, indeed! Look at the card! I don't have to draw you a picture; Lady Harris could hardly have been more explicit. The whole card is the Devil. A magnificent three-eyed Himalayan goat stands before a tree and its two great transparent globular roots. Perhaps most interesting are the figures in the testes.

In traditional tarot decks, the Devil trump shows a woman and a man standing beneath the Devil in curious attitudes of worship and bondage. These figures are translated in the Harris painting as four female forms in the left testicle and four male forms in the right. The top male form bears the classic horned head of the Devil, who appears to have fought his way to the top. The pairs of broken lines are insinuative of chromosomes, and the starry rays at the equator of the globes suggest cellular division. This is the Devil the world has been taught to fear. He is life itself, unrestrained, in mad love and seeking to grow and unite with absolutely everything.

> The formula of this card is then the complete appreciation of all existing things. He rejoices in the rugged and the barren no less than in the smooth

and the fertile. All things equally exalt him. He represents the finding of ecstasy in every phenomenon, however naturally repugnant; he transcends all limitations; he is Pan; he is All.[134]

In *The Wake World,* Crowley spins a charming fairytale of a little girl's initiatory trip up the Tree of Life. Her name is Lola, and her guide is her Holy Guardian Angel, whom she calls her Fairy Prince. When they reach path 26 (that of Ayin and the Devil) they attend a strange banquet on a desolate heath.

It was midnight, and the Devil came down and sat in the midst; but my Fairy Prince whispered: "Hush! it is a great secret, but his name is Yeheswah, and he is the Saviour of the World." And that was very funny, because the girl next to me thought it was Jesus Christ, till another Fairy Prince (my Prince's brother) whispered as he kissed her: "Hush! tell nobody ever, that is Satan, and he is the Saviour of the World."[135]

ATU XVI
THE TOWER

The Lord of the Hosts of the Mighty

Planetary Trump of Mars

Original Design: A tower struck by forked lightning. Human figures thrown thence suggest the
letter ע (Ayin) by their attitude.[136]

Hebrew Letter: Pé (mouth).

Tree of Life: Path 27, joining ❼ Netzach—Victory,
to ❽ Hod—Splendor.

Colors: Scarlet; Red; Venetian Red; Bright Red,
rayed azure or emerald.

*Break down the fortress of thine Individual
Self, that thy Truth may spring free from the
ruins!*[137]

The House of God appears to me as a vortex not a mouth, or is it yours
which can't be filled by mortal effort try as you may.[138]
                                        —Harris to Crowley, date uncertain.

Have you ever watched the phases of a large construction project? In the first phase,
the land is cleared by smoke-belching bulldozers. Trees are ruthlessly ripped from
their roots. Grass and vegetation is plowed under and raked away, then cut up or
burned. It is a scene of utter destruction and desolation. If you were to take a pho-
tograph of the site at the end of phase one, you would have a picture of a catastrophe. However, in a year or two, the picture changes. Construction has taken place,
and now there stands a magnificent building, landscaped with grass and trees and
flowers, and perhaps a beautiful little waterfall and lake with a swan or two.

In the Thoth Tarot, phase one is represented by Atu XVI, the Tower, and phase
two is represented by Atu XX, the Aeon. The Tower is not the end of the world; it
just looks like the end of the world. It is, quite simply, what Crowley calls "the manifestation of cosmic energy in its grossest form."[139]

The Tower is the planetary trump of Mars, and it incorporates most of the
images that characterize traditional versions—a blasted tower with human figures
falling from it. Most older versions, however, show the tower being struck by lightning from above, as if by some heavenly wrath. In Harris's vision, the tower is blasted

from below by flames belching from the mouth of the underworld (The Hebrew letter Pé means mouth). This is a most significant reverse in symbolic imagery. Another feature unique to the Harris version is the presence of a large eye at the top of the card that seems to radiate a zigzag of lightning or fire that may be the spark that has ignited the flames from the mouth below.

In *The Book of Thoth,* this eye, which Crowley refers to alternately as the Eye of Horus and the Eye of Shiva, causes him to wax quite philosophic. He even teases us with comments relating to sex magick and the eye:

> There is a special technical magical meaning, which is explained openly only to initiates of the Eleventh degree of the O.T.O.; a grade so secret that it is not even listed in the official documents. It is not even to be understood by study of the Eye in Atu XV. Perhaps it is lawful to mention that the Arab sages and the Persian poets have written, not always guardedly, on the subject.[140]

If all this "eye" stuff is so secret, why even bring up the subject? This is an extremely narrow and esoteric reference that Crowley knew full well would not be understood or appreciated by the vast majority of readers. Obviously, the eyes refer to various body openings and the psychic centers to which they are linked. While all this is very interesting from a clinical sex-magick point of view, it really doesn't help us too much in understanding the general meaning of this trump. The concept of the Eye of Shiva, on the other hand, does.

The Hindu Trinity of Brahma, Vishnu, and Shiva respectively create, sustain, and destroy the universe. Shiva is the God of Destruction and, to destroy the universe, Crowley, warns, he need only open his eye.

> Shiva is represented as dancing upon the bodies of his devotees. To understand this is not easy for most western minds. Briefly, the doctrine is that the ultimate reality (which is Perfection) is Nothingness. Hence all manifestations, however glorious, however delightful, are stains. To obtain perfection, all existing things must be annihilated.[141]

The traditional title of the Tower is "The House of God," or "Destruction of the House of God." In chapter I, verse 57, of *The Book of the Law,* the goddess Nuit makes a direct reference:

> Invoke me under my stars! Love is the law, love under will. Nor let the fools mistake love; for there are love and love. There is the dove, and there is the serpent. Choose ye well! He, my prophet, hath chosen, knowing the law of the fortress, and the great mystery of the House of God.

We see the dove and the serpent near the great eye at the top of the card. The dove has an olive branch in its mouth. Crowley desribes the image like this:

> The Serpent is portrayed as the Lion-Serpent Xnoubis or Abraxas. These represent the two forms of desire; what Schopenhauer would have called the Will to Live and the Will to Die. They represent the feminine and masculine impulses; the nobility of the latter is possibly based upon recognition of the futility of the former. This is perhaps why the renunciation of love in all the ordinary senses of the word has been so constantly announced as the first step towards initiation. This is an unnecessarily rigid view. This Trump is not the only card in the Pack, nor are the "will to live" and the "will to die" incompatible.[142]

Placed in perspective, this is not such a bad card after all. The citizen of the Aeon of Horus is no longer to fear natural processes depicted in the Tower. When the DuQuette's own Crowned and Conquering Child (our son, Jean-Paul) was four years old, he asked me what will eventually happen to the world. I told him that nobody knows for sure, but that the Hindus worship a God called Shiva who is responsible for destroying the universe. "All Shiva has to do is open his eye," I said, "and the universe is completely destroyed. What do you think of that?" Without a moment's hesitation he answered, "Then he closes his other eye."

I'm still thinking about that.

ATU XVII
THE STAR

The Daughter of the Firmament

The Dweller between the Waters

Zodiacal Trump of Aquarius

Saturn Rules, Neptune Exalted

Original Design: The figure of a water-nymph disporting herself. A woman, naked and kneeling on her left knee, pours from a vase in her right hand silver waters into a river, by which grow roses, the haunts of coloured butterflies. With her left hand, she pours golden waters over her head, which are lost in her long hair. Her attitude suggests the Swastika. Above flames a great star of seven rays.[143]

Hebrew Letter: Hé (window).

Tree of Life: Path 15, joining ❷ Chokmah—Wisdom to ❻ Tiphareth—Beauty.

Colors: Violet; Sky Blue; Bluish Mauve; White, tinged purple.

Pour water on thyself: thus shalt thou be
a Fountain to the Universe.

Find thou thyself in every Star!

Achieve thou every possibility![144]

> I think, looking at the finished cards you will remember all the sequences you have forgotten & I shall be crushed by alterations which will confuse the structural design & any spectator without your knowledge & so suffer little children to come unto thee & confuse them not by too much symbolism & stay thy hand from poor Frieda's tormented visions.[145]
> —Harris to Crowley, date uncertain.

Drawing from imagery found in the first chapter of *The Book of the Law*, the Star is one of the most intensely Thelemic cards in the deck. To truly appreciate its secrets, one must be familiar with the contents of that chapter and cognizant of its possible meanings. The central subject is Nuit (Nuith) herself. Here, she is not pictured as the infinite arch of the night sky (as we see her on the Stèle or Atu XX, the Aeon), but tangibly personified as a beautiful goddess.

The three seven-pointed stars that populate this card are versions of the Star of Babalon, and reveal to us (if we haven't already figured it out) that Nuit and Babalon are, to Crowley, two aspects of the same goddess: "Babalon," he tells us, "is yet a further materialization of the original idea of Nuith; she is the Scarlet Woman, the sacred Harlot who is the lady of Atu XI."[146] He also refers to the seven-pointed star as "the Star of Venus, as if declaring the principal characteristic of her nature to be Love."[147]

The abode of Babalon/Nuit on the Tree of Life is the third sephira, Binah, the Supernal Sother. In the great name, Yod Hé Vau Hé, the mother is the first Hé. It makes perfect sense to attribute Hé to this trump, which presents the sublime image of the goddess of infinite space.

The Harris Star is very faithful to the original description (see above). She even includes the roses and butterflies (seen in the lower right corner) that are absent in more traditional decks. The river, which is a bit hard to see, flows at the bottom of the card and is demarcated by hills on the distant shore. Perhaps the most exciting departure from the traditional versions of the Star is the huge celestial globe that dominates the card. This globe is often mistakenly identified as the Earth. If it were the Earth, it would dramatically diminish the spiritual and cosmic scale of this card.

The celestial globe represents the entire heavens surrounding the Earth. Therefore, all other images on this card that are placed outside of the celestial sphere must represent spiritual environments that transcend even the concept of infinite space. The largest and smallest of the three stars are found outside the celestial sphere: the former spins counterclockwise like a cosmic pinwheel in the upper left corner of the card; the latter tumbles clockwise like a tiny star-seed from the golden bowl in the goddess's right hand. The third star whirls counterclockwise on the celestial sphere itself.

The two cups in her hands, Crowley writes, are fashioned as breasts, "as it is written, 'the milk of the stars from her paps; yea, the milk of the stars from her paps.'" "From the golden cup," he continues, "she pours this ethereal water, which is also milk and oil and blood, upon her own head, indicating the eternal renewal of the categories, the inexhaustible possibilities of existence."[148] Crowley completes the description thus:

> The left hand, lowered, holds a silver cup, from which also she pours the immortal liquor of her life. (This liquor is the Amrita of the Indian philosophers, the Nepenthe and Ambrosia of the Greeks, the Alkahest and Universal Medicine of the Alchemists, the Blood of the Grail; or, rather, the nectar which is the mother of that blood."[148]

Traditionally, the Star is the card of hope—the promise of things unseen. What is the hope that Nuit offers us? What is the promise of our star goddess? I wish I could simply reprint the entire first chapter of *The Book of the Law* and show you, but this short excerpt might give you some idea:

> I give unimaginable joys on earth: certainty, not faith, while in life, upon death; peace unutterable, rest, ecstasy; nor do I demand aught in sacrifice.[149]

ATU XVIII
THE MOON

The Ruler of the Flux and Reflux

The Child of the Sons of the Mighty

Zodiacal Trump of Pisces

Jupiter Rules—Venus Exalted

Original Design: The waning Moon. Below, a path leads between two towers, guarded by jackals, from the sea, wherein a Scarabus marcheth landwards.[150]

Hebrew Letter: Qoph (back of head).

Tree of Life: Path 29, joining ❼ Netzach—Victory to ❿ Malkuth—Kingdom.

Colors: Crimson (ultra Violet); Buff, flecked silver White; Light translucent pinkish Brown; Stone color.

Let the Illusion of the World pass over thee,
unheeded, as thou goest from the Midnight
to the Morning.[151]

> In this Trump, her lowest avatar, she joins the earthy sphere of Netzach with Malkuth, the moon of witchcraft and abominable deeds. She is the poisoned darkness which is the condition of the rebirth of light.[152]

There is no doubt about it, this is a spooky card. It represents the light that darkness creates. It is the light that illuminates your dreams—and your nightmares.

We recall that the trump attributed to the Moon is Atu II, the Priestess. She is the waxing Moon and represents Luna in her higher aspect, that of forming a link between the human and the divine. (The path of the Priestess crosses the Abyss and joins Tiphareth and Kether.) Atu XVIII, the Moon, is a very different aspect of Luna, and the most cheerful thing I can think to say about it is, "It will change."

Now, before many of my brothers and sisters in the Craft take offence, let me hasten to point out that the "witchcraft" Crowley is referring to in the above quote is not the nature-loving and life-affirming religions of the neopagan movements that have proliferated around the world since his death in 1947. It is more the imagined witchcraft spawned in the tortured and obscene fantasies of the fanatic witch hunters.

The moonlight of Atu XVIII is that which illuminates the phantasmagoric nightmares of all of us who cannot acknowledge the dark horrors of our own fears. The Moon card shows a path through and beyond this nightmare, but it is not an easy path, and the myths of all ages and cultures prove that this journey through "the poisoned darkness" is an obligatory chapter in every hero's quest. As Crowley warns:

> This path is guarded by Tabu. She is uncleanliness and sorcery. Upon the hills are the black towers of nameless mystery, of horror and of fear. All prejudice, all superstition, dead tradition and ancestral loathing, all combine to darken her face before the eyes of men. It needs unconquerable courage to begin to tread this path.[153]

Harris's rendering is disturbingly haunting, but it is not too dissimilar to the traditional image. The path runs between two towers guarded by twin figures of the Egyptian god Anubus, god of embalming and guardian of cities of the dead. Poison blood drips from the dying Moon. The creature walking out of the water at the bottom of the card represents the scarab beetle, symbolic of the Egyptian god Kephra, who is the god of the Sun at midnight.

Traditional decks usually show a crawfish, or even a lobster, instead of the scarab, and the symbolism of the Lord of the Sun at midnight becomes somewhat lost in memories of melted butter. I must confess, Harris's scarab doesn't look very scaraby either. In fact, it is a water spider. Nevertheless, it carries the Sun out of the dark water and, by doing so, assures us that this awful night will eventually come to an end. In *The Book of Thoth*, Crowley also assures the courageous seeker in his last words concerning this card:

> One is reminded of the mental echo of subconscious realization, of that supreme iniquity which mystics have constantly celebrated in their accounts of the Dark Night of the Soul. But the best men, the true men, do not consider the matter in such terms at all. Whatever horrors may afflict the soul, whatever abominations may excite the loathing of the heart, whatever terrors may assail the mind, the answer is the same at every stage: "How splendid is the Adventure!"[154]

ATU XIX
THE SUN

The Lord of the Fire of the World

Planetary Trump of the Sun

Original Design: A Sun. Below is a wall, in front of which, in a fairy ring, two children wantonly and shamelessly embrace.[155]

Hebrew Letter: Resh (head).

Tree of Life: Path 30, joining ❽ Hod—Splendor to ❾ Yesod—Foundation.

Colors: Orange; Gold Yellow; Rich Amber; Amber, rayed red.

Give forth thy light to all without doubt:
the clouds and shadows are no matter for thee.

Make Speech and Silence, Energy and Stillness,
twin forms of thy play![156]

Every man and every woman is a star.[157]

In fortune telling traditions, the Sun is often interpreted as the card representing the querent, or the face the querent shows to the world. This indicates to me that, deep down inside, all of us are inherently aware that we are ultimately solar beings. Crowley explains:

> This is one of the simplest of the cards; it represents Heru-ra-ha, the Lord of the New Aeon, in his manifestation to the race of men as the Sun spiritual, moral, and physical. He is the Lord of Light, Life, Liberty and Love. This Aeon has for its purpose the complete emancipation of the human race.[158]

That is quite a statement, and I believe Crowley meant every word of it. Whenever I am asked to explain the philosophy or, if you prefer, the religion of Thelema, the first thing I usually tell people is, "It is a modern form of Sun worship." But then, I am quick to add, "And when I use the word 'Sun,' I am also referring to myself."

Whether or not Crowley would have agreed with my gross generalization is debatable. I believe, however, that it does describe in the most primitive terms the essence of Thelema. Now that human consciousness has been subtly "mutated" with the knowledge that Sun continually exists—that it neither dies at night nor plunges toward extinction in the autumn—we as a race are poised to identify our own consciousness with the same phenomenon. Just as sunlight is perpetual, consciousness is continuous. Death is an illusion every bit as much as night is an illusion. Immortality is simply consciousness of the continuity of existence.

Heru-ra-ha is a unique name for the two opposite and equal forms of the Egyptian god Horus. Hoor-pa-kraat, is the passive, innocent, god of silence and infinite potential, often portrayed as a baby curled in the fetal position, pressing his thumb or forefinger to his lips. Ra-Hoor-Khut[159] is the active, violent, hawk-headed avenger of the gods. Combined under the one name Heru-ra-ha, they are the divine expression of the passive/active dynamics of the element Spirit.[160] Harris depicts the classic Egyptian images of both these gods in Atu XX, the Aeon.

Why should the Sun, the ultimate symbol of unity and singularity in our solar system, be identified with this double nature? From time immemorial, the doctrine of twin suns has bubbled secretly in the sanctuaries of the mysteries. Ancient traditions speak of a twin of Earth's Sun about which it and our entire solar system rotate in a cycle dance of hundreds of millions of years. Early Gnostic Christians dubbed Satan the twin of Christ, suggesting a great solar mystery hidden in the relationship.

Whatever may have been the original circumstances and motives that created these ancient traditions, modern science affirms that the secret of the Sun is indeed the perpetual struggle of two titanic forces: the active, thermonuclear process that burns the Sun's fuel and radiates light and energy outward into space, and the passive, gravitational presence of the Sun's own mass. The former keeps the Sun from collapsing in upon itself; the later keeps the burning process perpetually contained and stable.

The twin babies in the Fool card, and the children and the bride and groom in the Lovers are earlier tarot incarnations of the two dancing children we find in the Sun card. According to Crowley:

> They represent the male and female, eternally young, shameless and innocent. They are dancing in the light, and yet they dwell upon the earth. They represent the next stage which is to be attained by mankind, in which complete freedom is alike the cause and the result of the new access of solar energy upon the earth.[161]

ATU XX
THE AEON

The Spirit of the Primal Fire

Elemental Trump of Fire and of Spirit

Original Design: Israfel blowing the last trumpet. The dead arising from their tombs. Angel blowing a trumpet, adorned with a golden banner bearing a white cross. Below, a fair youth rises from a sarcophagus in the attitude of the god Shu supporting the firmament. On his left, a fair woman, her arms give the sign of water—an inverted triangle on the breast. On his right a dark man gives the sign of fire—an upright triangle on the forehead.[162]

Hebrew Letter: Shin (tooth).

Tree of Life: Path 31, joining ❽ Hod—Splendor to ❿ Malkuth—Kingdom.

Colors for Fire: Glowing Orange Scarlet; Vermilion; Scarlet, flecked gold; Vermilion, flecked crimson; and Emerald.

Colors for Spirit: White merging into Grey; Deep Purple, nearly Black; The seven prismatic colors (violet outside); White, Red, Yellow, Blue, Black (this outside).

Be every Act an Act of Love and Worship!

Be every Act the Fiat of God!

Be every Act a Source of radiant Glory.[163]

Ra-Hoor-Khuit hath taken his seat in the East and the Equinox of the Gods.[164]

The traditional name of this card is Judgment, or The Last Judgment. The traditional design shows the Archangel Israfel blowing his trumpet to announce the end of the world as the dead arise from their tombs. In chapter 6, which is actually an expanded commentary on this card, I attempted to explain why Crowley replaced The Last Judgment with the Aeon in the Thoth Tarot. The reader who has not yet read that chapter is strongly advised to do so now. I will sum up what I wrote there simply by saying that, according to Crowley, the Last Judgment trump is now obsolete. The event that it depicted (the destruction of the world by fire) has already occurred. The world we are talking about, of course, is the spiritual Age of Osiris. the Aeon card of the Thoth Tarot depicts the spiritual forces that initiated the next age, the Aeon of Horus.

Crowley saw this event as a magical changing-of-the guard that was foreshadowed symbolically by one of the regular seasonal ceremonies of the Golden Dawn. Every six months, the ritual officers of that order were ceremonially promoted one chair up, and new secret passwords were issued. In that ritual, the officer who had formerly served as second-in-command (who, in that position, had magically assumed the identity of the Egyptian God Horus) was installed to serve as Hierophant (symbolized by Osiris) for the next six months. *The Book of the Law* calls the cosmic version of this ceremony The Equinox of the Gods.

Horus is the God of Force and Fire, and his ascension as Lord of the New Aeon spiritually destroys the old world by fire. It only looks like the end of the world to those of us who cannot accept the possibility that old spiritual points of view can ever be replaced by new ones.

As we learned in chapter 5, Crowley asserted that the latest Equinox of the Gods took place on March 20, 1904 e.v. in Cairo. Triggering the events that led up to this moment was the psychic possession of Crowley's wife, Rose, and their discovery of a twenty-fifth dynasty funeral stèle. Among many other features, the stèle shows the God Horus (Ra-Hoor-Khuit) on a throne. Before him is a table of offerings. Standing beside the table is the deceased, Ankh-af-na-Khonsu.

Nuit (Nut), the goddess of the night sky and infinite space, arches her body over the entire top section of the stèle. Directly beneath her heart is a winged solar disk that *The Book of the Law* refers to as the god Hadit.

In Atu XX, the Aeon, Harris interprets the stèle in one of the most colorful and aesthetically pleasing of all the trumps. The Goddess Nuit, her body filled with stars, her breasts alive with the milk of whirling galaxies, forms a beautiful blue omega as she bends in ecstasy around an immense egg containing the seated image of Ra-Hoor-Khuit. He holds the phoenix wand in his right hand. His left hand is empty. Standing as a transparent essence before Ra-Hoor-Khuit is his twin, Hoor-pa-kraat (see the Sun), his finger at his lips in the sign of silence. His head is shaven (except for his Horus lock) and crowned with two Uraeus serpents.

The God Hadit, pictured as the winged solar disk, is nearly camouflaged by the entire scene. This is most appropriate, for these are among his open words in *The Book of the Law*:

In the sphere I am everywhere the centre, as she, the circumference, is nowhere found. Yet she shall be known & I never.[165]

The Hebrew letter Shin is assigned to the Aeon, and a large Shin containing three embryonic figures appears at the bottom of the card. It flames in front of a very stylized set of scales, perhaps pointing to the Aeon that will follow the Aeon of Horus, that of Maat, the goddess of justice and balance.

Crowley ends his discussion of this card with a comparison of the world events of approximately two thousand years ago, at the advent and birth of the last Aeon. His words carry a chilling but ultimately hopeful message:

> The time for the birth of an Aeon seems to be indicated by great concentration of political power with the accompanying improvements in the means of travel and communication, with a general advance in philosophy and science, with a general need of consolidation in religious thought. It is very instructive to compare the events of the five hundred years preceding and following the crisis of approximately 2,000 years ago, with those of similar periods centred in 1904 of the old era. It is though far from comforting to the present generation, that 500 years of Dark Ages are likely to be upon us. But if the analogy holds, that is the case. Fortunately, to-day we have brighter torches and more torch-bearers.[166]

ATU XXI
THE UNIVERSE

The Great One of the Night of Time

Planetary Trump of Saturn

Elemental Trump of Earth

Original Design: Should contain a demonstration of the Quadrature of the Circle. An ellipse, composed of 400 lesser circles. At the corners of the card a man, an eagle, a bull, and a lion. Within the circle, a naked shining figure with female breasts, with closed eyes in the sign of Earth—right foot advanced, right hand advance and raised, left hand lowered and thrown back. The hands grip each a ray of dazzling light, spiral, the right hand being dextro- and the left hand lævo-rotary. A red scarf conceals the fact of male genital organs, and suggests by its shape the letter ב. Such is the conventional hieroglyph.[167]

Hebrew Letter: Tau (cross).

Tree of Life: Path 32, joining ❾ Yesod—Foundation to ❿ Malkuth—Kingdom.

Colors for Saturn: Indigo; Black; Blue-black; Black, rayed blue.

Colors for Earth: Citrine; Olive; Russet and Black; Amber; Dark Brown; Black, flecked Yellow.

Treat time and all conditions of Event as
Servants of thy Will, appointed to present the
Universe to thee in the form of thy Plan.

And: blessing and worship to the prophet of the lovely Star.[168]

> The elemental Cherubims are quite jolly but the Little Lady has twisted and turned 'til I am insane with the wiggling lines and I've done about forty drawings of her.[169]
>
> —Harris to Crowley, date uncertain.

For many years, the Universe has served as the cover image of Weiser editions of *The Book of Thoth*. It is without question one of the most recognizable cards of the

Thoth Tarot. Familiar as it is to us, it is one of the most complex and mysterious cards in the deck. There are several elements in the card I don't understand at all. For instance, what is the black crescent-shaped object in the goddess's right hand? I don't have a clue. I can't find any reference to it in *The Book of Thoth*. If Crowley explains it in any other writings, I confess it has escaped me completely. My best guess is that it is a sickle (not an inappropriate weapon for a Saturnian goddess). It looks like she is sticking the sharp end right in the middle of the big eye at the top of the card, perhaps causing it to erupt in glories of light—but I can't say for sure.

There are several other images in the card that I didn't see until I had the card enlarged and enhanced. I'll talk about those in a moment. First, let's start with what we know from Crowley's own comments:

> In the card itself there is consequently a glyph of the completion of the Great Work in its highest sense, exactly as the Atu of the Fool symbolizes its beginning. The Fool is the negative issuing into manifestation; the Universe is that manifestation, its purpose accomplished, ready to return. The twenty cards that lie between these two exhibit the Great Work and its agents in various stages. The image of the Universe in this sense is accordingly that of a maiden, the final letter of the Tetragrammaton[170]

Atu XXI, the Universe, represents both the planet Saturn and the element earth. We already know earth is in some ways a real second-class citizen in the Qabalistic universe. We also know that because earth is lowest, it ironically plays a pivotal role in the cosmic scheme of things.

Saturn is also very special. As Binah's representative, it is the only planetary sphere above the Abyss. In many ways, it is the highest of the high. At the same time, on the Tree of Life, the path of the Universe (32) leads from Yesod (the ninth and last true sephira on the Tree) down into Malkuth (which is only pendant to the Tree, a cosmic dingleberry). How strange that the highest high and the lowest low would be represented by the same card. The Universe must indeed hold many mysteries, something Crowley confirms in this passage:

> The first and most obvious characteristic of this card is that it comes at the end of all, and is therefore the complement of the Fool. It is attributed to the letter Tau. The two cards together accordingly spell the word Ath, which means Essence. All reality is consequently compromised in the series of which these two letters form the beginning and the end. This beginning was Nothing; the end must therefore be also Nothing, but Nothing in its complete expansion, as was previously explained.[171]

As we see from the original description, Atu XXI, the Universe, should contain a demonstration of the "Quadrature of the Circle." Good Luck! For centuries, it has been the quest of mystic mathematicians to square the circle or construct, by using only a compass and a straight edge, a square of precisely the same circumference as that of any given circle. It would be the geometric equivalent of building the New Jerusalem—the marriage of the eternal circle of heaven to the terrestrial square of Earth.

In 1882, German mathematician Carl Louis Ferdinand von Lindemann finally demonstrated that the perfect squaring of the circle is a mathematical impossibility. However, thousands of years of attempting the impossible has produced a body of graphic and architectural devices that have supplied the patterns and proportions for temples and cathedrals, sacred statuary, and paintings. It has also provided us with the blueprint for Atu XXI, the Universe.

Bold seekers have also introduced into this quest collateral data, such as the mysterious numbers that appear in the Old and New Testaments, and the estimated size and ratios of planetary orbits. The mental stimulation and ecstasy such mathematical gymnastics induce can be addictive, to the point of triggering emotional instability. British architect, William Stirling, author of the monumental work *The Canon: An Exposition of the Pagan Mystery Perpetuated in the Cabala as the Rule of All the Arts,* died most hideously while attempting to sever his own head from his body.[172] (One can think too much about such things.)

I confess that I become hopelessly lost whenever I try to follow the logic and numbers of transcendental mathematics. What I do understand is the aesthetic beauty of the figures such musings produce when translated into graphic designs, especially the diagram called, appropriately, the New Jerusalem. Because I cannot explain exactly why this diagram is an attempt to square the circle, I will instead try to show you how it is constructed and allow you decide whether or not to pursue its mysteries further. (But, please, try not to lose your head!)

The New Jerusalem and the Universe trump both start with a special oval called a *vesica piscis* (a fish bladder). We see the vesica in two places on the Universe card: as the large oval that touches the top, bottom, and sides of the card, and as the eye at the top right section of the large vesica. The small eye vesica appears either to be projecting the images on to the card, or drawing them all back inside itself.

It is very easy to create a vesica piscus, and the beginning of its construction employs Qabalistic concepts that by now should be familiar to you.

1. First, you must have two circles of equal size that intersect at their centers. (The first circle is Kether, which unites with its reflection, Chokmah, to create the opening, the Yoni of Mother Binah from which will issue all creation). The vesica was the floor plan of many cathedrals of the late Renaissance and early Baroque periods, structures that were nearly all dedicated to Our Lady.

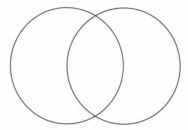

2. Next, enclose and center the vesica inside a third circle the same size as the other two (It is as though the supernal triad has made and positioned the vesica). It looks like an eye, doesn't it?

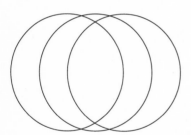 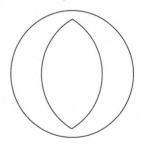

3. Enclose the vesica with a square that is the same length and breadth as the length of the vesica.

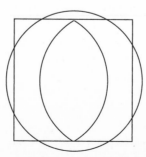

4. Draw four circles at the diagonal corners whose centers intersect the great circle, and whose circumferences touch the vesica.

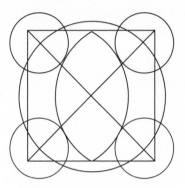

5. Finally, enclose all within a square.

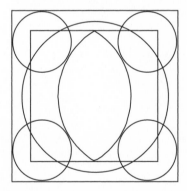

There it is. This is the basic model for both the traditional and the Crowley-Harris versions of the Universe. You may also recognize this design as pattern for many paintings and stained-glass windows that depict Christ, or the Holy Family, or the Trinity surrounded by the images of the angel or man, the lion, the bull, and the eagle. In the Harris-Crowley card, the four Kerubic creatures are placed in the corners in the same manner as in the Hierophant.

For reasons that have never been very clear to me, Christian believers are told these creatures represent respectively the four Evangelists: Mathew, Mark, Luke, and John. Jews naturally recognize them as the symbols for the four tribes of Israel, who were assigned the corner positions in the camp of the Israelites:[173] the man of the tribe of Reuben, the lion of Judah, the bull of Ephriam, and the eagle of Dan. We, of course, recognize them as the four Kerubic beasts.

Even though the original description states the vesica should be an ellipse composed of 400 lesser circles (a reference to the Hebrew letter Tau assigned to this card, which enumerates to 400), Lady Harris does well to give us seventy-two circles[174] (yes, I counted them), which provocatively suggest (to me at least) the ribbed skeleton of an infinitely huge serpent.

Now that we know that Lady Harris gave it the old college try to squaring the circle, let's get out our magnifying glass and look at the all the wonderful things she puts inside it. At the bottom point of the vesica is a skeletal structure that looks a bit like the blueprint of a building. That is exactly what it is—it is the house of matter. If the structure were projected in three dimensions, we would see a four-sided building and that each of the tiny vertical lines represents one of the ninety-two then known elements. They are ingeniously arranged in hierarchical order and joined by a series of diagonal lines that form a diagram of the chemical building blocks of the material universe. The model for this design first appeared in *The Bases of Modern Science*, by J. W. N. Sullivan.[175]

Impressive as this diagram is, Harris superimposes it upon a structure even more magnificent and mysterious. If you look carefully, you will see that Sullivan's house of matter is projected upon the largest of three pyramids suggestive of those at the Giza complex. Like the Great Pyramid at Giza, the apex of the large pyramid in the center of Harris's drawing is also covered with finishing stones, making it appear to swell a bit at the top.

Crowley makes no reference to these pyramids in *The Book of Thoth*, and my poor mind boggles at the possible implications. He does mention something we can't see—at least I can't see it:

> In the centre, a wheel of Light initiates the form of the Tree of Life, shewing the ten principal bodies of the solar system. But this Tree is not visible except to those of wholly pure heart.[176]

Well I guess I'm busted! Emperor Lon has no clothes! As if I really need the Master Therion to tell me I'm not wholly pure of heart! I'm really not surprised I can't see his damned Tree of Life in the center of this card.

What I can see is a beautiful green sphere upon which sits a complex Möbius strip.[177] Actually, it's not that complex. It's just a regular Möbius strip made from three half twists rather than just one. (Yes, I made one to be sure.) The endlessness of a Möbius strip makes it a perfect and beautiful glyph of the infinite, and it is my guess that Lady Harris replaced Crowley's invisible Tree of Life with this brilliantly appropriate device.

The main feature of the card is the beautiful "Little Lady" Crowley refers to in this passage:

In the present card she is represented as a dancing figure. In her hands she manipulates the radiant spiral force, the active and passive, each possessing its dual polarity. Her dancing partner is shown as Heru-Ra-Ha of Atu XIX.[178]

Is she Nuit/Babalon, goddess of the sphere of Saturn, Binah? Or is she the virgin princess of the sphere of earth, Malkuth? She is, in truth, both the great mother and the virgin daughter of eternity.

What could possibly serve as the model for this goddess who is at once the beginning and the end and all things in between? What vision could have emboldened Lady Harris to give such solid form to this formless and eternal process?

On the afternoon of December 6, 1909, between the hours of 2:00 and 4:15 p.m. in a lonely valley of fine sand in the desert near Bou-Sada, North Africa, Aleister Crowley, accompanied by the poet Victor Nueberg, who served as his servant and magical scribe, crossed the Abyss[179] and experienced the terrible vision of the tenth Enochian Aethyr. The details of this ordeal are chronicled in *The Vision and the Voice*,[180] and remain the central features of one of the most breathtaking and remarkable magical visions ever recorded.

The next evening, December 7, 1909, between 9:30 and 11:10 p.m., while his consciousness still thrilled with the bliss of that magical plateau, he experienced the vision of the next Aethyr, the ninth. I have excerpted a large portion of that vision, because I believe that there is nothing I or anyone else could say about Atu XXI, the Universe, that could be more profound or relevant. It is nothing less than an account of a face-to-face encounter with the goddess of Atu XXI, the Universe.

> She has very deep eye-lids, and long lashes. Her eyes are closed, or nearly closed. It is impossible to say anything about her. She is naked; her whole body is covered with fine gold hairs, that are the electric flames that are the spears of mighty and terrible Angels whose breast-plates are the scales of her skin. And the hair of her head, that flows down to her feet, is the very light of God himself. Of all the glories beheld by the seer in the Aethyrs, there is not one which is worthy to be compared with her littlest finger-nail. For although he may not partake of the Aethyr, without the ceremonial preparations, even the beholding of this Aethyr from afar is like the partaking of all the former Aethyrs.
>
> The Seer is lost in wonder, which is peace.
>
> And the ring of the horizon above her is a company of glorious Archangels with joined hands, that stand and sing: This is the daughter of BABALON the Beautiful, that she hath borne unto the Father of All. And unto all hath she borne her.
>
> This is the Daughter of the King. This is the Virgin of Eternity. This is she that the Holy One hath wrested from the Giant Time, and the prize of them that have overcome Space. This is she that is set upon the Throne of

Understanding. Holy, Holy, Holy is her name, not to be spoken among men. For Koré they have called her, and Malkah, and Betulah, and Persephone.

And the poets have feigned songs about her, and the prophets have spoken vain things, and the young men have dreamed vain dreams; but this is she, that immaculate, the name of whose name may not be spoken. Thought cannot pierce the glory that defendeth her, for thought is smitten dead before her presence. Memory is blank, and in the most ancient books of Magick are neither words to conjure her, nor adorations to praise her. Will bends like a reed in the tempests that sweep the borders of her kingdom, and imagination cannot figure so much as one petal of the lilies whereon she standeth in the lake of crystal, in the sea of glass.

    This is she that hath bedecked her hair with seven stars the seven breaths of God that move and thrill its excellence. And she hath tired her hair with seven combs, whereupon are written the seven secret names of God that are not known even of the Angels, or of the Archangels, or of the Leader of the armies of the Lord.

    Holy, Holy, Holy art thou, and blessed be Thy name for ever, unto whom the Aeons are but the pulsings of thy blood.[181]

And so we come to both the end and beginning of the trumps. I know that, for many of you, the trip has been pretty bumpy in spots. Perhaps you think that you've bitten off more than you can chew and that you will never completely understand the tarot (especially the Thoth Tarot). You're right. You will never completely under-stand. Nobody will. However, you do have the best teacher in the universe stand-ing by to be your mentor and guide for all areas of your spiritual life—your Holy Guardian Angel.

    Here, at the end of our discussion of Atu XXI, on the lowest path on the Tree of Life, it is especially appropriate that we remember our Holy Guardian Angel, because, whether we are aware of it or not, whether we have achieved knowledge and conversation of our HGA, or have just begun our initiatory journey, we are helped at every step of the way.

    In *The Wake World*,[182] at the very beginning of Lola's trip up the Tree of Life, she is frightened when she and her fairy prince (HGA) first enter path 32, the path of Tau and the Universe. Crowley describes how her Guardian Angel comforts her and gives her the best advice anyone on the initiatory path can receive:

Then he said: "Come on! This is only the Servants' Hall, nearly everybody stays there all their lives." And I said: "Kiss me!" So he said: "Every step you take is only possible when you say that."[183]

CHAPTER FIFTEEN

THE MINOR ARCANA

"Did the Tarot come from playing cards or did playing cards come from the Tarot?"
"Yes."[184]

As much as tarot fans would like to believe otherwise, modern playing cards did not come from the tarot. As a matter of fact, where the fifty-six cards of the Lesser Arcana are concerned, tarot came from playing cards. The game was called Mamluk, and we can easily trace its existence and popularity to fifteenth-century Turkey.

Mamluk cards had four suits, each numbered one through ten. The suits displayed images of polo sticks, cups, swords, and coins. Each suit also had a set of three male royalty figures, a King, an Emir, and a Wazir. The appearance of Mamluk cards in Europe in the 1370s predates the earliest known tarot by at least fifty years.

The revelation of Islamic roots of the Lesser Arcana gives ammunition to those who would suggest Qabalistic roots to the tarot. Mamluk's introduction to Europe almost certainly came through Moorish Spain, which, at the time, was a hotbed of Qabalistic activity. As I said concerning the Major Arcana, however, nothing can be proven to suggest anything more occult or mysterious than the natural congealing of the conventions of a popular game. Nevertheless, that phenomenon in itself may have profound implications concerning how the human mind is hardwired to respond to archetypal images.

CHAPTER SIXTEEN

THE SPIRIT
OF THE ACES

The Aces represent the roots of the four elements. They are quite above, and distinct from, the other small cards in the same way as Kether is said to be symbolized only by the topmost point of the Yod of Tetragrammaton. In these cards is no real manifestation of the element in its material form. They form a link between the small cards and the Princesses, who rule the Heavens around the North Pole . . . both in their appearance and in their meaning, the Aces are not the elements themselves, but the seeds of those elements.[185]

You may think it odd that I begin my examination of the fifty-six cards of the Minor Arcana by first examining the four aces instead of the court cards. After all, aren't the aces simply the first of the small cards? I hope I didn't hear anyone ask that question. To say the ace is just the lowest-numbered tarot small card of its suit is like saying Kether is just the first sephira on the Tree of Life.

Ultimately, there are not fifty-six cards in the Minor Arcana of the tarot. There are only four—the four aces. The other fifty-two cards (the sixteen court cards and the thirty-six small cards), live inside the four aces. As we learned in chapter 8, if we look at the ace of any suit under a magic microscope, we first see the four court cards of that suit living comfortably inside. Let's not stop there. If we increase the magnification level of our microscope, we see that the nine small cards of the suit are nestled neatly inside in three rows of three cards. Isn't that tidy?

What does Crowley mean when he tells us that the aces are not the elements themselves, but the seeds of those elements? Qabalistically, the most obvious answer deals with the fact that Kether, the first sephira of the Tree of Life, is the inscrutable singularity of its particular world. As head honcho of the supernal triad, it is above, and distinct from, the other sephiroth that actually do all the manifesting in (and

FIGURE 26. THE SMALL CARDS EMBEDDED IN THE ACE. IN 10° INCREMENTS, THE 2S, 3S, 4S REPRESENT THE CARDINAL ZODIAC SIGNS; THE 5S, 6S, 7S, REPRESENT THE FIXED ZODIAC SIGNS; THE 8S, 9S, 10S, REPRESENT THE MUTABLE ZODIAC SIGNS.

of) their respective worlds. Isn't that explanation kind of a cop-out, however? It sounds as if I'm just trying to explain something that is impossible to understand by giving an example of something else that is impossible to understand.

I didn't start to grasp this "root-of-the-elements" concept until I learned that physicists cannot properly define the nature of matter. They go as far as to tell us that the components of atoms (subatomic particles like protons, electrons, neutrons, and other strange things like quarks, and charm and quark-gluon plasma) aren't matter at all, but can only be described as nonmaterial "tendencies."

What a perfect description of Kether! What a perfect description of the ace! It is that supremely fundamental tendency underlying a particular element. The Ace of Wands is not fire, but the tendency, or grouping of tendencies, to be fire and the suit of Wands.

Physicists theorize that these tendencies likely existed in their pure state in nature under conditions of extreme heat such as might have existed in the first milliseconds after the Big Bang. Accurately or inaccurately, the words these men and women of science are currently tossing about to describe these premanifestation tendencies that floated free in the immeasurable heat of creation are enough to make mystics of all schools stand up and salute: words like dark matter, mana, urmatter, quintessence, and (are you ready for this?) spirit![186]

Tarot trump XX, the Aeon, represents the element of spirit. But, as we will see, it also does double duty on the Tree of Life and in tarot by representing the element fire. Perhaps this is the tarot's way of pointing to spirit's primordial home in the fire of creation itself, and how the aces can be the root of their element yet, as Crowley tells us, "quite above, and distinct from, the other small cards."[187]

As we know, each ace enjoys a unique and very important relationship with the Princess of its suit. We touched on that relationship in chapters 8 and 11. The Princess is the throne of her ace and, when we consider one, we must by necessity think of the other. Hopefully, this connection will become clearer when we examine the court cards and small cards.

In some card games, aces are considered just the cards that come before the twos in value. In tarot, the aces are the gods of their suits and deserve some real respect. Let's take a look at them.

CHAPTER SEVENTEEN

THE FOUR ACES

Do try & answer me about the Aces. I feel broody about them. I keep on thinking about those 4 elements & their mightiness & I feel drowned in water, burnt with fire, cut by the air & dug into the earth. The air feels to be the most solid & dead of them all, which is odd, as it is supposed to be so light. No blood I suppose.[188]

—Harris to Crowley, date uncertain.

ACE OF WANDS

With the Princess of Wands as its throne, the Ace of Wands rules the Cancer-Leo-Virgo Quadrant above the North Pole, and the area of Asia.

Original Title: The Root of the Powers of Fire.

Golden Dawn Model: A hand appears from clouds at the bottom of the card holding a three-branched flaming club. Three flames issue from the ends of the right and left branch, and four flames from the top central branch. The whole is surrounded by twenty-two red flames or Yods arranged as to suggest the paths on the Tree of Life.

Color: Brilliance.

This card represents the essence of the element of Fire it its inception. It is a solar-phallic outburst of flame from which spring lightnings in every direction.[189]

If that was how Crowley described his vision of this card to Harris, then we will have to admit that she did a magnificent job. The Golden Dawn model is more complex than its description might suggest. Some renditions I've seen are almost comical in their attempt to fulfill all the required images. Harris throws them all out the window and gives us the image of a huge Tree of Life ablaze with ten flaming sephiroth.

In a very real way, this image is telling us that, just as all the sephiroth of all four Trees of Life are only aspects of the one supreme Kether, just as all four Qabalistic worlds are really only aspects of the highest world, just as the Hé and the Vau and the final Hé of YHVH are really only aspects of the Yod, all the cards of the Minor Arcana ultimately live inside one card, the Ace of Wands.

Of course, it takes a Buddha to actually grasp that concept. It also leaves us with a pretty thin deck of tarot cards to play with. It's probably better for us to go along with the Qabalistic drill and view this card as representing Kether, of the Tree of Life that represents the highest of the Qabalistic worlds, Atziluth. That's a heavy enough concept as it is.

This card is the masculine compliment of the Ace of Cups and is derived from the Lingam and the Sun exactly as the Ace of Cups is from the Yoni and the Moon.[190]

ACE OF CUPS

With the Princess of Cups as its throne, the Ace of Cups rules the Libra-Scorpio-Sagittarius quadrant above the North Pole, and the area of the Pacific.

Original Title: The Root of the Powers of the Waters.

Golden Dawn Model: A hand appears from clouds at the bottom of the card supporting on its palm the cup of the Stolistes from which gush fountains of water. The Hebrew letter Hé is formed by the spray of the fountain. The water falls on all sides into a calm sea where lotuses and lilies grow.

Color: White Brilliance.

This card represents the element of Water in its most secret and original form. It is the feminine complement of the Ace of Wands, and is derived from the Yoni and the Moon exactly as that is from the Lingam and the Sun.[191]

This card is a stunning and vivid image of the cosmic Yoni. In Wagnerian terms, it is the Holy Grail to the Ace of Wands' sacred lance. The Golden Dawn model has more or less been discarded, and Crowley's description in *The Book of Thoth* is that of an earlier draft of this card, not Harris's finished product. This is, nonetheless, one of, if not the, most beautiful cards in the entire deck.

Scalloped radiations of light burst from the cup to meet and match the undulating waves of water at the horizon of the sea. Harris repeats the motif of scallops in the dress of the Princess of Cups, suggesting perhaps her relationship as throne of the ace.

The cup itself is a simple blue bowl with what appear to be two blue-green entwined serpents serving as handles. For reasons that are not altogether clear to me, Harris has placed three interlaced rings (the same as those that crowned the Hierophant's wand in Atu V) on the front of the cup. This symbol, which Crowley described as "representative of the three Aeons of Isis, Osiris and Horus with their interlocking magical formulae"[192] is not to be confused with the more complex Mark of the Beast, which we find on the Ace of Disks and the Prince and Five of Wands. One can only speculate why Harris was moved to apply this symbol to the cup.

ACE OF SWORDS

With the Princess of Swords as its throne, the Ace of Swords rules the Capricorn-Aquarius-Pisces quadrant above the North Pole and the area of the Americas.

Original Title: The Root of the Powers of the Air.

Golden Dawn Model: A hand appears from clouds at the bottom of the card holding the hilt of a great sword that penetrates at its point a radiant crown. An olive branch hangs from the right of the crown, a palm branch from the left. Six Hebrew Vaus fall from the sword point upon the top of the crown.

Color: White Brilliance.

The Ace of Swords is the primordial Energy of Air, the Essence of the Vau of the Tetragrammaton, the integration of the Ruach.[193]

The Ace of Swords is the root of the element air and represents the Ruach. Ruach is the intellect part of the soul, and (according to Eastern mystics) the mind is the great enemy. The mind violently resists identification with any higher levels of consciousness. Consequently, from out of the mind springs conflict, frustration, anxiety, worry, and sorrow. Is it any wonder the suit of Swords is filled with so many unpleasant cards? However, in the proper hands, the sword can be the weapon that cuts through the crap, and the Ace of Swords is the sword of the Magus, "crowned with the 22 rayed diadem of pure Light."[194] In *Magick, Liber ABA, Book Four,* Crowley describes the sword. I can offer no better description of this card.

The hilt of the Sword should be made of copper. The guard is composed of the two crescents of the waxing and the waning Moon—back to back. Spheres are placed between them, forming an equilateral triangle with the sphere of the pommel. The blade is straight, pointed, and sharp right up to the guard. It is made of steel to equilibrate with the hilt, for steel is the metal of Mars, as copper is of Venus. . . . The hilt is Venus, for Love is the motive of this ruthless analysis—if this were not so the Sword would be a Black Magical weapon. The pommel of the Sword is in Daäth, the guard extends to Chesed and Geburah; the point is in Malkuth.[195]

Upon the blade, Harris has engraved, in Greek, the word *Thelema* (Will) in Arabic Damascened work.

ACE OF DISKS

With the Princess of Disks as its throne, the Ace of Disks rules the Aries-Taurus-Gemini quadrant above the North Pole, and the area of Europe and Africa.

Original Title: The Root of the Powers of the Earth.

Golden Dawn Model: A hand appears from clouds at the bottom of the card holding the branch of a rose tree surmounted by a large disk composed of five concentric circles. The center is white, is adorned with a red Greek cross, and radiates twelve white rays that reach to the inner edge of the disk. Above this is a circled Maltese Cross with two white wings.

Color: White, flecked Gold.

> Steal not this Book for fear of shame!
> The Ace of Disks—the Author's name.[196]

To represent the root of the element earth and the material world Assiah, Lady Harris gives us the ultimate coin of the realm centered upon money-green layers of the vegetal embellishments that historically have adorned the world's paper currency.

A tarot tradition dating back to sixteenth-century Italy (where decks of cards were stamped and taxed by local authorities) dictates that the creator of the deck place his or her mark or signature on the Two or the Ace of Disks. Crowley was obviously aware of this tradition, and I think we can be confident that he supervised its execution very carefully. The Ace of Disks is nothing less than Crowley's own magical signature. His motto, TO ΜΕΓΑ ΘΗΡΙΟΝ To Mega Therion, Greek for the Great Beast, is displayed on the perimeter of the disk, and his personal seal is placed in the very center of all.

A decagon fits snugly within the outer ring and seems to create ten facets that reach toward the center and curiously end at the points of two five-sided polygons. Within the two polygons is a heptagram (Thelema's Star of Babalon), and within the heptagram we find the Mark of the Beast.

The Mark of the Beast is made up of three intersecting circles. The uppermost circle contains a dot at its center, creating the astrological symbol of the Sun. Cradling the Sun circle from below is an upturned crescent Moon. Together, they are the Sun and Moon conjoined, the symbol of so many things that I would be an idiot to even start a footnote. The number 666, the number of the Sun and of the Beast is written across the two lower circles. This symbol is rich in magical and Qabalistic symbolism. One can also, with very little imagination, see a bird's-eye view of the three main characters of male genitalia. Perfect Crowley!

CHAPTER EIGHTEEN

THE CRAZY MIXED-UP WORLD OF COURT CARDS

The convenience of these arrangements is that these cards are suitable as being descriptive, in a rough and empirical fashion, of divers types of men and women. One may say briefly that any of these cards is a picture of the person whose Sun, or whose rising sign at his nativity, falls within the Zodiacal attribution of the card.[197]

We tend to treat the four aces as if they were each the pure representatives of their element. That is not altogether correct. It is true that they are the purest representatives of their element, but, if they did not contain some minute quantities (and qualities) of the other three elements, they would be unable to combine to form the matter and energy that creates and sustains the phenomenal universe. Simply put, there would be no creation at all if the individual elements remained pure and set completely apart from one another. Water would not be able to combine with air if it didn't have a bit of air already in it to serve as an attractor, and vice versa. In order to manifest a universe, things have to be shaken up. The court cards make four very mixed-up families.

MIX-UP #1: SIXTEEN SUBELEMENTS

Remember that, when we put an ace under our magick microscope, we saw the four court cards of the suit living inside? As the four aces represent the four elements of fire, water, air, and earth, the four court cards in each suit represent the same four elements in subdivisions of their suit. The Knights are the fire subdivision; the Queens are the water subdivision; the Princes are the air subdivision; and the Princesses are the earth subdivision. This gives us sixteen members of the court-card family and sixteen subelemental characteristics that Crowley identifies as types of human beings.

Modern tarot scholars, in particular Linda Gail Walters,[198] have done a remarkable job of applying the Jungian personality types as defined by the famous Myers-Briggs type indicators[199] to the sixteen court cards. So has psychologist Arthur Rosengarten, who, in his groundbreaking text, *Psychology and Tarot*,[200] discusses these same parallels. I firmly believe that, had the Myers-Briggs concepts been available to Crowley at the time of his writing *The Book of Thoth*, he would most certainly have referred to them, because they bolster his own theories concerning the personality characteristics of the court cards.

Just as each of our personalities has been molded by an elaborate mixture of factors, including genetics, environment, education, and experience, so each court card is a complex mixture of elemental, planetary, and zodiacal factors. When considering what follows, keep in mind that it is the duty of the elements to "mix" (see tables 14 and 15).

MIX-UP #2: PRINCESSES—QUADRANTS OF SPACE— NOT QUADRANTS OF TIME

The Princesses are the earth subelement of their suits and enjoy a special relationship with their aces. For this reason, they are considered separately from the rest of their families. They and their aces rule quadrants of space (see chapter 11).

The Ace/Princess of Wands rules the celestial quadrant of Cancer/Leo/Virgo and the area of Asia; Ace/Princess of Cups rules Libra/Scorpio/Sagittarius and the Pacific; Ace/Princess of Swords rules Capricorn/Aquarius/Pisces and the area of the Americas; and the Ace/Princess of Disks rules Aries/Taurus/Gemini and the areas of Europe and Africa.

MIX-UP #3: KNIGHTS, QUEENS, PRINCES— QUADRANTS OF TIME

Each Knight, Queen, and Prince rule 30° of the zodiacal year. Chauvinistic logic would suggest that the Knights should predominate in cardinal signs, Queens in fixed signs, and Princes in mutable signs of the zodiac—but chauvinistic logic would be wrong!

To mix things up, the knights dominate the mutable signs: (Knight of Wands, Sagittarius; Knight of Cups, Pisces; Knight of Swords, Gemini; Knight of Disks, Virgo). It is the queens who dominate the cardinal signs: (Queen of Wands, Aries; Queen of Cups, Cancer; Queen of Swords, Libra; Queen of Disks, Capricorn). The princes dominate the fixed signs: (Prince of Wands, Leo; Prince of Cups, Scorpio; Prince of Swords, Aquarius; Prince of Disks, Taurus). Very mixed up.

MIX-UP #4: KNIGHTS, QUEENS, PRINCES—THE ADOPT-A-NEIGHBOR'S-DECAN PROGRAM[201]

The mixing up doesn't end here. You will notice that I used the words "predominate" and "dominate," rather than "rule." That is because each of these twelve court cards isn't allowed to completely rule any of the signs of the zodiac; it can only mostly rule a sign of the zodiac. To be precise, each court card rules from 20° of one sign to 20° of the next (see table 14). Even though the Knight of Wands dominates the first 20° (or ²/₃) of the mutable fire sign, Sagittarius, he is also forced by the admixture law of the tarot to back up a bit on the zodiac belt and adopt the last decan (period of 10°) of the sign that preceeds Sagittarius. This means the fiery Knight of Wands has to adopt the last decan of the fixed water sign, Scorpio.

The Queen of Cups dominates the first 20° of the cardinal sign Cancer, but she also has to play hostess to (and be colored by) the last 10° of the mutable sign Gemini. This is how the Knights, Queens, and Princes literally knit the zodiacal year together.

Planets are also assigned to each 10° division (decan) of the zodiac and further influence the character of these twelve court cards, but I will talk about the planets in chapter 19.

NOW I'M MIXED UP

I know this might at first appear rather complicated and beyond the scope of interest of many of you. If that is the case, I commend you for your patience and willingness to wade through this technical discussion of the complexities of the court cards. Please take comfort in the knowledge that, for the moment, it is not as important for you to completely master all these details as it is for you realize that, if you really wanted to, you could master them.

So, as a reward for your forbearance, I'm going to share with you a little shortcut to understanding the court cards and making them immediately usable in a tarot reading. It starts with Crowley's quote that I used to head this chapter:

> The convenience of these arrangements is that these cards are suitable as being descriptive, in a rough and empirical fashion, of divers types of men and women. One may say briefly that any of these cards is a picture of the person whose Sun, or whose rising sign at his nativity, falls within the Zodiacal attribution of the card.

The characteristics of people are a lot easier to remember and understand than the theoretical characteristics of Qabalistic and astrological abstractions. It is enough to remember that each Knight, each Queen, and each Prince is somebody's birthday card. Start with yourself. What court card are you? Do my comments describe you? Do Crowley's? If not, feel free to disregard them and give that card your own definition, based on what you know about yourself.

Next, learn the birthdays of people you know—family members, friends, co-workers, enemies, even celebrities or historical characters about whom you know a great deal. Using their date of birth, determine which court cards they are. Chances are that the character traits you and the others exhibit are very similar to the classic descriptions of the cards. What if they are not, however? Hey! Maybe the cards are wrong. After all, people are real characters in a real world; tarot cards are just pieces of painted paper in a box.

To prime the pump for this kind of meditation, I have, in discussing the court cards, included the names of a few stereotypical celebrities and historical personages whose birth dates make them a Knight, Queen, or Prince of the appropriate suit. I realize only too well that these digressions smack of pop-culture dilettantism, and represent a shocking breach of my vow to keep things as "Crowley" as possible. To all the Crowley purists who are affronted by this un-Crowley offering, I offer my sincere apology. To everyone else—have fun.

KNIGHT OF WANDS
Fire of Fire

20° Scorpio to 20° Sagittarius

November 13 to December 12

Rules 7 of Cups; 8 of Wands; 9 of Wands

Original Titles: The Lord of the Flame and the Lightning; The King of the Spirits of Fire King of the Salamanders.

Crest: Winged black horse's head.

Symbols: Black horse, waving flames. Club. Scarlet gold cloak.

Hair: Red-gold.

Eyes: Grey or Hazel.

> The moral qualities appropriate to this figure are activity, generosity, fierceness, impetuosity, pride, impulsiveness, swiftness in unpredictable actions. If wrongly energized, he is evil-minded, cruel, bigoted and brutal. He is in either case ill-fitted to carry on his action; he has no means of modifying it according to circumstances. If he fails in his first effort, he has no resource.[202]

Representing fire of fire, the Knight of Wands certainly has the potential of being the strongest member of the court cards. He represents the Yod subdivision of the Yod (of YHVH.) However, it is well for us to remember that, where court cards are concerned, representing something is not the same as being something.

Harris translates the Golden Dawn description into a magnificent and thrilling image that almost leaps off the card. Did I say leap? *Explodes* is perhaps a better word. The forward thrust of the horse's mane and tail and the hair and beard of the Knight suggests that they aren't so much in the act of jumping as being blown from behind by some unimaginably strong explosive force. It is the portrait of someone who is riding a rocket, and that can be very risky. If the rocket isn't aimed properly, he or she misses the target. If there is not enough fuel, he or she crashes. If there is too much fuel, the person explodes. But if everything goes well, it is the most spectacular of successes.

Robert Fulton, Indira Gandhi, Robert Kennedy, Frank Sinatra, and Mary Queen of Scots all were Knights of Wands.

Fiery reds, yellows, and gold dominate this card as they do all the Wand court cards.

QUEEN OF WANDS
WATER OF FIRE

20° Pisces to 20° Aries

March 11 to April 10

Rules 10 of Cups; 2 of Wands; 3 of Wands

Original Titles: The Queen of the Thrones of Flame; Queen of the Salamanders.

Crest: Winged leopard.

Symbols: Leopard. Steady flames. Wand with heavy head or end.

Hair: Red-gold.

Eyes: Blue or Brown.

> The Characteristics of the Queen are adaptability, persistent energy, calm authority which she knows how to use to enhance her attractiveness. She is kindly and generous, but impatient of opposition. She has immense capacity for friendship and for love, but always on her own initiative.[203]

The top portion of the card projects such a powerful image of supreme feminine strength and nobility that one could easily see it chiseled in stone as the façade of a great public building or monument. Unfortunately, beautiful as she is, she is somewhat of a façade herself. Crowley goes so far as to suggest she is somewhat of a snob.

When H. Rider Haggard wrote the classic science fiction story *She*, he must have had the Queen of Wands in mind. The title character is Ayesha, a beautiful, immortal queen who rules a land where she is known as "She Who Must Be Obeyed." She is a just but ruthless queen who seems to take offense quite easily. She loves her people (in a selfish sort of way), but she is so self-absorbed that, when the opportunity for her to experience true love presents itself, she becomes a cruel, tyrannical, savage monster. This, naturally, results in her unhappiness and eventual destruction. Describing the character represented by this card, Crowley uses a wonderful expression, "when she misses her bite, she breaks her jaw!"[204]

But that's the downside of this lovely lady. She also can be everything the world needs in a strong woman.

Actress Ursula Andress, who portrayed Queen Ayesha in the 1965 film *She*, is a Queen of Wands. So was Joan Crawford (a real-life She Who Must Be Obeyed). Two other Queens of Wands (whose laws we obey) were Albert Einstein and Wyatt Earp (although, I probably wouldn't have told Wyatt Earp he was the Queen of anything.)

Fiery reds, yellows, and gold dominate this card, as they do all the Wand court cards.

PRINCE OF WANDS
AIR OF FIRE

20° Cancer to 20° Leo

July 12 to August 11

Rules 4 of Cups; 5 of Wands; 6 of Wands

Original Titles: The Prince of the Chariot of Fire; Prince and Emperor of the Salamanders.

Crest: Winged lion's head.

Symbols: Wand and salient flames. Fire wand of Zelator Adeptus Minor.

Hair: Yellow.

Eyes: Blue Grey.

He is romantic especially in matters of history and tradition, to the point of folly, and may engineer "stunts" or play elaborate practical jokes.[205]

The Ascendant (or the rising sign) in one's astrological natal chart is second only to the Sun sign in importance. Among other things, it represents the native's personality and how they appear to others in the world. Crowley's Ascendant was 3° Leo; consequently, he identified strongly with Leo and with the Prince of Wands, who rules 20° Cancer to 20° Leo.

This card is Crowley's idealized image of himself. First of all, we find his personal seal, the Mark of the Beast, emblazoned upon the breast of the Prince. This device appears in only two other places in the Thoth Tarot—on the Five of Wands (which represents 0° to 10° Leo), and the Ace of Disks, which, by tradition, is the signature card of the deck's creator. The Prince is even seated in Crowley's favorite yogic posture, the Thunderbolt asana.[206] Crowley, because he felt he knew himself so well, has a great deal to say about the moral qualities and intellectual paradoxes of this card:

> He is often violent, especially in the expression of an opinion, but he does not necessarily hold the opinion about which he is so emphatic. . . . His character is intensely noble and generous. He may be an extravagant boaster, while slyly laughing both at the object of his boast and at himself for making

it. . . . His courage is fanatically strong, and his endurance indefatigable. He is always fighting against odds, and always wins in the long—the very long—run.[207]

While Crowley identifies with this card because of his rising sign, it also describes a few other notables whose Sun sign makes them Princes of Wands: Julius Caesar, John Dee, Nelson Mandela, Mick Jagger, Jacqueline Kennedy, Madam Blavatsky, and Christopher Hyatt.

Fiery reds, yellows, and gold dominate this card, as they do all the Wand court cards.

PRINCESS OF WANDS
EARTH OF FIRE

Together with the Ace of Wands, rules the Cancer/Leo/Virgo celestial quadrant above the North Pole and the area of Asia.

Original Titles: The Princess of the Shining Flame; The Rose of the Palace of Fire; Princess and Empress of the Salamanders. Throne of the Ace of Wands.

Crest: Tiger's head.

Symbols: Tiger, leaping flames. Gold Altar, long club, largest at bottom.

Hair: Red-gold.

Eyes: Blue.

I am a bit worried. The princess is behaving most queer! She won't have any nice tidy lines & I really don't know if she will be alright. She is certainly no relation of the first sample submitted. I think when I have smacked her, I shall have to post her to you, & you can tear her up or retain her as she strikes you. Oh dear I am tired. I have battled with her blaring wriggles till the eye falls out & she has burnt my throat & I can't swallow. [208]

> —Harris to Crowley, date uncertain.

The Princesses share a special status among the court cards, and Harris seems to have given all four of them the special attention they deserve. They are all breathtakingly beautiful. Placed side by side, they are the four pin-up girls of the Thoth Tarot. The Princess of Wands is especially stunning, and is one more reason the Crowley-Harris deck is banned contraband within so many prisons. Crowley wrote, "This card may be said to represent the dance of the virgin priestess of the Lords of Fire."[209]

As the earth subelement of the suit of fire, she not only officiates before the ram's-headed altar as Princess of the flaming sacrifice, but is herself the fuel of the fire. We recognize her in people we meet who are so energetically self-assured, so independent and irrationally audacious that, while inspirational and thrilling, they can be downright dangerous to be around.

When ill-dignified, she is the ultimate drama queen, who is so shallow and self-absorbed that it never occurs to her that nobody is sympathizing with her. If left unchecked, the Princess of Wands gone bad will not only incinerate herself need-lessly, in doing so she will also set fire to the whole neighborhood. She can be "cruel, unreliable, faithless and domineering."[210] Know anyone like that?

Princesses do not rule degrees of the zodiacal year, so we have no examples of celebrated personalities who are/were Princesses of Wands.

Fiery reds, yellows, and gold dominate this card, as they do all the Wand court cards.

KNIGHT OF CUPS
FIRE OF WATER

20° Aquarius to 20° Pisces

February 9 to March 10

Rules 7 of Swords; 8 of Cups; 9 of Cups

Original Titles: Lord of the Waves and the Waters; The King of the Hosts of the Sea; King of Nymphs or Undines.

Crest: Peacock with open wings.

Symbols: White horse, crab issuing from cup. Sea.

Hair: Fair.

Eyes: Blue.

> Swiftness and violence ill suit a character naturally placid; it is rare indeed to meet a person who has succeeded in harmonizing these conflicting elements.[211]

I've got to be careful with this one. Both my wife and son are the Knights of Cups. Of course, none of the negative qualities of this card pertain to either of them.

Leaping out of the card in the opposite direction than that of the Knight of Wands, the Knight of Cups is a cool contrast to his brother. Fire of water brings to mind water in action—a pelting rain, a gushing spring—and the more patient actions whereby water erodes and dissolves things.

Like most of the court cards, Harris's version respectfully contains all the major features of the Golden Dawn model, including a most beautiful and subtle peacock that seems to be fashioned from a plume of pure water created by the wake of the Knight's movement.

I think Crowley rather liked this fellow, and after all, what's not to like? "He is amiable in a passive way. He is quick to respond to attraction, and easily becomes enthusiastic under such stimulus; but he is not very enduring."[212]

We can probably blame the influence of mutable Pisces for throwing her wet blanket on the white horse of our otherwise fiery lord of the waves and the waters. This makes the Knight of Cups a pretty nice guy. He's just not very deep. In fact, the worst name we can call him is "shallow water." He has a natural innocence and purity that make him likeable, but he's often just not deep enough for those virtues to easily manifest as profound nobility of character. As Crowley says, "His name is writ in water."[213]

While this may be somewhat true for natives such as Sonny Bono, Mia Farrow, and Burt Reynolds, there must also be something in the character of this card that engenders the likes of George Washington, Abraham Lincoln, Susan B. Anthony, and Thomas Edison.

Cool blues and blue-greens dominate this card, as they do the other Cups court cards.

QUEEN OF CUPS
WATER OF WATER

20° Gemini to 20° Cancer

June 11 to July 11

Rules 10 of Swords; 2 of Cups; 3 of Cups

Original Titles: The Queen of the Thrones of Water; Queen of the Nymphs or Undines.

Crest: Ibis

Symbols: Crayfish issuing from River.

Hair: Gold-brown.

Eyes: Blue.

Her image is of extreme purity and beauty, with infinite subtlety; to see the Truth of her is hardly possible, for she reflects the nature of the observer in great perfection.[214]

The Queen of Cups is my birthday court card, so please be warned that the objectivity of my comments may be obscured by clouds of narcissism, but honestly, who am I to argue with Crowley?[215]

Harris's Queen of Cups bears striking similarities to Atu II, the High Priestess. As a matter of fact, if you were to trim the borders of the two cards and place the Queen of Cups upside down above the High Priestess, you would see that they match in a dizzying display of synthetic projective geometry. Both cards present the image of a great cup, the stem of which is formed by the body of a goddesss. Atu II is the cup of the virginal goddess of the Moon; the Queen of Cups is that of the great mother goddess.

Water of water is tantamount to saying reflection of reflection, or mirror to mirror. The Queen of Cups is popular and makes friends easily because, when others look at her, they see only themselves. Crowleys tells us that "She is the perfect agent and patient, able to receive and transmit everything without herself being affected thereby."[216] To liberals, she looks like a liberal; to conservatives, she looks like a conservative, when in truth she may be neither. If ill dignified, she can be dangerous and cruel, distorting the reflections she casts back on her unsuspecting victims, who then see only monsters in the mirror.

My fellow Queens of Cups include Paul McCartney, Jacques Cousteau, John D. Rockefeller, Nikola Tesla, George Orwell, and Gerald Gardner.

Cool blues and blue-greens dominate this card, as they do the other Cups court cards.

PRINCE OF CUPS
Air of Water

20° Libra to 20° Scorpio

October 13 to November 12

Rules 4 of Swords; 5 of Cups; 6 of Cups

Original Titles: The Prince of the Chariot of the Waters: Prince and Emperor of the Nymphs or Undines.

Crest: Eagle.

Symbols: Scorpion, eagle-serpent issuing from lake.

Hair: Brown.

Eyes: Grey or Brown.

> The moral characteristics of the person pictured in this card are subtlety, secret violence, and craft. He is intensely secret, an artist in all his ways. . . . He is in fact perfectly ruthless.[217]

With style worthy of a comic book cover, Harris's Prince of Cups makes a spectacular entrance by bursting straight at us from a crashing wave, his chariot drawn by an enormous black eagle. His left hand grasps a cup out of which rises a coiled a snake. In his right hand, he holds an enormous lotus blossom.

I have to believe that Crowley had an unpleasant experience with a Prince of Cups. If everyone born between October 13 and November 12 manifested all the dark and chilling qualities Crowley ascribes to this card, then ¹/₁₂ of the population of the planet would be melodrama villains. While that may have been true of Princes of Cups Lee Harvey Oswald and Leon Trotsky, there is still great strength and potential in this card.

Libra passing over to Scorpio is a very strong moment, but the active characteristics of air in the passive environment of water makes an uneasy combination. Like foaming bubbles exploding from an underchilled bottle of champagne, these two elements do not care if they ruin the party or the furniture; they just want to get out and away from each other. Maybe that is why Crowley describes the Prince of Cups as "completely without conscience in the ordinary sense of the word, and is therefore usually distrusted by his neighbors."[218]

I've known several Princes of Cups, including my father, and I must say they were indeed men of immense abilities who could not be, as Crowley noted, "relied upon to work in harness."[219] The same could be said of fellow Princes Martin Luther, Oscar Wilde, Friedrich Nietzsche, Timothy Leary, and Pablo Picasso.

Cool blues and blue-greens dominate this card, as they do the other Cups court cards.

PRINCESS OF CUPS
EARTH OF WATER

Together with the Ace of Cups, rules the Libra/Scorpio/Sagittarius celestial quadrant above the North Pole, and the area of the Pacific.

Original Titles: The Princess of the Waters; Lotus of the Palace of the Floods; Princess and Empress of the Nymphs or Undines. Throne of the Ace of Cups.

Crest: Swan.

Symbols: Dolphin, Lotus. Sea with spray, turtle from cup.

Hair: Brown.

Eyes: Blue or Brown.

> The character of the Princess is infinitely gracious. All sweetness, all voluptuousness, gentleness, kindness and tenderness are in her character. She lives in the world of Romance, in the perpetual dream of rapture.[220]

I cannot overemphasize the importance of the relationship between the ace of each suit and its Princess. The ace may be beautiful to look at, but, because it is the root—the hidden germ—of its suit and element, it is impossible to understand. The Princess, on the other hand, represents the end product, the crystallization and materialization of what was purely potential in the ace. In the language of religion, the ace may be worshipped, but the Princess can be adored. That being so, it would not be inappropriate for the herald of this card to cry out, "All fall down before Princess of the Waters; Lotus of the Palace of the Floods; Throne of the Holy Grail!" You my think I'm laying it on a bit thick for this young lady, but I assure you, not half as thick as Mr. Crowley did. She's not all dreams, either. As earth of water, she literally can ground vaporous and romantic ideas into manifestation, and provide a fixed and fertile medium where the water-nourished life of ideas can flourish.

Harris's image is one of graceful fluid movement. The water is alive with large smooth waves that suggest the heavy environment of ocean's depth. The Princess is dancing, her eyes closed, her head thrown back, an expression of pure rapture on her face reminiscent of Bernini's *The Ecstasy of Saint Theresa*. The scallops of her dress are the same motif found on the Ace of Cups, and the hem is adorned with clear water crystals.

Princesses do not rule degrees of the zodiacal year, so we have no examples of celebrated personalities who are/were Princesses of Cups.

Cool blues and blue-greens dominate this card, as they do the other Cups court cards.

KNIGHT OF SWORDS
Fire of Air

20° Taurus to 20° Gemini

May 11 to June 10

Rules 7 of Disks; 8 of Swords; 9 of Swords

Original Titles: The Lord of the Winds and Breezes; King of the Spirits of Air; King of the Sylphs and Sylphides.

Crest: Winged Hexagram.

Symbols: Winged brown horse, driving clouds, drawn brown sword.

Hair: Dark Brown.

Eyes: Dark.

> I have done as you suggested to the Swords. Thank you Mr Crowley. You were quite right.[221]
>
> —Harris to Crowley, date uncertain.

Swords are the suit of air and, as we begin our examination of these cards, I must point out a design motif that appears repeatedly in all the cards of this suit—wings. Lady Harris incorporates angular and highly stylized wings everywhere! They may not always look like wings, but that is what they are.

Beginning with the Knight of Swords, we see that what appear at first to be four propeller blades spinning atop his pointed helmet are actually four triangular wings sprouting from his back. They are transparent and veined, like those of a dragonfly. Perhaps there are only two wings that are moving so fast they appear as four. Please take a moment and look at the Queen, Prince, and Princess of Swords, and locate the marvelous angular wings on these figures. Now look at all the small cards of the suit and see the backgrounds festooned with these stylized wings—some balanced, almost pinwheel in form; some twisted, broken, stretched, and distorted.

It has been suggested that these figures represent magical sigils drawn from planetary kameas, or magical squares. Anyone familiar with the extent (or should I say the limits) of Lady Harris's magical education at the time would not even suggest such a thing.

The Knight of Swords is fire of air, suggestive of a violent wind. The general divinatory meaning of the card can be summed up in one word—*attack*. "The moral qualities of person thus indicated," Crowley warned, "are activity and skill, subtlety and cleverness. He is fierce, delicate and courageous but altogether the prey of his idea, which comes to him as an inspiration without reflection."[222]

Famous Knights of Swords include Baron Münchhausen, Arthur Conan Doyle, Pope John Paul II, Malcolm X, Queen Victoria, John Wayne, John F. Kennedy, Marilyn Monroe, and Cher.

Sky blues, yellows, and white cirrus clouds dominate this card, as they do the Queen of Swords.

QUEEN OF SWORDS
Water of Air

20° Virgo to 20° Libra

September 12 to October 12

Rules 10 of Disks; 2 of Swords; 3 of Swords

Original Titles: The Queen of the Thrones of Air; Queen of the Sylphs and Sylphides.

Crest: Winged child's head.

Symbols: Head of man severed. Cumulous clouds. Drawn sword.

Hair: Grey.

Eyes: Light Brown.

> The person symbolized by this card should be intensely perceptive, a keen observer, a subtle interpreter, and intense individualist, swift and accurate at recording ideas; in action confident, in spirit gracious and just.[223]

This card represents Crowley's Sun sign and so, naturally, it is the most intimidating card in the deck. One look at this lady tells us she means business. Water of air is suggestive of clouds that promise either life-giving rain or the threat of a torrential cloudburst. She holds the severed head of a bearded man in her left hand and the sword that probably did the job in her right. One may think this grisly touch is just another gruesome Crowleyism. It is not. This image is the classic Golden Dawn description of the Queen of Swords, and makes a fundamental Qabalistic statement.

The suit of Swords represents Yetzirah, the formative world—the mind's eye of deity. Swords' and Yetzirah's counterpart in the human soul is the Ruach, the intellect, which is centered in the brain—the human head. Using the sword of discretion and reason, the Queen has separated the higher faculties of the intellect from the influences of the lower nature (the Nephesh, the animal soul). She is quite literally, Crowley points out, the "Liberator of the Mind."[224] The head is that of a bearded man (the Hermit of Virgo perhaps?), the eyes closed peacefully, the face suggesting the trance of deep meditation.

The influence of Virgo moving into Libra gives the Queen of Swords the practicality and grace of a great monarch. This native "should be intensely perceptive, a keen observer, a subtle interpreter, an intense individualist, swift and accurate at recording ideas; in action confident, in spirit gracious and just. Her movements will be graceful, and her ability in dancing and balancing exceptional."[225] If ill-dignified, she can be as cruel and dangerous as she looks.

Crowley's fellow Queens of Swords include Mahatma Gandhi, Eleanor Roosevelt, H. G. Wells, and Stephen King.

Sky blues, yellows, and white cumulus clouds dominate this card.

PRINCE OF SWORDS
Air of Air

20° Capricorn to 20° Aquarius

January 10 to February 8

Rules 4 of Disks; 5 of Swords; 6 of Swords

Original Titles: The Prince of the Chariot of the Winds; Prince and Emperor of Sylphs and Sylphides.

Crest: Winged angel's head.

Symbols: Arch Fairies winged. Dark clouds, nimbi, drawn swords.

Hair: Grey.

Eyes: Dark.

It is easy to be deceived by such people; for the manifestation itself has enormous potency: it is as if an imbecile offered one the dialogues of Plato. They may in this way acquire a great reputation both for depth and breadth of mind.[226]

An earlier version of this card paints a kinder, gentler picture of the Prince of Swords and the arch fairies who draw his chariot. The final version is full of mad, seemingly futile movement. The geometrical wings of the Prince and the children are enclosed in bright yellow bubbles—air of air. The children pull the chariot "irresponsibly in any direction that takes their fancy; they are not reined, but perfectly capricious. The chariot consequently is easy enough to move, but quite unable to progress in any definite direction except by accident. This is a perfect picture of the Mind."[227]

Like a madman whose brain creates only to destroy, we see the Prince with the sword in his right hand, with which he creates ideas and images, and the sickle in his left hand, with which he immediately cuts them down. This sounds like madness, but we are doing the same thing every moment of our waking lives. When the mind is given a creative outlet for this process, such as music, literature, or film making, we discover great genius. Mozart and Mendelssohn were Princes of Swords, as were the great film directors D. W. Griffith and Federico Fellini, and the visionary Emmanuel Swedenborg.

Crowley heaps great praise upon the pure intelligence of the Prince of Swords, but he cannot avoid discussing the futility of thinking about thinking. "He is full of ideas and designs which tumble over each other," he points out. "He is a mass of fine ideal unrelated to practical effort."[228]

The great actor James Dean was a Prince of Swords, and while Jim Stark (the character he played so brilliantly in the film *Rebel without a Cause*) was fictitious, Dean nonetheless gave profound life to that role. In my mind, it was the perfect tortured portrayal of the frustrations inherent in this card—a performance that I believe, in all likelihood, would have been appreciated by fellow Prince of Swords, Edgar Allan Poe.

Clouds of sharp white ice crystals, yellows, and metallic greens dominate this card.

PRINCESS OF SWORDS
EARTH OF AIR

Together with the Ace of Swords, rules the Capricorn/Aquarius/Pisces celestial quadrant above the North Pole, and the area of Americas.

Original Titles: The Princess of the Rushing Winds; The Lotus of the Palace of Air; Princess and Empress of the Sylphs and Sylphides. Throne of the Ace of Swords.

Crest: Medusa's head.

Symbols: Silver altar, smoke. Cirrus clouds. Drawn brown sword.

Hair: Light Brown.

Eyes: Blue.

The character of the Princess is stern and revengeful. Her logic is destructive. She is firm and aggressive, with great practical wisdom and subtlety in material things. She shews great cleverness and dexterity in the management of practical affairs, especially where they are of a controversial nature. She is very adroit in the settlement of controversies.[229]

Rising out of a cloud of dust, Crowley's paradoxical Princess of Swords, earth of air, appears like a beautiful avenging angel. Her head is crowned with the Medusa-headed helmet, which mercifully is turned away from our view. For if we were to gaze upon its awful face, we would surely be turned to stone. Turning things to stone ("fixation of the volatile"—"materialization of Idea"[230]) is just part of the job description for Princess of Swords, however.

The suit of Swords (as Ruach, the intellect) is a wonderful aspect of our being because, when we identify with the Ruach, we rise above and separate ourselves from our lower nature, the animal soul (the Nephesh). However, when we identify with the Ruach, we also separate ourselves from the higher parts of our souls that represent greater realities and levels of consciousness than our Ruach is incapable of comprehending. Consequently, the Ruach does everything it can to keep its grasp on our identity. This is why the Eastern mystics warn us that the mind is a great enemy. It must be defeated in battle. When the battle begins, the Ruach naturally sends its finest swordswoman into the field—a warrior-princess who manifests everything that is inherent, yet hidden, in her lord, the ace, a mighty champion of the mind—a Minerva, an Artemis, a Valkyrie,—the Princess of Swords.

Swirling clouds of gray-black dust and violent windbursts darken the heavens and almost completely dominate and obscure what once was the yellows and blues of this suit.

Since Princesses do not rule degrees of the zodiacal year, we have no examples of celebrated personalities who are/were Princesses of Swords.

KNIGHT OF DISKS
FIRE OF EARTH

20° Leo to 20° Virgo

August 12 to September 11

Rules 7 of Wands; 8 of Disks; 9 of Disks

Original Titles: The Lord of the Wide and Fertile Land; The King of the Spirits of Earth; King of the Gnomes.

Crest: Winged stag's head.

Symbols: Light brown horse. Ripe corn land. Scepter with Hexagram of Zelator Adeptus Minor.

Hair: Dark.

Eyes: Dark.

I am doing the King of Pantacles. I didn't like what I had done. Someone has lent me a genuine flail—it is like this [manuscript drawing of flail] a lovely instrument of solid wood. Most difficult to manage.[231]
—Harris to Crowley, November 3, 1939.

The Knight of Disks is unique among his brother Knights. He appears to be the shortest in stature. He rides a workhorse that seems to be more concerned with eyeing the lush grass than with conveying his rider. His helmet is completely raised, and he gazes at the fertile fields and hills, as if in contemplation of harvest, not battle. His flail dangles near the grasses, suggesting the thrashing of wheat rather than the thrashing of heads, and his shield is a disk that could double as a dish that could hold enough food to feed a village. Am I making this up just because I'm hungry and dinner is late? Not at all. Crowley writes that the function of the Knight of Disks "is entirely confined to the production of food."[232]

I am sure there are many geniuses and intellectually brilliant individuals whose birthdays fall between August 12 to September 11 (Napoleon Bonaparte, Cardinal Richelieu, Louis the XIV, Bill Clinton, Madonna, and H. P. Lovecraft to name a few). Nonetheless, the natural character of this card is not that of a rocket scientist. The Knight of Disks keeps his nose to the grindstone, and takes little interest in (and has little respect for) intellectual musings or the finer aspects of culture or civilization. If ill-aspected, he will even make ignorance a virtue and take obstinate pride in his own lack of sophistication and subtlety.

Davey Crockett, Annie Oakley, and Country and Western stars Buck Owens, Porter Wagoner, Patsy Cline, and Jim Reeves were all Knights of Disks.

Rich browns, greens, and golden yellow dominate this card.

QUEEN OF DISKS
WATER OF EARTH

20° Sagittarius to 20° Capricorn

December 13 to January 9

Rules 10 of Wands; 2 of Disks; 3 of Disks

Original Titles: The Queen of the Thrones of Earth; Queen of the Gnomes.

Crest: Winged goat's head.

Symbols: Barren land. Light falls on only one side of her face. Scepter with golden orb.

Hair: Dark.

Eyes: Dark.

> Persons signified by this card possess the finest of the quieter qualities. They are ambitious, but only in useful directions.[233]

Life-giving water to a thirsty Earth. What a beautiful concept. What a beautiful tarot card. Her dress alone is worth looking at with a magnifying glass.

The genteel author, Jane Austen, is an ideal model for Crowley's characterization of this card, and matches his description in *The Book of Thoth* perfectly. She was quietly passive—but passivity, Crowley claims, "in its highest aspect."[234] She and many of her characters were "quiet, hard-working, practical, sensible, domesticated."[235]

Like Austen herself, however, there is much more to the Queen of Disks than needlepoint and country dances. I believe, at least on one level, Aleister Crowley was having us on when he wrote, "They are not intellectual, and not particularly intelligent; but instinct and intuition are more than adequate for their needs."[236] I think he was getting closer to the truth when he wrote, "She thus represents the ambition of matter to take part in the great work of Creation."[237]

Think about that for a moment. That is a force to be reckoned with.

Water of earth manifests in very complex and diverse ways, and these are reflected in the broad spectrum of personalities who can embody the ambition of matter to take part in the great work of creation. A Queen of Disks can be strong and charismatic like her sister Joan of Arc, or just talented and charismatic like Elvis Presley. She can be ruthless and manipulative like Catherine of Aragon, Joseph Stalin, Mao Tse-tung, and Richard Nixon; or sensitive and idealistic like Woodrow

Wilson, George Washington Carver, or Carl Sandburg. She can possess instinctual, intuitive, and superior intelligence like Nostradamus, Johannes Kepler, Isaac Newton, and Stephen Hawking; or she can be a giant of creative force like Ludwig Van Beethoven, J. R. R. Tolkien, or Steven Spielberg.

Dark greens and rich browns dominate the foreground of this card.

PRINCE OF DISKS
AIR OF EARTH

20° Aries to 20° Taurus

April 11 to May 10

Rules 4 of Wands; 5 of Disks; 6 of Disks

Original Titles: The Prince of the Chariot of Earth; Prince and Emperor of the Gnomes.

Crest: Winged bull's head.

Symbols: Flowery land. Bull. Dark scepter with orb and cross. Orb held downward.

Hair: Dark Brown.

Eyes: Dark.

> The Prince of Disks is a devil. I've been a whole week on him & he is engendering a nervous breakdown in me coupled with starvation as he gives me no time to eat. He is a bastard. However, I hope I have caught him today. He swells & swells & I can't get him in the picture with all the farm produce & bulls you suggest.[238]
>
> —Harris to Crowley, date uncertain.

A devil indeed! But what a devil! I don't think it's a good idea to put too many Princes of Disks in the same room. These fellows change the world with their "great energy brought to bear upon the most solid of practical matters."[239] Consider this short roster of Princes of Disks: Marcus Aurelius, William Shakespeare, Catherine the Great, Thomas Jefferson, Robespierre, Ulysses S. Grant, Sigmund Freud, Karl Marx, Nikolai Lenin, Adolf Hitler, Emperor Hirohito, Robert Oppenheimer, Harry Truman, Golda Meir, and Saddam Hussein.

You and I, however, are more likely to run into what I call the "garden variety" Prince of Disks—and by "garden variety" I mean just that. Harris's Prince is seated in a chariot filled with globular seeds that seem to be ready to burst into plants at any moment. He is a very cool character. His eyes are closed in meditation, as if he were mentally directing the brooding fecundity of the entire universe. He is the picture of someone who is in control on the material plane. He may seem a bit dull and emotionless, but he's not. He's just not a snob, and he doesn't bother with things he considers impractical. He's the ultimate handyman. Crowley confirms that assessment, telling us that "He is competent, ingenious, thoughtful, cautious, trustworthy, imperturbable; he constantly seeks new uses for common things."[240]

This is the darkest card of the suit of Disks, full of rich browns and blacks.

PRINCESS OF DISKS
Earth of Earth

Together with the Ace of Disks, rules the Aries/Taurus/Gemini celestial quadrant above the North Pole, and the area of Europe and Africa.

Original Titles: The Princess of the Echoing Hills; The Rose of the Palace of Earth; Princess and Empress of the Gnomes. Throne of the Ace of Disks.

Crest: Winged ram's head.

Symbols: Grass. Flowers, grove of trees. Scepter with disk. Disk is as others.

Hair: Rich Brown.

Eyes: Dark.

> The Princess is now on the stocks. I wish she would not insist on being pregnant. She just will, so now I have let her get on with it. She chatters to me about being mixed up with the Virgin Mary.[241]
> —Harris to Crowley, December 11, 1942.

We do not know for certain which card of the Thoth Tarot Lady Harris painted last, but the date of the above note suggests she was working on the Princess of Disks toward the very end of the project. If she did complete the deck with this card, she certainly saved the best for last. For me, the Princess of Disks is the most beautiful female figure in the entire Thoth Tarot. "She is strong and beautiful," Crowley affirms, "with an expression of intense brooding, as if about to become aware of secret wonder."[242] To be embarrassingly honest, I am most profoundly (and most hopelessly) in love with her. I am not alone in my sloppy adoration of her divine image. Enlargements of this card adorn the living-room walls of many of my colleagues, and it is one of the most frequently reproduced cards of the deck.

I now ask the reader to recall the Qabalistic fairytale we discussed in chapter 11, and the importance of the Princess as carrier of the essence of the highest high and the lowest low. As earth of earth, she is the lowest court card of the lowest suit. She is the ultimate princess. Not only is she pregnant with the highest high/ lowest low (and everything in between) of the suit of Disks, she is pregnant with the highest high/lowest low (and everything in between) of all the suits. She is the Malkuth of Malkuths and carries within her body the potential of all possible possibilities, and the key to perpetuating the life of the universe.

As a priestess of Demeter, she arises in her glory from out of the Earth itself and establishes her altar in the midst of a grove of barren and dying trees that her fertile presence will now restore to green health. Her magic wand is the diamond-tipped rod, symbolic of the essence of Kether, the highest high, and whose tetrahedral form is the basic structure of all carbon-based life. She is wrapped in an enormous cape of what appears to be animal fur and is crowned with the head and horns of a ram. Her disk is a giant seed composed of thirty-six sections, perhaps suggesting the source of the thirty-six small cards of the tarot to follow. The central germ of the seed is the Chinese yin-yang. Dark yellows and browns radiate a warm and almost humid atmosphere for this card. Textured grays combine to make this card almost tactile.

All this Qabalistic cosmology and Eleusinian mythology is fine and good, but Crowley told us at the beginning of our discussion of the court cards that "these cards are suitable as being descriptive, in a rough and empirical fashion, of divers types of men and women."[243] In a tarot reading, what kind of person does the Princess of Disks represent? Because her potential is limitless, Crowley writes that she might have the reputation of "bewildering inconsistency."[244] He uses the example of a lottery, where it does not matter how many times a particular number has been drawn in the past, each future draw provides the same odds of it being drawn or not drawn again. In the old days of male chauvinism, this quality might have been summed up in the somewhat sexist term "woman's prerogative." That might have been where Crowley was coming from when he wrote that the Princess of Disks represents "Womanhood in its ultimate projection."[245]

As he concludes his comments on this card in *The Book of Thoth*, Crowley writes as if he were ending the entire book. In a way, he was, because the Princess of Disks is, in many ways, the last tarot card. I too would like to end our discussion of the Court cards with his wonderful of benediction:

> Let every student of this Essay, and of this book of Tahuti, this living Book that guides man through all Time, and leads him to Eternity at every page, hold fast this simplest, most far-reaching Doctrine in his heart and mind, inflaming the inmost of His Being, that he also, having explored each recess of the Universe, may therein find the Light of Truth, so come to the Knowledge and Conversation of the Holy Guardian Angel, and accomplish the Great Work, attain the Summum Bonum, true Wisdom and perfect Happiness![246]

CHAPTER NINETEEN

THE SMALL CARDS

Hang on. It's easier than you think![247]

Now we turn our attention to the thirty-six small cards. In the ancient decks, these cards were called "pips" and were seldom more complex than simple geometrical arrangements of Wands, Cups, Swords, or Disks. Sometimes, the number of the card was printed on one or more corners, much like our modern playing cards. This changed dramatically with the introduction of secret images taught to initiates of the Golden Dawn, and the published deck suggested by Arthur Edward Waite and executed by Pamela Coleman Smith. Suddenly, the small cards had images that evoked feelings and emotions the same way the trumps did.

There is a big difference between the Golden Dawn images and those of the Waite/Smith deck. Waite, an influential member of the Golden Dawn, felt bound by his oaths of secrecy to the order never to reveal the correct and esoteric images and meanings of the tarot. The deck that he and Smith produced was created as a vehicle to introduce the mysteries, not to reveal them. They certainly succeeded. It is difficult to develop a complex or overly esoteric dogma around the deck, and for this I must admit Waite did a good job of not violating his vows. What I am not sure he foresaw was the fact that, over the years, the deck would become so wildly popular that its images would engender a perfectly viable self-referential divinatory device of its own. In other words, the Waite/Smith deck may not be the perfect Qabalistic tarot, but it is perfect whatever it is.

RECIPE FOR THE SMALL CARDS

The small cards of the Thoth Tarot take the Golden Dawn model as their basic standard and, when considering them, we are immediately confronted with the question of their titles and meanings. Why is the Two of Cups called Love and the Seven of Cups called Debauch? Why is the Ten of Wands Oppression and the Ten of Disks Wealth? Why are so many of the Swords horrible cards?

The answer is a simple formula containing two Qabalistic and two astrological factors. The formula is:

$$(\text{n of s}) + (\text{p in zs}) = \text{sc}$$
$$(\underline{N}\text{umber of Suit}) + (\underline{P}\text{lanet in } \underline{Z}\text{odiac Sign}) = \underline{S}\text{mall } \underline{C}\text{ard})$$

In chapter 9, we learned the basics concerning the ten sephiroth, YHVH, and the four Qabalistic Worlds. Now let's look at the astrological factors.

Let's start with the signs of the zodiac and their divisions by quadruplicities and triplicities.

QUADRUPLICITIES OF THE ZODIAC
The twelve signs of the zodiac are categorized, according to element into quadruplicities (four groups of three signs; see table 9). The four tarot suits are assigned to each as follows:

Wands: Fire signs (Aries, Leo, Sagittarius)
Cups: Water signs (Cancer, Scorpio, Pisces)
Swords: Air signs (Libra, Aquarius, Gemini)
Disks: Earth signs (Capricorn, Taurus, Virgo)

TRIPLICITIES OF THE ZODIAC
The twelve signs of the zodiac are categorized according to modes into triplicities (three groups of four signs; see table 10). The nine small cards of each suit are assigned in groups of three to each as follows:

Twos, Threes, Fours: Cardinal signs (Aries, Cancer, Libra, Capricorn)
Fives, Sixes, Sevens: Fixed signs (Leo, Scorpio, Aquarius, Taurus)
Eights, Nines, Tens: Mutable signs (Sagittarius, Pisces, Gemini, Virgo)

When we put the zodiac signs in order, we see the small cards are ordered in four repeating patterns of 2 through 10 (see table 11). Each small card represents one decan (period of 10°) of the zodiac, and approximately ten days of the year (see table 12).

Table 9. Small Cards Suits, Zodiac Signs and Elements

The small cards are allocated to the signs of the zodiac according to the element of their suit
(*Wands to the Fire Signs; Cups to the Water Signs; Swords to the Air Signs; Disks to the Earth Signs*)

WANDS
Wands are attributed to three Fire Signs
(Aries, Leo, Sagittarius)

♈ ARIES	♌ LEO	♐ SAGITTARIUS
FIRE SIGN	FIRE SIGN	FIRE SIGN

CUPS
Cups are attributed to three Water Signs
(Cancer, Scorpio, Pisces)

♋ CANCER	♏ SCORPIO	♓ PISCES
WATER SIGN	WATER SIGN	WATER SIGN

SWORDS
Swords are attributed to three Air Signs
(Libra, Aquarius, Gemini)

♎ LIBRA	♒ AQUARIUS	♊ GEMINI
AIR SIGN	AIR SIGN	AIR SIGN

DISKS
Disks are attributed to three Earth Signs
(Capricorn, Taurus, Virgo)

♑ CAPRICORN	♉ TAURUS	♍ VIRGO
EARTH SIGN	EARTH SIGN	EARTH SIGN

Table 10. Cardinal Signs, Fixed Signs, and Mutable Signs

The 2-3-4s of each suit represent the **Cardinal** Signs; The **5-6-7s**, the **Fixed** Signs; the **8-9-10s**, the **Mutable** Signs

CARDINAL SIGNS
(Aries, Cancer, Libra, Capricorn)

♈ ARIES Cardinal fire	♋ CANCER Cardinal Water	♎ LIBRA Cardinal Air	♑ CAPRICORN Cardinal Earth
2 3 4	2 3 4	2 3 4	2 3 4
of WANDS	of CUPS	of SWORDS	of DISKS

FIXED SIGNS
(Leo, Scorpio, Aquarius, Taurus)

♌ LEO Fixed Fire	♏ SCORPIO Fixed Water	♒ AQUARIUS Fixed Air	♉ TAURUS Fixed Earth
5 6 7	5 6 7	5 6 7	5 6 7
of WANDS	of CUPS	of SWORDS	of DISKS

MUTABLE SIGNS
(Sagittarius, Pisces, Gemini, Virgo)

♐ SAGITTARIUS Mutable Fire	♓ PISCES Mutable Water	♊ GEMINI Mutable Air	♍ VIRGO Mutable Earth
8 9 10	8 9 10	8 9 10	8 9 10
of WANDS	of CUPS	of SWORDS	of DISKS

Table 11. Small Cards in Four Repeating Patterns of 2 Through 10

When we put the zodiac signs in order, we see the small cards are ordered in four repeating patterns of 2 through 10.

♈ ARIES Cardinal Fire	♉ TAURUS Fixed Earth	♊ GEMINI Mutable Air	♋ CANCER Cardinal Water	♌ LEO Fixed Fire	♍ VIRGO Mutable Earth	♎ LIBRA Cardinal Air	♏ SCORPIO Fixed Water	♐ SAGITTARIUS Mutable Fire	♑ CAPRICORN Cardinal Earth	♒ AQUARIUS Fixed Air	♓ PISCES Mutable Water
2 3 4	5 6 7	8 9 10	2 3 4	5 6 7	8 9 10	2 3 4	5 6 7	8 9 10	2 3 4	5 6 7	8 9 10
of WANDS	*of* DISKS	*of* SWORDS	*of* CUPS	*of* WANDS	*of* DISKS	*of* SWORDS	*of* CUPS	*of* WANDS	*of* DISKS	*of* SWORDS	*of* CUPS

Table 12. Progression of the Small Cards Through the Zodiacal Year

Each small card represents 1 decan (period of 10 degrees) of the zodiac, and approximately 10 days of the year.

Sign	Suit	Card	Degrees	Dates
♈ ARIES Cardinal Fire	WANDS	2	0°–10°	MAR 21–30
		3	10°–20°	MAR 31 APR 10
		4	20°–30°	APR 11–20
♉ TAURUS Fixed Earth	DISKS	5	0°–10°	APR 21–30
		6	10°–20°	MAY 1–10
		7	20°–30°	MAY 11–20
♊ GEMINI Mutable Air	SWORDS	8	0°–10°	MAY 21–30
		9	10°–20°	JUN 1–10
		10	20°–30°	JUN 11–20
♋ CANCER Cardinal Water	CUPS	2	0°–10°	JUN 21 JUL 1
		3	10°–20°	JUL 2–11
		4	20°–30°	JUL 12–21
♌ LEO Fixed Fire	WANDS	5	0°–10°	JUL 22 AUG 1
		6	10°–20°	AUG 2–11
		7	20°–30°	AUG 12–22
♍ VIRGO Mutable Earth	DISKS	8	0°–10°	AUG 23 SEP 1
		9	10°–20°	SEP 2–11
		10	20°–30°	SEP 12–22
♎ LIBRA Cardinal Air	SWORDS	2	0°–10°	SEP 23 OCT 2
		3	10°–20°	OCT 3–12
		4	20°–30°	OCT 13–22
♏ SCORPIO Fixed Water	CUPS	5	0°–10°	OCT 23 NOV 1
		6	10°–20°	NOV 2–11
		7	20°–30°	NOV 13–22
♐ SAGITTARIUS Mutable Fire	WANDS	8	0°–10°	NOV 23 DEC 2
		9	10°–20°	DEC 3–12
		10	20°–30°	DEC 13–20
♑ CAPRICORN Cardinal Earth	DISKS	2	0°–10°	DEC 21–30
		3	10°–20°	DEC 31 JAN 9
		4	20°–30°	JAN 10–19
♒ AQUARIUS Fixed Air	SWORDS	5	0°–10°	JAN 20–29
		6	10°–20°	JAN 30 FEB 8
		7	20°–30°	FEB 9–18
♓ PISCES Mutable Water	CUPS	8	0°–10°	FEB 19–28
		9	10°–20°	FEB 1–10
		10	20°–30°	MAR 11–20

Table 13. Assignment of the Planets to the Small Cards

Starting at 0° Leo, planets are assigned in the following repeating order: Saturn, Jupiter, Mars, Sol, Venus, Mercury, Luna. This is the descending order of the planetary spheres on the Tree of Life. Mars repeats at the end of winter and the beginning of spring —an extra dose of energy to overcome winter.

Sign	Suit	Card	Degrees	Dates	Planet
♈ ARIES Cardinal Fire	WANDS	2	0°–10°	MAR 21–30	♂
		3	10°–20°	MAR 31 APR 10	☉
		4	20°–30°	APR 11–20	♀
♉ TAURUS Fixed Earth	DISKS	5	0°–10°	APR 21–30	☿
		6	10°–20°	MAY 1–10	☽
		7	20°–30°	MAY 11–20	♄
♊ GEMINI Mutable Air	SWORDS	8	0°–10°	MAY 21–30	♃
		9	10°–20°	JUN 1–10	♂
		10	20°–30°	JUN 11–20	☉
♋ CANCER Cardinal Water	CUPS	2	0°–10°	JUN 21 JUL 1	♀
		3	10°–20°	JUL 2–11	☿
		4	20°–30°	JUL 12–21	☽
♌ LEO Fixed Fire	WANDS	5	0°–10°	JUL 22 AUG 1	♄
		6	10°–20°	AUG 2–11	♃
		7	20°–30°	AUG 12–22	♂
♍ VIRGO Mutable Earth	DISKS	8	0°–10°	AUG 23 SEP 1	☉
		9	10°–20°	SEP 2–11	♀
		10	20°–30°	SEP 12–22	☿
♎ LIBRA Cardinal Air	SWORDS	2	0°–10°	SEP 23 OCT 2	☽
		3	10°–20°	OCT 3–12	♄
		4	20°–30°	OCT 13–22	♃
♏ SCORPIO Fixed Water	CUPS	5	0°–10°	OCT 23 NOV 1	♂
		6	10°–20°	NOV 2–11	☉
		7	20°–30°	NOV 13–22	♀
♐ SAGITTARIUS Mutable Fire	WANDS	8	0°–10°	NOV 23 DEC 2	☿
		9	10°–20°	DEC 3–12	☽
		10	20°–30°	DEC 13–20	♄
♑ CAPRICORN Cardinal Earth	DISKS	2	0°–10°	DEC 21–30	♃
		3	10°–20°	DEC 31 JAN 9	♂
		4	20°–30°	JAN 10–19	☉
♒ AQUARIUS Fixed Air	SWORDS	5	0°–10°	JAN 20–29	♀
		6	10°–20°	JAN 30 FEB 8	☿
		7	20°–30°	FEB 9–18	☽
♓ PISCES Mutable Water	CUPS	8	0°–10°	FEB 19–28	♄
		9	10°–20°	FEB 1–10	♃
		10	20°–30°	MAR 11–20	♂

Table 14. The Court Cards Rule the Small Cards

Twelve of the Court Cards "rule" the Small Cards.
The Knights, Queens, and Princes "rule" from 20° of one sign to 20° of the next.

Sign (Element)	Suit	Degrees	Dates	Planet	Card	Court Card Ruler
♈ ARIES (Cardinal Fire)	WANDS	0°–10°	MAR 21–30	♂	2	Queen of Wands
♈ ARIES	WANDS	10°–20°	MAR 31 / APR 10	☉	3	Queen of Wands
♈ ARIES	WANDS	20°–30°	APR 11–20	♀	4	Prince of Disks
♉ TAURUS (Fixed Earth)	DISKS	0°–10°	APR 21–30	☿	5	Prince of Disks
♉ TAURUS	DISKS	10°–20°	MAY 1–10	☽	6	Prince of Disks
♉ TAURUS	DISKS	20°–30°	MAY 11–20	♄	7	Knight of Swords
♊ GEMINI (Mutable Air)	SWORDS	0°–10°	MAY 21–30	♃	8	Knight of Swords
♊ GEMINI	SWORDS	10°–20°	JUN 1–10	♂	9	Knight of Swords
♊ GEMINI	SWORDS	20°–30°	JUN 11–20	☉	10	Queen of Cups
♋ CANCER (Cardinal Water)	CUPS	0°–10°	JUN 21 / JUL 1	♀	2	Queen of Cups
♋ CANCER	CUPS	10°–20°	JUL 2–11	☿	3	Queen of Cups
♋ CANCER	CUPS	20°–30°	JUL 12–21	☽	4	Prince of Wands
♌ LEO (Fixed Fire)	WANDS	0°–10°	JUL 22 / AUG 1	♄	5	Prince of Wands
♌ LEO	WANDS	10°–20°	AUG 2–11	♃	6	Prince of Wands
♌ LEO	WANDS	20°–30°	AUG 12–22	♂	7	Knight of Disks
♍ VIRGO (Mutable Earth)	DISKS	0°–10°	AUG 23 / SEP 1	☉	8	Knight of Disks
♍ VIRGO	DISKS	10°–20°	SEP 2–11	♀	9	Knight of Disks
♍ VIRGO	DISKS	20°–30°	SEP 12–22	☿	10	Queen of Swords
♎ LIBRA (Cardinal Air)	SWORDS	0°–10°	SEP 23 / OCT 2	☽	2	Queen of Swords
♎ LIBRA	SWORDS	10°–20°	OCT 3–12	♄	3	Queen of Swords
♎ LIBRA	SWORDS	20°–30°	OCT 13–22	♃	4	Prince of Cups
♏ SCORPIO (Fixed Water)	CUPS	0°–10°	OCT 23 / NOV 1	♂	5	Prince of Cups
♏ SCORPIO	CUPS	10°–20°	NOV 2–11	☉	6	Prince of Cups
♏ SCORPIO	CUPS	20°–30°	NOV 13–22	♀	7	Knight of Wands
♐ SAGITTARIUS (Mutable Fire)	WANDS	0°–10°	NOV 23 / DEC 2	☿	8	Knight of Wands
♐ SAGITTARIUS	WANDS	10°–20°	DEC 3–12	☽	9	Knight of Wands
♐ SAGITTARIUS	WANDS	20°–30°	DEC 13–21	♄	10	Queen of Disks
♑ CAPRICORN (Cardinal Earth)	DISKS	0°–10°	DEC 22–30	♃	2	Queen of Disks
♑ CAPRICORN	DISKS	10°–20°	DEC 31 / JAN 9	♂	3	Queen of Disks
♑ CAPRICORN	DISKS	20°–30°	JAN 10–19	☉	4	Prince of Swords
♒ AQUARIUS (Fixed Air)	SWORDS	0°–10°	JAN 20–29	♀	5	Prince of Swords
♒ AQUARIUS	SWORDS	10°–20°	JAN 30 / FEB 8	☿	6	Prince of Swords
♒ AQUARIUS	SWORDS	20°–30°	FEB 9–18	☽	7	Knight of Cups
♓ PISCES (Mutable Water)	CUPS	0°–10°	FEB 19–28	♄	8	Knight of Cups
♓ PISCES	CUPS	10°–20°	MAR 1–10	♃	9	Knight of Cups
♓ PISCES	CUPS	20°–30°	MAR 11–20	♂	10	Queen of Wands

Table 15. Princesses: Thrones of the Aces and Rulers of Quadrants of Space

Princess of Disks
Throne of the Ace of Disks
Rules the ♈♉♊ Quadrant above the North Pole

Sign	♈ ARIES	♉ TAURUS	♊ GEMINI
Suit	WANDS	DISKS	SWORDS
Cards	2 3 4	5 6 7	8 9 10
Court	Queen of Wands / Prince of Disks	Prince of Disks	Knight of Swords

Princess of Wands
Throne of the Ace of Wands
Rules the ♋♌♍ Quadrant above the North Pole

Sign	♋ CANCER	♌ LEO	♍ VIRGO
Suit	CUPS	WANDS	DISKS
Cards	2 3 4	5 6 7	8 9 10
Court	Queen of Cups	Prince of Wands	Knight of Disks

Princess of Cups
Throne of the Ace of Cups
Rules the ♎♏♐ Quadrant above the North Pole

Sign	♎ LIBRA	♏ SCORPIO	♐ SAGITTARIUS
Suit	SWORDS	CUPS	WANDS
Cards	2 3 4	5 6 7	8 9 10
Court	Queen of Swords	Prince of Cups	Knight of Wands

Princess of Swords
Throne of the Ace of Swords
Rules the ♑♒♓ Quadrant above the North Pole

Sign	♑ CAPRICORN	♒ AQUARIUS	♓ PISCES
Suit	DISKS	SWORDS	CUPS
Cards	2 3 4	5 6 7	8 9 10
Court	Queen of Disks	Prince of Swords	Knight of Cups / Queen of Wands

Now let's turn our attention to the planets.

THE PLANETS

Starting at 0° Leo, planets are assigned in the following repeating order:

Saturn
Jupiter
Mars
Sol
Venus
Mercury
Luna

This is the descending order of the planetary spheres on the Tree of Life (see table 13).[248]

Astrologically speaking, an interesting and symbiotic relationship exists between the signs of the zodiac and the planets. First, each planet rules (or bestows its particular nature and character on) one or more signs of the zodiac. (For example; warlike and fiery Mars rules aggressive Aries and passionate Scorpio.) Second, there are certain signs of the zodiac that exalt a specific planet, almost as if it were an honored guest upon whom much attention and preference is bestowed. (For example: Aries, the ram of spring, exalts the Sun and welcomes its return from winter darkness.)

Because of the way the planets are allotted to the signs of the zodiac throughout the thirty-six small cards, we are bound to have some planets happy in their zodiacal homes and some zodiacal homes happy to host their planets. Conversely, some planets are decidedly unhappy in their zodiacal homes and some zodiacal homes are equally unhappy to host their planets. This astrological harmony or disharmony is a major factor in determining the characteristic meaning of a small card. It is great fun to peruse a good astrology book and match the aspects of the individual small cards with the descriptions of the character of people who have the same aspect in their natal charts. A perfect example is the Seven of Cups, which, in the Thoth Tarot, is called Debauch. It is Venus in Scorpio. Venus is not well dignified in Scorpio. Astrologer Joan Quiqley wrote of this aspect:

> Common types with Venus in Scorpio dissipate relentlessly and are frequently degenerates or drunks. Most of you overdo when it comes to sex.[249]

What a perfect description of a tarot card whose traditional title is "Lord of Illusionary Success," and that Crowley simply calls Debauch.

GOOD NEWS/BAD NEWS

Now we can couple the astrological factors with everything we've learned about the Tree of Life and the four Qabalistic worlds, and begin working out the nature of each small card. Unfortunately, while the formula is very simple, the interpretation is rather complex. As a matter of fact, it is very much like one of those jokes that starts out "I've got some good news, and I've got some bad news."

Take the Seven of Disks, Failure, as an example:

- The good news is—we have Saturn in Taurus. Saturn is very happy in Taurus. It is one of the most stable match-ups of sign and planet imaginable.
- The bad news is that Saturn and Taurus find themselves in the seventh sephira, Netzach, and Netzach holds a horribly imbalanced position on the Tree of Life.

On the other hand:

- The good news is that Netzach is the sphere of Venus and Venus rules Taurus.
- The bad news is that all this is in Assiah, the lowest of the Qabalistic worlds, an environment so earthy that poor Venus is totally dethroned from her accustomed place in heaven. Add to that the fact that this is happening so low on the Tree of Life that the bad news is amplified to such a disastrous level that the good news is just not good enough to make any difference . . . and so we have FAILURE.

Or how about the Nine of Swords, Cruelty?

- The good news is that we find ourselves on the very stable ninth sephira, Yesod.
- The bad news is that Swords rule the mind and reason. Yesod is so low on the Tree of Life that all that good intellect has degenerated to heartless passion.

On the other hand:

- The good news is that we have very active Mars in very active Gemini.
- The bad news is that Mars and Gemini do not agree about how to be active. Mars is focused and directed; he attacks with the forward thrusts of a warrior. Gemini, on the other hand, is scattered and operates best while flitting around. This is very frustrating to Mars, who now, because he is

totally unrestrained by intellect and reason, becomes downright mean. Voila! Cruelty!

In this chapter, I will talk briefly about each of the thirty-six small cards. As before, I will not hesitate to quote liberally from *The Book of Thoth*. But, as much as I respect Crowley's genius (and my own twisted insights), I want to encourage you to use the formula (n of s) + (p in zs) = sc to work out your own new and more innovative meanings for the small cards yourself. The more you learn about the Qabalah and astrology, the deeper your understanding of these cards will become. Go ahead. It's easier than you think.

TWO OF WANDS
DOMINION

(Mars in Aries)

0° to 10° Aries

March 21 to March 30

Original Title: Lord of Dominion.

Golden Dawn Model: A hand appears from clouds and grasps two crossed wands. Flames appear where wands meet.

King Scale for Chokmah: Pure soft Blue.

The Four Scales for Mars: Scarlet; Red; Venetian Red; Bright Red, rayed Azure or Emerald.

The Four Scales for Aries: Scarlet; Red; Brilliant Flame; Glowing Red.

Formula: 2 (Chokmah) of Wands (Atziluth) + Mars in Aries = DOMINION

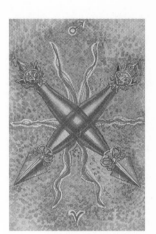

Following the basic Mathers design, the Two of Wands exhibits a textbook use of the color scale—the reds of Aries upon an explosive background of martial reds, azure, and emerald. The colors inform us in no uncertain terms that Mars is very happy in Aries and that Aries is happy to play host to Mars.

Crowley oberves that this strong astrological marriage in Chokmah (where the elements first manifest) makes the Two of Wands "fire in its best and highest form"[250] and represents what he calls "Will in its most exalted form . . . ideal Will, independent of any given object."[251]

The Wands are demon-headed Tibetan Dorjes.[252] Like the thunderbolt of Zeus, the Dorje represents the directed power of the gods, and serves as the instrument of divine destruction that must, of necessity, precede the creative cycle. "The virgin ovum," Crowley claims, "must be broken in order to fertilize it."[253] The six flames bursting behind the Dorjes allude to the Sun,[254] which is exalted in Aries and very happy to be there.

See chapter 20 for the general divinatory meanings of this card.

THREE OF WANDS
VIRTUE

(Sol in Aries)

10° to 20° Aries

March 31 to April 10

Original Title: Lord of Established Strength.

Golden Dawn Model: A hand (as in the Two of Wands) appears from clouds, and grasps three wands in the center (two crossed, the third upright). Flames appear where wands meet.

King Scale for Binah: Crimson.

The Four Scales for Sol: Orange; Gold Yellow; Rich Amber; Amber, rayed Red.

The Four Scales for Aries: Scarlet; Red; Brilliant Flame; Glowing Red.

Formula: 3 (Binah) of Wands (Atziluth) + Sol in Aries = VIRTUE

Graphically, this card is one of the simplest in the entire deck, and holds closely to the Golden Dawn model. Harris skillfully uses each of the ten colors of the scales to present three gold-and-amber lotus wands trimmed in scarlet and set upon an orange background of brilliant flames. The effect is one, not only of brilliance, but of immense heat. It represents the primal solar energy that first penetrates the soil in spring to awaken seeds that have slumbered all winter.

Along with the aces and twos (the other two cards representing the supernal triad of the Tree of Life), Crowley holds all the threes in particular veneration. The aces are the unmanifest roots of their element and suit, and the twos represent the element and suit manifested as ideas. But with the threes, Crowley argues, "The idea has become fertilized; the triangle has been formulated. In each case, the idea is of a certain stability which can never be upset, but from which a child can issue."[255] In tarot, that child is the remaining small cards, fours through tens.

What a truly noble and well-aspected card this is. The Sun is in Aries, the sign of his exaltation, and couldn't be happier. Furthermore, this harmonious and energetic marriage takes place in the third sephira, Binah, adding sublime understanding to the mix. The great power (and the will to use that power) that we saw represented by the Two of Wands has now become fertilized and expressed in terms of character as Virtue.

See chapter 20 for the general divinatory meanings of this card.

FOUR OF WANDS
COMPLETION

(Venus in Aries)

20° to 30° Aries

April 11 to April 20

Original Title: The Lord of Perfected Work.

Golden Dawn Model: Two hands appear from clouds right and left of the card and clasp in the center with the grip of the First Order. They hold four wands or torches crossed. Flames appear where wands meet.

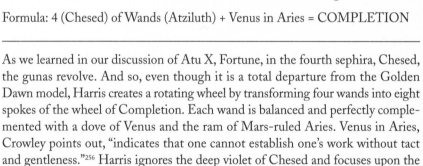

King Scale for Chesed: Deep Violet.

The Four Scales for Venus: Emerald Green; Sky Blue; Early Spring Green; Bright Rose or Cerise, rayed Pale Green.

The Four Scales for Aries: Scarlet; Red; Brilliant Flame; Glowing Red.

Formula: 4 (Chesed) of Wands (Atziluth) + Venus in Aries = COMPLETION

As we learned in our discussion of Atu X, Fortune, in the fourth sephira, Chesed, the gunas revolve. And so, even though it is a total departure from the Golden Dawn model, Harris creates a rotating wheel by transforming four wands into eight spokes of the wheel of Completion. Each wand is balanced and perfectly complemented with a dove of Venus and the ram of Mars-ruled Aries. Venus in Aries, Crowley points out, "indicates that one cannot establish one's work without tact and gentleness."[256] Harris ignores the deep violet of Chesed and focuses upon the greens and reds of this planet and sign.

Chesed is fourth sephira, but it is the first one below the Abyss. Consequently, the fours of the tarot represent the first solid manifestation of their suits. This is the classic characteristic of the Demiurge (Demiourgos)—a god who, as we learned in chapter 8, is, by all appearances, the first principal and creator of its universe, but who, in reality, is only the fourth principal and completely unaware of the three abstract principals (gods) that preceded it.

Zeus, Ammon, Jupiter, Jove, and Jehovah are classic examples of the Demiurge, who thinks he is god, but who is really only the visible manifestation of the invisible primal forces that created him. Nevertheless, the Demiurge brings order and the rule of law to the universe, a characteristic that is shared by all the small-card fours.

See chapter 20 for the general divinatory meanings of this card.

FIVE OF WANDS
STRIFE

(Saturn in Leo)

0° to 10° Leo

July 22 to August 1

Original Title: Lord of Strife.

Golden Dawn Model: Two hands (one from each side of the card) appear from clouds and clasp in the center with the grip of the First Order. They hold four wands, crossed two over two. A third hand appears from a cloud at the lower part of the card, holding an upright wand, which passes between the others. Flames flash where wands meet.

King Scale for Geburah: Orange.

The Four Scales for Saturn: Indigo; Black; Blue-black; Black, rayed Blue.

The Four Scales for Leo: Yellow (greenish); Deep Purple; Grey; Reddish Amber.

Formula: 5 (Geburah) of Wands (Atziluth) + Saturn in Leo = STRIFE

In *The Book of Thoth*, Crowley writes more about the Five of Wands than any other small card in this suit. Could it be because this card represents the first decan of Leo, which happens to be where we find the Ascendant in Crowley's astrological natal chart? Crowley identified strongly with Leo. His signature even bore the astrological sign of Leo in place of the "A" of Aleister.

This is one of only three cards on which Crowley literally left his mark. If we look closely at the orb of the winged solar disk atop the large version of the Chief Adept's wand in the center of the card, we find the image of Crowley's personal magical device, the Mark of the Beast upon the seven-pointed star of Babalon. This symbol is the device of the Ace of Disks (by tradition, one of the cards that most often bears the signature of the deck's creator) and the Prince of Wands, who also rules the 30° period in which we find Crowley's Ascendant.

Like Crowley himself, this card is a wild mix of profound contradictions: fiery Leo is happy enough in fiery Geburah, and Geburah implies motion and offers an environment of strength and activity. Saturn, on the other hand, presents a heavy and constant resistance to all this. This card is a picture of hot, pressurized magma struggling to reach the surface of the volcano, but frustrated by the sheer weight of the mountain itself.

See chapter 20 for the general divinatory meanings of this card.

SIX OF WANDS
VICTORY

(Jupiter in Leo)

10° to 20° Leo

August 2 to August 11

Original Title: Lord of Victory.

Golden Dawn Model: Two hands appear from clouds right and left of the card and clasp in the center with the grip of the First Order. They hold six wands, crossed three and three. Flames appear where wands meet.

King Scale for Tiphareth: Clear Pink Rose.

The Four Scales for Jupiter: Violet; Blue; Rich Purple; Bright Blue, rayed Yellow Emerald.

The Four Scales for Leo: Yellow (greenish); Deep Purple; Grey; Reddish Amber.

Formula: 6 (Tiphareth) of Wands (Atziluth) + Jupiter in Leo = VICTORY

The Six of Wands is called Victory; the Six of Cups is Pleasure; the Six of Swords is Science; and the Six of Disks is Success. All the sixes are wonderful cards. What gives? Are the four sixes special? You bet they are!

On the Tree of Life, Tiphareth is the direct reflection of Kether. It is the Son of the Father. It is perfectly balanced, left to right and top to bottom. It is the heart center of our psychic bodies and the Ruach of our souls. It rules as the central Sun King, surrounded by the spheres of the planets: Chesed (Jupiter), Geburah (Mars), Netzach (Venus), Hod (Mercury), Yesod (Moon), and even Binah (Saturn). Consequently, no matter how incompatible the card's planetary and zodiacal relationship may be, if that card is a six, we are in Tiphareth, and if we are in Tiphareth we're looking good.

In the case of the Six of Wands, we are doubly blessed with the happy marriage of expansive, boisterous, and generous Jupiter in powerful Sun-ruled Leo. This is the recipe for triumphant Victory.

This card is a relatively faithful version of the Golden Dawn model. The wands are a bit more elaborate and represent those used by various GD officers. The two topped with winged solar disks are those of the Chief Adept, the others are clearly Phoenix and Lotus wands.

See chapter 20 for the general divinatory meanings of this card.

SEVEN OF WANDS
VALOUR

(Mars in Leo)

20° to 30° Aries

August 12 to August 22

Original Title: Lord of Valour.

Golden Dawn Model: Two gripped hands holding
six wands, three are crossed. A third hand appears
from a cloud at the lower part of the card, holding
an upright wand, which passes between the others.
Flames flash where wands meet.

King Scale for Netzach: Amber.

The Four Scales for Mars: Red; Venetian Red;
Bright Red, rayed Azure or Emerald.

The Four Scales for Leo: Yellow (greenish); Deep Purple; Grey; Reddish Amber.

Formula: 7 (Netzach) of Wands (Atziluth) + Mars in Leo = VALOUR

The background of the Seven of Wands is deep purple, but, other than that, this card
is a near carbon copy of the Six of Wands. A crude seventh wand, more like a club,
overshadows the other six and delivers a sobering message: "The four Sevens are
not capable of bringing any comfort; each one represents the degeneration of the
element. Its utmost weakness is exposed in every case."[257]

There is still enough power and energy in the Seven of Wands to slug it out.
But the situation has degenerated into such a mess that nobody is sure with whom
to slug it out! It may be that a blow here or there will find its mark, but, more times
than not, it's a waste of energy. Crowleys sums it up aphoristically, "Patriotism, so
to speak, is not enough."[258]

Warlike Mars may find a measure of moral support in proud and fiery Leo,
but machismo is a tragic joke this far down the Tree of Life in the weak and unbalanced environment of Netzach (natural home of sensitive, peace-loving Venus).
The high art of battle has been replaced with the chaos of a mindless melee. "The
army," Crowley observes, "has been thrown into disorder; if victory is to be won, it
will be by dint of individual valour—a 'soldiers' battle."[259]

See chapter 20 for the general divinatory meanings of this card.

EIGHT OF WANDS
SWIFTNESS

(Mercury in Sagittarius)

0° to 10° Sagittarius

November 23 to December 2

Original Title: Lord of Swiftness.

Golden Dawn Model: Four hands (two from each side of the card) appear from clouds; clasped in two pairs in the center with the grip of the First Order. They hold eight wands, crossed four with four. Flames appear where wands meet.

King Scale for Hod: Violet.

The Four Scales for Mercury: Yellow; Purple; Grey; Indigo, rayed Violet.

The Four Scales for Sagittarius: Blue; Yellow; Green; Dark vivid Blue.

Formula: 8 (Hod) of Wands (Atziluth) + Mercury in Sagittarius = SWIFTNESS

If this card doesn't electrocute you, it may tickle you to death. Harris departs dramatically from the Golden Dawn model, and offers us a portrait of energy becoming matter: "Light-wands turned into electrical rays, sustaining or even constituting Matter by their vibrating energy."[260] Without mentioning Einstein or the formula $e=mc^2$, Crowley goes so far as to state, "This card, therefore, represents energy of high velocity, such as furnishes the master-key to modern mathematical physics."[261]

Swiftness is the perfect title for this card, because it represents everything that requires speed and a high-frequency level to hold together, whether that be a business endeavor, a romance, or the sum of all the matter in the universe. All this is fine and good, but what does all that mean when this card appears in a tarot reading? Let's look at the formula.

Mercury is in Sagittarius, where the element fire has become stabilized, and is eminently comfortable. This partnership is doubly energized by being in Hod, the sphere of Mercury. Even Hod's low and unbalanced position on the Tree of Life does little to diminish the intense activity of this almost overly stimulated coupling. This card is like two people who have had too much coffee who stay up all night, talking simultaneously. A lot may be said. A lot may be learned. But, inevitably, they are both going to crash.

See chapter 20 for the general divinatory meanings of this card.

NINE OF WANDS
STRENGTH

(Moon in Sagittarius)

10° to 20° Sagittarius

December 3 to December 12

Original Title: Lord of Great Strength.

Golden Dawn Model: Four hands (two from each side of the card) appear from clouds; clasped in two pairs in the center with the grip of the First Order. They hold eight wands, crossed four over four. A fifth hand appears from the bottom center of the card holding a ninth wand upright, which crosses the point of junction with the others. Flames flash where wands meet.

King Scale for Yesod: Indigo.

The Four Scales for Moon: Blue; Silver; Cold Pale Blue; Silver, rayed Violet.

The Four Scales for Sagittarius: Blue; Yellow; Green; Dark vivid Blue.

Formula: 9 (Yesod) of Wands (Atziluth) + Moon in Sagittarius = STRENGTH

Holding very close to the Golden Dawn description and color scales, the Nine of Wands tells its story in almost quiet simplicity. Eight of the wands are arrows, each of which has a crescent Moon as the head and eight Moons for feathers. The great central wand, with the Sun at its top and the Moon at its bottom, represents the path of Sagittarius on the Tree of Life, which joins Tiphareth (Sun) to Yesod (Moon). "Here the Moon," Crowley writes, "the weakest of the planets, is in Sagittarius, the most elusive of the Signs; yet it dares call itself Strength."[262]

The source of this confident strength is the card's position in Yesod on the Tree of Life. Not only is Yesod the natural sephira of the Moon (making our Moon here very comfortable—even if it is in Sagittarius), it is also the Foundation, the "seat of the great crystallization of Energy."[263] As Crowley observes, "The Nine represents always the fullest development of the Force in its relation with the Forces above it."[264]

This card indicates great strength, but its strength lies in its ability to change perpetually. Crowley gave what is perhaps the simplest meaning of this card when he wrote: "Defense, to be effective, must be mobile."[265]

See chapter 20 for the general divinatory meanings of this card.

TEN OF WANDS
OPPRESSION

(Saturn in Sagittarius)

20° to 30° Sagittarius

December 13 to December 21

Original Title: Lord of Oppression.

Golden Dawn Model: Four hands (two from each side of the card) appear from clouds; clasped in two pairs in the center with the grip of the First Order. They hold eight wands, crossed four with four. A fifth hand appears from the bottom center of the card holding a ninth and tenth wand upright, which cross the point of junction with the others. Flames flash where wands meet.

King Scale for Malkuth: Yellow.

The Four Scales for Saturn: Indigo; Black; Blue-black; Black, rayed Blue.

The Four Scales for Sagittarius: Blue; Yellow; Green; Dark vivid Blue.

Formula: 10 (Malkuth) of Wands (Atziluth) + Saturn in Sagittarius = OPPRESSION

All factors conspire to make this an altogether unpleasant card. Saturn's iron heel brutally pins poor Sagittarius (the lightest and most ethereal of the fire signs) to the floor of inflexible Malkuth. If zodiac signs could dream, the Ten of Wands would be Sagittarius's worst nightmare. Harris basically follows the Golden Dawn model with this card, and is meticulously faithful to the color scales. That, however, is where the similarities end. Her Ten of Wands is an explosive and suffocating image of oppression and repression.

Crowley writes that Malkuth, "depends from the other nine Sephiroth, but is not directly in communication with them. It is become a blind Force; so, the most violent form of that particular energy, without any modifying influences."[266] Blind force, Crowley points out, in the suit of Wands means "Fire in its most destructive aspect."[267]

Harris ingeniously illustrates this by transforming the two Dorjes (which in the Two of Wands were the symbols of celestial power) into dark iron prison bars. Crowley describes the card thus:

> The whole picture suggests oppression and repression. It is a stupid and obstinate cruelty from which there is no escape. It is Will which has not understood anything beyond its dull purpose, its "lust of result", and will devour itself in the conflagrations it has evoked.[268]

See chapter 20 for the general divinatory meanings of this card.

TWO OF CUPS
LOVE

(Venus in Cancer)

0° to 10° Cancer

June 21 to July 1

Original Title: Lord of Love.

Golden Dawn Model: From cloud and water at the bottom, a hand appears holding by a single stem two lotuses, one rising vertically from the other. Upon the stem between the lotuses two dolphins cross. Two fountains of water (silver to the left, gold to the right) spring from the top lotus and fall upon the dolphins then down into two cups, which in turn overflow and flood the bottom of the card.

Queen Scale for Chokmah: Grey.

The Four Scales for Venus: Emerald Green; Sky Blue; Early Spring Green; Bright Rose or cerise, rayed Pale Green.

The Four Scales for Cancer: Amber; Maroon; Rich bright Russet; Dark Greenish Brown.

Formula: 2 (Chokmah) of Cups (Briah) + Venus in Cancer = LOVE

The Two of Cups is perhaps the most beautiful of the small cards of the Thoth Tarot. While Harris doesn't completely ignore the color scales, she does give herself room for innovation. The calm green sea, the rose-colored lotuses, and the amber dolphins (or are they Koi?) conform nicely, but she breaks rank a bit by giving us a violet sky. The card is magnificently beautiful and a fitting representative of the first manifestation of the element water. It is the energy of water in its best and highest form.

Harris shows her appreciation of the card by sharing a perhaps apocryphal event involving the card: "Also [at the exhibition] a little person aged 2, scuttling & crawling, was asked which picture: Straight she went to No. 2 Cups, Love. I thought she would forget & asked her again 10 minutes later & she toddled off to the same Picture. "That" she said again.[269]

Because the number two (Chokmah on the Tree of Life) is particularly expressive of Will, Crowley wrote:

> This card might really be renamed the Lord of Love under Will for that is its full and true meaning. It shows the harmony of the male and the female: interpreted in the largest sense. It is perfect and placid harmony, radiating an intensity of joy and ecstasy.[270]

See chapter 20 for the general divinatory meanings of this card.

THREE OF CUPS
ABUNDANCE

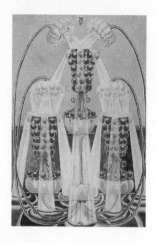

(Mercury in Cancer)

10° to 20° Cancer

July 2 to July 11

Original Title: Lord of Abundance.

Golden Dawn Model: A hand appears from clouds at the bottom of the card, and grasps the stems of four lotuses or water lilies. Two flowers rise to the right and left and overhang two cups. The third and fourth flowers arise between the lower two and overhang and pour water into a single cup at the top of the card. The top cup overflows in two streams that fill and overflow the lower two cups.

Queen Scale for Binah: Black.

The Four Scales for Mercury: Yellow; Purple; Grey; Indigo, rayed Violet.

The Four Scales for Cancer: Amber; Maroon; Rich bright Russet; Dark Greenish Brown.

Formula: 3 (Binah) of Cups (Briah) + Mercury in Cancer = ABUNDANCE

The three factors of our formula conspire to create a marriage made in heaven. "Mercury is the Will or Word of the All-Father," Crowley states. "Here its influence descends upon the most receptive of the Signs."[271]

In an exuberant interpretation of the Golden Dawn model, Harris fills the surface of the Three of Cups to overflowing. The images crowd to the very edges of the card. Her choice of colors is drawn directly from the dictated scales with one stunning exception—the bright red pomegranate cups. They are elevated above a tranquil sea by lotuses and filled with living water by other overhanging lotus blossoms. Crowley calls this the card of Demeter and Persephone and "the fulfillment of the Will of Love in abounding joy. It is the spiritual basis of fertility."[272]

One could not ask for a more perfect picture of sensuous pleasure and plenty. The imagery of the pomegranates, however, carries a subtle warning. Abundance has its price. Because she swallowed a few seeds of the pomegranate, Persephone was obliged to spend part of every year in the dark realms of her husband, Pluto, the Lord of the Dead. None of the Gods of Olympus, not even great Zeus, could break the spell. Crowley interprets it thus: "The lesson seems to be that the good things of life, although enjoyed, should be distrusted."[273]

See chapter 20 for the general divinatory meanings of this card.

FOUR OF CUPS
LUXURY

(Moon in Cancer)

20° to 30° Cancer

July 12 to July 21

Original Title: Lord of Blended Pleasure.

Golden Dawn Model: A hand appears from clouds at the bottom of the card grasping three stems of a lotus. Two green leaves grow from the right and left stems, forming a cross between four cups arranged as a square. The center stem flowers at the top of the card. Two streams of water flow right and left from the flower, filling the top two cups, which overflow and fill the two lower cups.

Queen Scale for Chesed: Blue.

The Four Scales for Moon: Blue; Silver; Cold Pale Blue; Silver, rayed Sky Blue.

The Four Scales for Cancer: Amber; Maroon; Rich bright Russet; Dark Greenish Brown.

Formula: 4 (Chesed) of Cups (Briah) + Moon in Cancer = LUXURY

This card is really loaded. As a matter of fact, it borders on being too much of a good thing. Just look at the formula: four is Chesed, the sphere of generous, expansive, and beneficent Jupiter. Jupiter is exalted in Cancer, and Cancer is ruled by the Moon. Can the components of one card get any cozier? No, but, in this case, familiarity is starting to breed contempt and eventually enough will be enough. When this card appears in a reading, enjoy the moment, but don't expect it to last forever.

The sea that was so still in the Three of Cups is now restless. The Cups have become heavy, the bottom two have sunk to the water's surface and are resting precariously on the lotus stems themselves; the upper two cups have actually flattened out the lotus blossoms and are threatening to collapse the entire plant. The source of the water, the single blossom at the top of the card, is wilted and has lost several petals. It gives the appearance that it is about to run out of juice. I believe it is.

Like the Demiurge itself, the Four of Cups, in its self-absorbed arrogance, thinks Luxury is the god of the suit of Cups—all the while never dreaming that it owes its very existence to the sublime true gods of the supernal triad, the Ace, Two, and Three of Cups.

See chapter 20 for the general divinatory meanings of this card.

FIVE OF CUPS
DISAPPOINTMENT

(Mars in Scorpio)

0° to 10° Scorpio

October 23 to November 1

Original Title: Lord of Loss in Pleasure.

Golden Dawn Model: A hand appears from clouds at the bottom of the card holding lotuses or water lilies. Flowers fall right and left and overhang five cups arranged as a square with one in the center. The lotus stem ascends between the cups as a fountain. No water comes from the flowers. All the cups are empty.

Queen Scale for Geburah: Scarlet Red.

The Four Scales for Mars: Scarlet; Red; Venetian Red; Bright Red, rayed Azure or Emerald.

The Four Scales for Scorpio: Green Blue; Dull Brown; Very dark Brown; Livid Indigo Brown.

Formula: 5 (Geburah) of Cups (Briah) + Mars in Scorpio = DISAPPOINTMENT

With this card, the suit of Cups takes a dramatic and sinister turn. This is very disappointing, because the Five of Cups had so much going for it. Discarding the configuration of the Golden Dawn model that displays five empty cups arranged as a square with one cup in the center, Crowley has Harris arrange her cups as an inverted pentagram, symbol (in this place) of the triumph of matter over spirit.

What is it that turns this card sour? Mars rules Scorpio and is very happy to be there. Not only that: all this is in Geburah, the hometown, the sphere of Mars. So where's the problem?

The problem stems from the fact that Mars is too happy to be here. He gets himself too excited to indulge in foreplay. This makes Scorpio nervous. He ends up prematurely blowing such a fiery blast upon the relationship that it retards what might have otherwise been the slow processes of passionate decay that Scorpio uses to devour and liberate her lovers. Who among us cannot understand this?

Water no longer pours into the cups; the lotus blossoms have been completely blown away by the hot martial wind that has turned the sky red. The sea is now a stagnating pool. Now we can see where the earlier small cards in this suit were taking us. Love leads to Abundance, which (left uncontrolled) leads to Luxury, which (left uncontrolled) leads to decadence, boredom, frustration and— Disappointment.

See chapter 20 for the general divinatory meanings of this card.

SIX OF CUPS
PLEASURE

(Sol in Scorpio)

10° to 20° Scorpio

November 2 to November 12

Original Title: Lord of Pleasure.

Golden Dawn Model: A hand appears from clouds at the bottom of the card and holds a group of stems of lotuses or water lilies, from which six flowers bend, one over each cup. Water flows from these flowers into the cups as if from a fountain. The cups are not yet full.

Queen Scale for Tiphareth: Yellow (gold).

The Four Scales for Sol: Orange; Gold Yellow; Rich Amber; Amber, rayed Red.

The Four Scales for Scorpio: Green Blue; Dull Brown; Very dark Brown; Livid indigo Brown.

Formula: 6 (Tiphareth) of Cups (Briah) + Sun in Scorpio = PLEASURE

Balance returns to the suit as the Six of Cups, Pleasure, finds a most delightful home in Tiphareth, the sphere of the Sun. The Four and Five of Cups seem like bad dreams (probably brought on by consuming too much rich food and wine), and we now awaken to the giddy realization that we are the card that is the direct reflection of the Ace of Cups on the Tree of Life. The Sun is outrageously happy to be in Tiphareth and shines with double warmth and pleasantness on the sensuous and fun-loving side of Scorpio. If this is the first card you draw in a tarot reading, you may want to stop right there and quit while you're ahead. This is a terrific card. Crowley agrees:

> Pleasure, in the title of this card, must be understood in its highest sense: it implies well-being, harmony of natural forces without effort or strain, ease, satisfaction. Foreign to the idea of the card is the gratification of natural or artificial desires. Yet it does represent emphatically the fulfillment of the sexual Will, as shown by the ruling Sephira, planet, element, and sign.[274]

The sea is alive with broad gentle waves, and the lotuses actually dance, leaving stem trails of perfectly symmetrical patterns and arcs. Water is again pouring into the cups from lotus blossoms, but, as yet, the cups are not filled. Four of the cups are tilted and appear ready to fall, but they are pressed securely against the stems by the generous water pressure from above.

See chapter 20 for the general divinatory meanings of this card.

SEVEN OF CUPS
DEBAUCH

(Venus in Scorpio)

20° to 30° Scorpio

November 13 to November 22

Original Title: Lord of Illusionary Success.

Golden Dawn Model: The cups are arranged as two descending triangles above a point: a hand holds lotus stems, which arise from a central lower cup. The hand is above this cup and below the middle one. With the exception of the central lower cup, each is overhung by a lotus flower, but no water falls from any of the flowers. All the cups are empty.

Queen Scale for Netzach: Emerald.

The Four Scales for Venus: Emerald Green; Sky Blue; Early Spring Green; Bright Rose or Cerise, rayed Pale Green.

The Four Scales for Scorpio: Green Blue; Dull Brown; Very dark Brown; Livid Indigo Brown.

Formula: 7 (Netzach) of Cups (Briah) + Venus in Scorpio = DEBAUCH

Crowley is definitely not a fan of the Seven of Cups:

> This is one of the worst ideas that one can have; its mode is poison, its goal madness. It represents the delusion of Delirium Tremens and drug addiction; it represents the sinking into the mire of false pleasure. There is something almost suicidal in this card.[275]

Just look at this card—if you can. Yuck! What happened to all that great Cup stuff higher up on the Tree of Life? Doesn't sexy Venus like to show off in sexy Scorpio? She does. She likes to show off everywhere! Venus, however, is not well dignified in Scorpio and often embarrasses herself when she visits.

You ask, shouldn't she be happy in Netzach, the sphere of Venus? Sure she is! She's so happy she's making herself sick. This is much-too-much of what was once a good thing and, this low on the tree and this far off balance, there isn't a single influencing factor left to remind her the party's over.

This card seems like the next logical step in the Abundance, Luxury, Disappointment sequence. Three martinis is abundantly enough; four is just the luxury of showing off; five is disappointing because you're not getting high any more, you're just getting smashed. But after seven—oh dear! The Seven of Cups is a stumbling dash to the lavatory just moments after you thought you were being irresistible to an attractive stranger.

See chapter 20 for the general divinatory meanings of this card.

EIGHT OF CUPS
INDOLENCE

(Saturn in Pisces)

0° to 10° Pisces

February 19 to February 28

Original Title: Lord of Abandoned Success.

Golden Dawn Model: From clouds at the bottom of the card a hand appears, holding the stems of lotuses or water lilies. There are only two flowers that bend over and fill to overflowing the two central cups. The overflow pours into (but does not fill) the three lowest cups. There are three cups above the two central cups, which remain empty.

Queen Scale for Hod: Orange.

The Four Scales for Saturn: Indigo; Black; Blue-black; Black, rayed Blue.

The Four Sales for Pisces: Crimson (ultra Violet); Buff, flecked silver White; Light Translucent pinkish Brown; Stone color.

Formula: 8 (Hod) of Cups (Briah) + Saturn in Pisces = INDOLENCE

Much to my wife's disappointment (this is her birthday card), Crowley didn't have much nice to say about the Eight of Cups. In fact, he called it "the German Measles of Christian Mysticism."[276] and "the very apex of unpleasantness."[277]

Is it any wonder? This card has a bad attitude (Sorry, Dear). Saturn is a heavy and hard-nosed downer and, this far down the Tree of Life, delicate Pisces doesn't have enough juice left to put up any kind of fight. This card will have you "playin' solitaire till dawn, with a deck of 51."[278]

Crowley's description of this unfortunate blending of forces is priceless:

> This card represents a party for which all preparations have been made; but the host has forgotten to invite the guests; or the caterers have not delivered the good cheer. There is this difference, though, that it is in some way or other the host's own fault.[279]

Harris's interpretation of Indolence is perfect—a stagnant pool, drooping blossoms. The top three cups and one at the bottom of the card are empty; the two in the center are spilling half their contents back into the sea.

See chapter 20 for the general divinatory meanings of this card.

NINE OF CUPS
HAPPINESS

(Jupiter in Pisces)

10° to 20° Pisces

March 1 to March 10

Original Title: Lord of Material Happiness.

Golden Dawn Model: A hand appears from clouds at the bottom of the card holding the stem of lotuses or water lilies, one flower of which over-hangs each of nine cups arranged in three rows of three.

Queen Scale for Yesod: Violet.

The Four Scales for Jupiter: Violet; blue; rich Purple; Bright Blue, rayed Yellow.

The Four Sales for Pisces: Crimson (ultra Violet); Buff, flecked silver White; Light Translucent pinkish Brown; Stone color.

Formula: 9 (Yesod) of Cups (Briah) + Jupiter in Pisces = HAPPINESS

Is everybody happy? Yes!

See what happens when we return to the stability of the middle pillar? This is one of the best cards in the deck. Pisces, being the mutable sign of water, tends to stabilize the element. She is most welcome in Yesod, the sphere of the watery Moon. Yesod is also the Foundation, the sephira that stabilizes the entire Tree of Life. This provides a most cozy and satisfying environment for loveable Jupiter to happily enjoy the good life as only Jupiter and his friends can.

Jupiter also has an affinity to water. Chesed, the sphere of Jupiter, Crowley affirms, "represents Water in its highest material manifestation."[280]

Everybody is, literally, happy!

Harris follows the color scales and pumps up the Golden Dawn model by straightening her streams of flowing water as if they were spurting from the lotus flowers and gushing under pressure into large-bowled cups. The whole image is one of voluptuous, surreal Victorian clutter. There is hardly room for her to include the symbols of Jupiter and Pisces at the top and bottom of the card.

See chapter 20 for the general divinatory meanings of this card.

TEN OF CUPS
SATIETY

(Mars in Pisces)

20° to 30° Pisces

March 11 to March 20

Original Title: Lord of Perfected Happiness.

Golden Dawn Model: A hand appears from clouds at the bottom of the card, holding the stem of lotus or water lilies whose flowers pour water into all the cups, which all spill over. The top cup is held sideways by another hand, and pours water into the left-hand upper cup. A single lotus flower rises above the top cup, and is the source of the water that fills it.

Queen Scale for Malkuth: Citrine; Olive; Russet; and Black.

The Four Scales for Mars: Scarlet; Red; Venetian Red; Bright Red, rayed azure or emerald.

The Four Scales for Pisces: Crimson (ultra Violet); Buff, flecked silver White; Light Translucent pinkish Brown; Stone color.

Formula: 10 (Malkuth) of Cups (Briah) + Mars in Pisces = SATIETY

Crowley advised Harris on the composition of this card, writing:

> The background; it ought to look menacing. There is something very sinister about this card. It suggests the morbid hunger which springs from surfeit. The craving of a drug addict is the idea. At the same time, of course, it is this final agony of descent into illusion which renders necessary the completion of the circle by awakening the Eld of the All-Father.[281]
> —Crowley to Harris, December 19, 1939.

Had enough? The Ten of Cups could have been filled with the realization of the potential of the suit of Cups. Instead, it is just filled with the concept of fullness. The cups have runneth over and are staining the carpet.[282] Crowley blames this on Mars in Pisces:

Mars is the gross, violent and disruptive force which inevitably attacks every supposed perfection. His energy displays the greatest possible contrast with that of Pisces, which is both peaceful and spiritualized.[283]

This is the end of the line for the suit of water. Harris ignores the Golden Dawn model and coloring guidelines and creates a Tree of Life from ten rather disturbed and tipsy cups.

See chapter 20 for the general divinatory meanings of this card.

TWO OF SWORDS
PEACE

(Moon in Libra)

0° to 10° Libra

September 23 to October 2

Original Title: Lord of Peace Restored.

Golden Dawn Model: Two hands appear from clouds at the right and left side of the card. They hold two swords like the air dagger of a Zelator Adeptus Minor. The swords cross in the center of the card. A red rose with five petals blooms where the swords touch. The rose emits white rays.

Prince Scale for Chokmah: Blue pearl gray, like mother of pearl.

The Four Scales for Moon: Blue; Silver; Cold Pale Blue; Silver, rayed Sky Blue.

The Four Scales for Libra: Emerald Green; Blue; Deep Blue-Green; Pale Green.

Formula: 2 (Chokmah) of Swords (Yetzirah) + Moon in Libra = PEACE

Harris has not strayed very far from the basic Golden Dawn model in this card. She has replaced the red rose with a deep blue-green blossom (Libra), and she forms a stylized Greek cross using the geometrical wings we first encountered on the Princess of Swords. These wings also festoon the backgrounds of the other cards of this suit.

Astrologers tell us that people who were born with Moon in Libra criticize and make judgments from a position of enviable equilibrium. They weigh every problem and proposition with the utmost fairness. This fortunate union of sign and planet finds a predictably dignified home in Chokmah. The result is one of the few cards in the suit of Swords that doesn't evoke groans when it appears in a tarot reading.

That is not to say that it is all goodness and light. We must remember that the natural vocation of a sword is to fight, to cut, to pierce, to kill. It is an instrument of action. Just like the mind, just like the Ruach, the intellectual part of the soul, it is in constant movement.

Eastern mystics tell us that the mind is the great enemy. If we are to achieve profound levels of consciousness, the mind must be overcome. Fearful that its existence and control will end, the mind resists these efforts at all costs. This is why so many cards in the suit of Swords seem so frustrated, anxious, nervous, even tortured.

In the case of the Two of Swords, Peace, it seems we've dodged a bullet. We must always remember, however, that for the sharp and dangerous sword, peace is just an uncharacteristic and temporary interruption from war.

See chapter 20 for the general divinatory meanings of this card.

THREE OF SWORDS
SORROW

(Saturn in Libra)

10° to 20° Libra

October 3 to October 12

Original Title: Lord of Sorrow.

Golden Dawn Model: Three hands holding three swords appear from clouds at the bottom of the card. The image is that of the Two of Swords, but the right and left swords are violently parted by a central third sword. The rose is destroyed and its five petals are dispersed into the air. There are no white rays.

Prince Scale for Binah: Dark Brown.

The Four Scales for Saturn: Indigo; Black; Blue-black; Black, rayed Blue.

The Four Scales for Libra: Emerald Green; Blue; Deep Blue-Green; Pale Green.

Formula: 3 (Binah) of Swords (Yetzirah) + Saturn in Libra = SORROW

Harris is strongly affected by the Three of Swords.

> Please don't frighten me with the Sword suit. I have obeyed in every way. I can't see how they can be wrong. The 3 was a fair horror & great suffering.[284]
> —Harris to Crowley, date uncertain.

I wrote earlier that, because they reside in the supernal triad above the Abyss, all the aces, twos, and threes are happy. Obviously Sorrow does not sound like a happy card. It is very difficult for us to understand the nature of consciousness above the Abyss, where the actuality of things does not exist. In this abstract atmosphere, there are no things or even forms of things—nothing but pure potential. The "sorrow" of this card is not the same kind of sorrow evoked by, say, the death of a loved one or the loss of a lover. It is a profound state of consciousness that, from our below-the-abyss point of view, we can only attempt to describe. Sorrow falls pitifully short of an accurate description, but it is probably the best word the English language can offer us.

Ignoring for a moment the astrological aspects of the card, let's consider the unique Qabalistic factors that make the Three of Swords happy to be Sorrow.

- Swords represent Yetzirah, the formative world—oh, but sorry! There can be no forms in Binah or anywhere above the Abyss.
- Swords also represent Ruach, the human intellect—oh, but sorry! Intellect and reason cannot exist above the Abyss in Binah.

Without forms or reason, the mind must give way to a consciousness higher than itself. The Three of Swords represents the wondrous trance of sorrow that first enlightened the Buddha. We should all be so lucky to draw Sorrow from the deck.

See chapter 20 for the general divinatory meanings of this card.

FOUR OF SWORDS
TRUCE

(Jupiter in Libra)

20° to 30° Libra

October 13 to October 22

Original Title: Lord of Rest from Strife.

Golden Dawn Model: The Four of Swords is exactly like the Two of Swords (including the rose of five petals and the white rays), except the hands that appear from clouds at the right and left hold two swords each.

Prince Scale for Chesed: Deep Purple.

The Four Scales for Jupiter: Violet; Blue; rich Purple; Bright Blue, rayed Yellow.

The Four Scales for Libra: Emerald Green; Blue; Deep Blue-Green; Pale Green.

Formula: 4 (Chesed) of Swords (Yetzirah) + Jupiter in Libra = TRUCE

The Four of Swords is perhaps the most beautiful of the small-card Swords. Harris executes a textbook use of the color scales and offers us a portrait of balance and order. She writes to Crowley: "I think it would be a good plan if you could arrange to come here one day next week & see the Swords. I have a superstitious horror of bringing them all unbalanced to London.[285]

Chesed is the sphere of Jupiter and serves as a gracious but authoritative host to Jupiter in Libra. Equilibrium and justice are definitely key words for this card, but Crowley tells us that it also brings with it the "establishment of dogma, and the law concerning it."[286] Swords are weapons, and weapons discharge their design by virtue of the disciplines of war, not of peace. The kind of "truce" the Four of Swords monitors is a peace enforced by the threat of violence, and as such will be short lived.

The four swords are arranged as a St. Andrew's cross, suggesting to Crowley "Fixation and rigidity."[287] Their points meet at the center of a large rose of forty-nine petals that Crowley tells us represents "social harmony."[288] It is the concord of conformity and compromise, however, that characterizes a culture that would rather blindly surrender to authority than to face the challenges of liberty.

See chapter 20 for the general divinatory meanings of this card.

FIVE OF SWORDS
DEFEAT

(Venus in Aquarius)

0° to 10° Aquarius

January 20 to January 29

Original Title: Lord of Defeat.

Golden Dawn Model: Three hands appear from clouds at the bottom card. The right and left hands hold two swords each, the center hand one. The image is that of the Three of Swords, but, in this case, the two swords to the right and to the left are violently parted by a central fifth sword. The rose is destroyed and its five petals are dispersed into the air. There are no white rays.

Prince Scale for Geburah: Bright Scarlet.

The Four Scales for Venus: Emerald Green; Sky Blue; Early Spring Green; Bright Rose or Cerise, rayed Pale Green.

The Four Scales for Aquarius: Violet; Sky Blue; Bluish Mauve; White, tinged Purple.

Formula: 5 (Geburah) of Swords (Yetzirah) + Venus in Aquarius = DEFEAT

This card presents five unmatched, bent, and damaged swords forming an averse pentagram. This pentagram of Defeat is projected upon a field of Harris's geometric and wildly asymmetric wings, some of which form swastikas. As this card was painted at the very height of England's struggle with Nazi Germany, it is easy to speculate that Harris was either consciously or unconsciously projecting magical defeat on this hated enemy. Her concern with the design is clear in her words to Crowley: "I only hope the Swords are alright for I can't do them again. I have followed your instructions with meticulous care."[289]

Popular opinion holds that the averse pentagram is an evil symbol. The Golden Dawn even cautioned its initiates never to use it magically. Be that as it may, it is the pinnacle of superstition to believe that any symbol, in and of itself, can be either good or evil. The averse pentagram can be used to symbolize an infinite number of perfectly innocuous concepts. However, in this card it really does mean trouble.

Venus rules Aquarius and, for a moment, she is very happy to have him as her date. After all, they're both pacifists. They are a friendly, mellow, and sentimental couple. Unfortunately, this sensitive pair has shown up at the wrong party. A terrible fight has broken out in a very rough and well-armed area of Qabalahville—Geburah, the house of Mars, which is located in Yetzirah (the world of Swords).

Naturally, Venus and Aquarius volunteer to be peacemakers, but they are just too nice, too peaceful, too weak to handle themselves in this violent neighborhood. The inevitable result is Defeat. Sorry kids. I hear things are quieter down in Tiphareth.

See chapter 20 for the general divinatory meanings of this card.

SIX OF SWORDS
SCIENCE

(Mercury in Aquarius)

10° to 20° Aquarius

January 30 to February 8

Original Title: Lord of Earned Success.

Golden Dawn Model: Two hands appear from
clouds at the right and left side of the card. They
each hold three swords like the air dagger of a
Zelator Adeptus Minor. The swords cross in the
center of the card. A red rose with five petals blooms
where the swords touch. The rose emits white rays.

Prince Scale for Tiphareth: Rich Salmon.

The Four Scales for Mercury: Yellow; Purple; Grey; Indigo, rayed Violet.

The Four Scales for Aquarius: Violet; Sky Blue; Bluish Mauve; White, tinged
Purple.

Formula: 6 (Tiphareth) of Swords (Yetzirah) + Mercury in Aquarius = SCIENCE

In chapter 8, we were introduced to the small Rose Cross at the heart of the Hermetic
Rose Cross. I presumptuously labeled it the Rose Cross of Being. In the Six of
Disks, this figure is found at the very center of the card, and six matched and balanced swords focus their powers of analysis and discrimination upon the mysteries
of being. This is Science.

The conservative beauty of this card announces that the shining balance of
Tiphareth brings a much-needed measure of nobility and clear-headedness to the
suit of Swords. The formula that creates the character of this card couldn't be more
auspicious for the suit of Swords. In the human soul, the counterpart of Yetzirah is
the Ruach, or the intellect. On the Tree of Life, the center of the Ruach radiates from
Tiphareth. Finally, an air planet, Mercury, finds itself in the fixed air sign of Aquarius.

Someone with Mercury in Aquarius in his or her natal horoscope is said to
have a keen, analytical mind and an extraordinary ability to concentrate. He or she
is also intensely curious and enjoys examining both sides of a question. Sounds like
a scientist, doesn't it?

See chapter 20 for the general divinatory meanings of this card.

SEVEN OF SWORDS
FUTILITY

(Moon in Aquarius)

20° to 30° Aquarius

February 9 to February 18

Original Title: Lord of Unstable Effort.

Golden Dawn Model: Two hands appear from clouds at the right and left side of the card. They each hold three swords like the air dagger of a Zelator Adeptus Minor. A third hand holds up a single sword in the center. The points of all the swords touch each other, the central sword not altogether dividing them. The rose of five petals blooms on the blade of the center sword.

Prince Scale for Netzach: Bright Yellow Green.

The Four Scales for Moon: Blue; Silver; Cold Pale Blue; Silver, rayed Sky Blue.

The Four Scales for Aquarius: Violet; Sky Blue; Bluish Mauve; White, tinged Purple.

Formula: 7 (Netzach) of Swords (Yetzirah) + Moon in Aquarius = FUTILITY

For me, the Seven of Swords is often difficult to interpret in a tarot reading. One would think that a Sword card in Netzach would be absolutely awful. There are, however, embedded complexities in our formula that relieve this card of some of the more tortuous burdens that afflict the other sevens. For example, the very name of the seventh sephira is Victory. This may seem like grasping at straws, but Swords resonate well to words like victory. The Moon in Aquarius adds elements of change and the possibility of compromise. Crowley observes: "It is like a rheumatic boxer trying to "come back" after being out of the ring for years."[290] Nonetheless, it is well to remember that, sometimes, even old boxers get in a lucky punch.

Harris chose to illustrate this as a planetary battle: six planets versus the Sun. Look closely at the swords. The hilts of the six small swords arrayed in a crescent near the top of the card carry the symbols of (from left to right) the Moon, Venus, Mars, Jupiter, Mercury, and Saturn. The large central sword is the Sun itself, outnumbered and battle-scarred. The entire arrangement, however, is orderly and restrained, almost suggestive of a moment when a negotiated settlement might be arranged.

I wouldn't bet on it.

See chapter 20 for the general divinatory meanings of this card.

EIGHT OF SWORDS
INTERFERENCE

(Jupiter in Gemini)

0° to 10° Gemini

May 21 to May 31

Original Title: Lord of Shortened Force.

Golden Dawn Model: Four hands appear from clouds, each holding two swords, points upward; all the points touch near the top of the card. Hands issue, two at each bottom angle of the card. The rose is reestablished in the center.

Prince Scale for Hod: Red-russet.

The Four Scales for Jupiter: Violet; Blue; rich Purple; Bright Blue, rayed Yellow.

The Four Scales for Gemini: Orange; Pale Mauve; New Yellow leather; Reddish Grey inclined to Mauve.

Formula: 8 (Hod) of Swords (Yetzirah) + Jupiter in Gemini = INTERFERENCE

Harris outdid herself in strict adherence to the color scales in this card. One would not expect a marriage of these colors to appear in art prior to the psychedelic black-light styles of the 1960s. The blades of the swords seem actually to glow in the dark. As in most of the small cards of this suit, the swords appear upon of field of stylized wings—here looking almost like pinwheels.

Actually, this card is not as bad as it looks or its title implies. Jupiter in Gemini indicates an element of luck in intellectual pursuits. Hod is the sphere of Mercury, who rules Gemini. As it does to the eights of the other suits, however, Hod's imbalanced and lowly position on the Tree of Life throws a wet blanket on what otherwise might have been a fortunate coupling. There is not enough Mercurial energy left to put up much of a fight, and in the suit of Swords, fighting is what it is all about. Crowley says, "the Will is constantly thwarted by accidental interference."[291]

The Eight of Swords does not show us much patience or persistence. If its influence is to be overcome, those qualities will need to be developed and introduced into the equation. Otherwise, everything will most definitely serve to interfere.

See chapter 20 for the general divinatory meanings of this card.

NINE OF SWORDS
CRUELTY

(Mars in Gemini)

10° to 20° Gemini

June 1 to June 10

Original Title: Lord of Despair and Cruelty.

Golden Dawn Model: From out of clouds on the left and right, four hands appear, each holding two swords nearly upright but with the points falling away from each other. From the bottom of the card, a fifth hand appears holding a ninth sword upright in the center, as if it had struck them apart. No rose at all is shown, seemingly having been utterly destroyed.

Prince Scale for Yesod: Very dark Purple.

The Four Scales for Mars: Scarlet; Red; Venetian Red; Bright Red, rayed Azure or Emerald.

The Four Scales for Gemini: Orange; Pale Mauve; New Yellow leather; Reddish Grey inclined to Mauve.

Formula: 9 (Yesod) of Swords (Yetzirah) + Mars in Gemini = CRUELTY

Oh, dear! Nobody expects the Spanish Inquisition! If you have a hangover, don't look at the Nine of Swords. You won't be ready to deal with this one. Who knows what Harris was doing with the colors, but she succeeded in making them perfectly nauseating. As if to underscore the degeneration of the suit, the pinwheel wings are being washed down the wall of the background by what look like drops of poison. The whole scene induces dizziness. I can almost taste the drops of rusty blood dripping from the swords.

It is kind of a surprise to find this horrible mess in middle-pillar Yesod. After all, the other nines are perfectly lovely fellows. But even the balance and stability of Yesod can't come to the rescue of all-action Mars—in all-talk Gemini—in the lowest burned-out region of Yetzirah, the world of thought. Watch out! It is, Crowley warns, "agony of mind."[292]

The only outlet for expression for this card is just ugly meanness. There is not even enough subtlety of mind left, Crowley points out, to take sadistic pleasure from its own cruelty: "Consciousness has fallen into a realm unenlightened by reason. This is the world of the unconscious primitive instincts, of the psychopath, of the fanatic."[293]

See chapter 20 for the general divinatory meanings of this card.

TEN OF SWORDS
RUIN

(Sol in Gemini)

20° to 30° Gemini

June 11 to June 20

Original Title: Lord of Ruin.

Golden Dawn Model: Four hands holding eight swords, as in the Nine of Swords, the points falling away from each other. Two hands hold two swords crossed in the center, as though their junction had disunited the others. No rose, flower, or bud is shown.

Prince Scale for Malkuth: Citrine; Olive; Russet; and Black; all with Gold, flecked Black.

The Four Scales for Sol: Orange; Gold Yellow; Rich Amber; Amber, rayed Red.

The Four Scales for Gemini: Orange; Pale Mauve; New Yellow leather; Reddish Grey inclined to Mauve.

Formula: 10 (Malkuth) of Swords (Yetzirah) + Sol in Gemini = RUIN

Can you find ten swords in the Ten of Swords? It's very difficult. Crowley tries to help us:

> The hilts of the Swords occupy the positions of the Sephiroth, but points One to Five and Seven to Nine touch and shatter the bright central sword (six) which represents the Sun, the Heart, the child of Chokmah and Binah. The tenth sword is also in splinters."[294]

There are three swords that form the middle pillar, the lowest having a crescent Moon on the handle. The next sword is placed upon the blade of the first and has an orb as part of its handle. The blade of the second sword is place upon the heart-shaped pommel of the central sword, whose blade is broken into three pieces.

It is difficult to put a good spin on this card. Harris herself reports, "I have done the 10 of Swords & promptly Russia takes up arms."[295] Along with the other tens, the Ten of Swords can't degenerate any lower without completely changing suits. Sol in Mercury-ruled Gemini brings a complete identification with the mind and the intellect, which, in this card, are in the very process of being destroyed. "It is the ruin of the Intellect," Crowley intones, "and even of all mental and moral qualities."[296] Ouch!

See chapter 20 for the general divinatory meanings of this card.

TWO OF DISKS
CHANGE

(Jupiter in Capricorn)

0° to 10° Capricorn

December 22 to December 30

Original Title: Lord of Harmonious Change.

Golden Dawn Model: In the center, a green and gold serpent with its tail in its mouth forms a figure 8. A hand appears from clouds on the left side of card and grasps the serpent where the two loops intersect. Within each loop is a disk, similar to that of the ace. There are no roses in this card.

Princess Scale for Chokmah: White-flecked red, Blue and Yellow.

The Four Scales for Jupiter: Violet; Blue; rich Purple; Bright Blue, rayed yellow.

The Four Scales for Capricorn: Indigo; Black; Blue-black; Cold Dark Grey, nearing Black.

Formula: 2 (Chokmah) of Disks (Assiah) + Jupiter in Capricorn = CHANGE

Even though Jupiter and Capricorn are not usually happy with each other, this high up on the Tree of Life, their differences are more or less forgiven. Crowley calls this card "the picture of the complete manifested Universe, in respect of its dynamics."[297]

Like the twos of the other suits, this card, not the ace, represents the first manifestation of its element. Disks being earth and, as we recall, earth being the throne of spirit, we have in a very real sense completed a great cosmic circuit. "[H]aving got to the bottom, Crowley explains, "one immediately comes out again at the top. Hence, the card manifests the symbolism of the serpent of the endless band."[298] Crowley sings in his Liber LXV:

> Then I beheld myself compassed about with the Infinite Circle of Emerald that encloseth the Universe.[299]

As if to suggest the nuclei of the first dividing cells of what will soon be the material universe, two yin-yangs whirl in the center of the two coils of the serpent; the top rotates to the left and contains within itself the symbols of fire and water; the bottom one rotates to the right and contains within itself the symbols of air and earth. Harris tells Crowley that she paid particular attention to the colors:

> No 2 Disks is on the stocks, is the serpent's eye to be red? It is a bit awkward as there are several colours introduced in the card which do not belong to Jupiter and Capricorn, I mean the 4 elements colours and they make inharmonious patches. Did you say anything about jewels on the serpent? I think you will like him."[300]

See chapter 20 for the general divinatory meanings of this card.

THREE OF DISKS
WORK

(Mars in Capricorn)

10° to 20° Capricorn

December 31 to January 9

Original Title: Lord of Material Works.

Golden Dawn Model: From clouds at the bottom of the card, a hand appears holding a branch of a rose tree. Three disks are arranged as an upright equilateral triangle. Crowning the top disk are two white rosebuds. The two lower disks appear right and left at the tips of green leaves.

Princess Scale for Binah: Grey, flecked Pink.

The Four Scales for Mars: Scarlet; Red; Venetian Red; Bright Red, rayed Azure or Emerald.

The Four Scales for Capricorn: Indigo; Black; Blue-black; Cold Dark Grey, nearing Black.

Formula: 3 (Binah) of Disks (Assiah) + Mars in Capricorn = WORK

Although in *The Book of Thoth* Crowley consistently refers to this card as Work, the title that appears on Lady Harris's painting (and consequently the published editions of the Thoth Tarot) is Works. In either case, the factors that determine its character (Binah of Assiah, Mars in Capricorn) make this card, among all the abstract supernal triad small cards, the most *un*-abstract. In a very real way, the Three of Disks is the material heart of the three-stroke engine that drives the universe that we discussed in Atu X. Crowley says it is "the material establishment of the idea of the Universe, the determination of its basic form."[301]

The image is an aerial view of a pyramid or tetrahedron firmly fixed on a desolate desert representing the great sea of Binah. The gray sand dunes seem to have been formed by blasts of energy emanating from the structure, which itself is supported by three great wheels. Although they are very small and difficult to see, the symbols of the alchemical elements mercury, sulfur, and salt appear in the hubs of the three wheels, suggesting the eternal universe-sustaining competition of the three gunas of the Hindu system.[302]

See chapter 20 for the general divinatory meanings of this card.

FOUR OF DISKS
POWER

(Sol in Capricorn)

20° to 30° Capricorn

January 10 to January 19

Original Title: Lord of Earthly Power.

Golden Dawn Model: From clouds at the bottom of the card, a hand appears holding a branch of a rose tree. There are no flowers or buds other than one white rose in the center in full bloom. Disks are arranged as if on the points of a square.

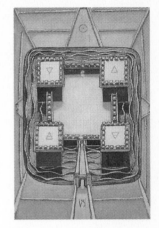

Princess Scale for Chesed: Deep Azure, flecked Yellow.

The Four Scales for Sol: Orange; Gold Yellow; Rich Amber; Amber, rayed Red.

The Four Scales for Capricorn: Indigo; Black; Blue-black; Cold Dark Grey, nearing Black.

Formula: 4 (Chesed) of Disks (Assiah) + Sol in Capricorn = POWER

This card is well named. It is Sol in Capricorn, and to the ancients, the greatest display of celestial power occurred each year when the Sun entered Capricorn and conquered death by reversing its southward plunge into darkness. In *The Book of Thoth*, Crowleys describes how "Chesed shows the establishment of the Universe in three dimensions, that is, below the Abyss."[303] In "The Rite of Saturn," he calls it "The Fortress that is upon the Frontier of the Abyss."[304] This is a perfect description of the Four of Disks.

To properly view this card, we must imagine ourselves hovering hundreds of feet above a foursquare walled citadel surrounded by a wide moat. We are approaching from the bottom of the card and are not yet above dead center. Four tall watchtowers crowned with battlements displaying the symbols of the elements rise from the corners and tower far above the walls. The main entrance to the fortress is seen at the bottom of the card; a fortified bridge crosses the moat. From this angle, we can only see one other entrance, a tiny opening (that does not lead to a bridge) in the opposite wall. Similar openings may exist in the walls on the right and left, but, from our aerial position, it is impossible to tell. However, we are tantalized by what appear to be roads leading up to the moat from the three other quarters, possibly an indication of other openings. The imagery of this card certainly leaves us with many mysteries unsolved.

See chapter 20 for the general divinatory meanings of this card.

FIVE OF DISKS
WORRY

(Mercury in Taurus)

0° to 10° Taurus

April 21 to April 30

Original Title: Lord of Material Trouble.

Golden Dawn Model: From clouds at the bottom of the card, a hand appears holding a branch of a white rose tree. The roses are falling, leaving no buds on the tree. Four disks similar to the ace are arranged in the form of a square with a fifth disk in the center.

Princess Scale for Geburah: Red, flecked Black.

The Four Scales for Mercury: Yellow; Purple; Grey; Indigo, rayed Violet.

The Four Scales for Taurus: Red Orange; Deep Indigo; Deep warm Olive; Rich Brown.

Formula: 5 (Geburah) of Disks (Assiah) + Mercury in Taurus = WORRY

Despite Mercury's active nature and Taurus's tendency to be a bit sluggish, this is not an overly difficult match. People with this aspect in their natal horoscopes are often very patient, practical, and conservative. However, Geburah throws a disturbing and stressful monkeywrench into the mechanism of this otherwise stable device. The natural result is worry, the kind of worry that has you asking, "Am I being pulled into a predicament I can't get out of? Am I in over my head? Will I be crushed by the blind momentum of this situation?

The surface of this card cannot contain the full images of five ponderous gear wheels laid one upon another like the inner workings of a huge and grotesque clock. What appear as five disks in the center of the card are actually only the hubs of these massive wheels. The five hubs are arranged as an averse pentagram, each containing one of the five Hindu tattva symbols of the elements: red triangle of fire, silver crescent of water, blue circle of air, yellow square of earth, and the black egg of spirit. If we look closely, we see that the black egg of spirit is upon the downward point of the pentagram. It is clear that the Five of Disks is pointing to the more nasty meaning of the averse pentagram, that of the triumph of matter over spirit.[305]

See chapter 20 for the general divinatory meanings of this card.

SIX OF DISKS
SUCCESS

(Moon in Taurus)

10° to 20° Taurus

May 1 to May 10

Original Title: Lord of Material Success.

Golden Dawn Model: From clouds at the bottom of the card, a hand appears holding a rose branch with white roses and buds, each of which touches a disk. Disks are arranged in two columns of three each, thus:

✪ ✪

✪ ✪

✪ ✪

Princess Scale for Tiphareth: Gold Amber.

The Four Scales for Moon: Blue; Silver; Cold Pale Blue; Silver, rayed Sky Blue.

The Four Scales for Taurus: Red Orange; Deep Indigo; Deep warm Olive; Rich Brown.

Formula: 6 (Tiphareth) of Disks (Assiah) + Moon in Taurus = SUCCESS

All things considered, things don't get any better than this in the suit of Disks. The Moon is exalted in Taurus and eminently happy to be there. As change is the Moon's primary characteristic, however, we may not have much time to enjoy our success. On the other hand, Tiphareth, as always, comes to the rescue:

> It represents consciousness in its most harmonized and balanced form; definitely in form, not only in idea, as in the case of the number Two. In other words, the Son is an interpretation of the Father in terms of the mind.[306]

For this reason, it is interesting to compare this card with the Ace of Disks, because, in a very real sense, the Six of Disks is an interpretation of the Ace of Disks in terms of the mind. In this, the most earthy and material suit, six (Tiphareth) applies its noble and stable influence toward practical ends—it is a brief reward for the tireless (if somewhat mindless) hands-on labor of the entrepreneur.

The basic image is that of the hexagram we found on the white section of the lower arm of the Hermetic Rose Cross (see chapter 8)—the Sun surrounded by the other six planets of the ancients. Here the Sun of Tiphareth is represented by the rose of forty-nine petals crucified upon a cross of five squares. This device, long associated with the Sun in magical and Masonic symbolism, is surrounded by three concentric rings of golden yellow, salmon-pink, and amber, which, in some reproductions, are hard to see.

In a tarot reading, this card acts somewhat like a Midas touch—bringing to neighboring cards the prospect of actually manifesting their qualities on the material plane.

See chapter 20 for the general divinatory meanings of this card.

SEVEN OF DISKS
FAILURE

(Saturn in Taurus)

20° to 30° Taurus

May 11 to May 20

Original Title: Lord of Success Unfulfilled.

Golden Dawn Model: From clouds at the bottom of the card, a hand appears holding a rose branch. There are only five buds, which overhang, but do not touch the five uppermost disks. The disks are arranged thus:

Princess Scale for Netzach: Olive, flecked Gold.

The Four Scales for Saturn: Indigo; Black; Blue-black; Black, rayed Blue.

The Four Scales for Taurus: Red Orange; Deep Indigo; Deep warm Olive; Rich Brown.

Formula: 7 (Netzach) of Disks (Assiah) + Saturn in Taurus = FAILURE

This card presents an image of cold, stark beauty. That, I'm afraid, is the best thing that can be said about it. Try as I may, I can't find one kind word from Crowley concerning Failure. But honestly, have any of the sevens really thrilled us? We have to hand it to Lady Harris, though. She did a marvelous job of setting seven leaden coins ("They suggest bad money," Crowleys explains.[307]) struck with the symbols of Saturn and Taurus in a world of dead and blackened vegetation. They form the geomantic figure Rubeus, which Crowley describes as "the most ugly and menacing of the Sixteen."[308]

One look at our formula tells us we are in for trouble. Netzach, the sphere of dreamy-eyed prima donna Venus has, as Crowley puts it, "its customary enfeebling effect."[309] And cold, heavy Saturn, in slow, earthy Taurus adds jack-booted insult to unimaginative injury. Crowley summarizes the dark imagery of the card:

> There is no effort here; not even dream; the stake has been thrown down, and it is lost. That is all Labour itself is abandoned; everything is sunk in sloth.[310]

When the Seven of Disks shows up in a tarot reading, you better hope your question was "What's going to happen to my worst enemy?"
See chapter 20 for the general divinatory meanings of this card.

EIGHT OF DISKS
PRUDENCE

(Sol in Virgo)

0° to 10° Virgo

August 23 to September 1

Original Title: Lord of Prudence.

Golden Dawn Model: From clouds at the bottom of the card, a hand appears grasping a branch of a rose tree with four white roses on it. They touch only the four lowermost disks. Leaves touch the four uppermost disks. The disks are arranged thus:

Princess Scale for Hod: Yellowish-Brown, flecked White.

The Four Scales for Sol: Orange; Gold Yellow; Rich Amber; Amber, rayed Red.

The Four Scales for Virgo: Green (yellowish); Slate Grey; Green Grey; Plum color.

Formula: 8 (Hod) of Disks (Assiah) + Sol in Virgo = PRUDENCE

Why is the Eight of Disks, Prudence, so inoffensive, while the Seven of Disks, Failure, is so perfectly awful? Both cards are low on the Tree of Life, and off the middle pillar. The formula explains it all.

Hod is the sphere of Mercury. Mercury both rules and is exalted in Virgo. Virgo is the mutable zodiac sign (and therefore the stabilizing influence) of Earth. Earth is the element of Assiah and the suit of Disks. (Isn't this cozy?) And finally, the Sun radiates its life-giving rays upon all this mental (Mercury) fertility (Virgo/earth).

Of course, everything isn't perfect. The number eight position is still unbalanced and weak. There are enough mitigating factors, however, to make Crowley comment that this card "signifies intelligence lovingly applied to material matters, especially those of the agriculturist, the artificer and the engineer."[311]

The disks are plum-colored blossoms of a thick-stalked tree firmly planted in the earth. Like the disks in the Golden Dawn model, they are arranged to suggest the figure Populus, which is one of two geomantic symbols representing the Moon. In all candor, I am unsure why this is so. Perhaps because of the Moon's association with the planting of crops.

This card is well named, for prudence is a passive activity. It is calculating. Plant and wait. Wait and see. Bet—but only if you've fixed the game.

See chapter 20 for the general divinatory meanings of this card.

NINE OF DISKS
GAIN

(Venus in Virgo)

10° to 20° Virgo

September 2 to September 11

Original Title: Lord of Material Gain.

Golden Dawn Model: From clouds at the bottom of the card, a hand appears holding a rose branch with nine white roses, each of which touches a disk. The disks are arranged thus:

Princess Scale for Yesod: Citrine, flecked azure.

The Four Scales for Venus: Emerald Green; Sky Blue; Early Spring Green; Bright Rose or Cerise, rayed Pale Green.

The Four Scales for Virgo: Green (yellowish); Slate Grey; Green Grey; Plum color.

Formula: 9 (Yesod) of Disks (Assiah) + Venus in Virgo = GAIN

Oh, how happy I am to see this card when the question concerns material matters! I don't care how unspiritual it sounds, I love this card! Six small coins, stamped with remarkably detailed and imaginative personifications of the planets, surround a large unmarked solar orb that is interlaced with two companion disks of the same size. Few cards of the Thoth Tarot bear less resemblance to Crowley's description in *The Book of Thoth* than this one. I have to conclude that his words were part of his original instructions to Harris and not an account of the finished product.

Be that as it may, the Nine of Disks is a balanced and beautiful interpretation of what most people on this planet think of as good luck. Crowley even uses the words "good luck" twice in his comments:

This card is ruled by Venus in Virgo. It shows good luck attending material affairs, favour and popularity . . . the mingling of "good luck and good management."[312]

Yesod of Assiah is such a low position in the lowest of the four Qabalistic worlds that its lowness is actually an asset. We are talking big-time payoff on the material plane, and we are blissfully insensitive to concerns and anxieties that plagued us throughout the cards of the other suits. "The suit of Disks," Crowley observes, "is much too dull to care; it reckons up its winnings; it does not worry its head about whether anything is won when all is won."[313]

See chapter 20 for the general divinatory meanings of this card.

TEN OF DISKS
WEALTH

(Mercury in Virgo)

20° to 30° Virgo

September 12 to September 22

Original Title: Lord of Wealth.

Golden Dawn Model: From clouds at the bottom
of the card, a hand appears holding the branch of a
rose tree whose roses touch all the disks. No buds,
however, are shown. The disks are arranged thus:

Princess Scale for Malkuth: Black, rayed with Yellow.

The Four Scales for Mercury: Yellow; Purple; Grey; Indigo, rayed Violet.

The Four Scales for Virgo: Green (yellowish); Slate Grey; Green Grey; Plum
color.

Formula: 10 (Malkuth) of Disks (Assiah) + Mercury in Virgo = WEALTH

The Ten of Disks represents the climax of the descent of matter and is the signal
for the redintegration by spirit. Crowley calls this card "a hieroglyph of the cycle
of regeneration."[314] It is, after all, the last tarot card. It represents the lowest sphere
(Malkuth-Earth) of the lowest Qabalistic world (Assiah-the material plane). The
tens of the other suits have somewhere to go. They simply cooperate with gravity
and degenerate into the next lower suit. For the Ten of Disks, there is no place to
descend, no place to grow, no place to go. The Ten of Disks is forced to do something that no other small card is called upon to do. From its position at the bottom
of the cosmos, it has somehow to form a link with the secret of creation, then actually reincarnate fresh and new at the very top of the tarot cycle.

In other words, it must regenerate the world. That's some trick, and it's going to take the biggest trickster in the universe to help pull it off. But let's first take a look at the card.

Lady Harris's interpretation is almost comically poignant: a Tree of Life made entirely of massive and heavy coins, its Malkuth bulging at the bottom as if the forces and energies of all the tarot cards, all the sephiroth and paths, all the Qabalistic worlds have settled into it like the tired sediment of the entire universe. For lack of a more gentile allusion, this card is the portrait of cosmic constipation. A magical laxative will need to be administered to prevent this stagnant wealth of energy, experience, and matter from putrefying and poisoning the body.

Is there a doctor in the house?

Yes! The best doctor in the universe—the god of physicians and magicians, the god who, tradition informs us, invented the tarot—Thoth-Hermes-Mercury!

This is perfect! For a job like this, his credentials are amazing. First of all, as Mercury, the Magus, he knows his way around the supernal triad. (Remember that the path of Mercury is above the Abyss and joins Kether to Binah.) As Hermes, he descended to the lowest region of the Land of the Dead and returned to Olympus with Persephone to regenerate the cycle of seasons. If he could do that, jump-starting the Ten of Disks is going to be a piece of cake! His greatest credential is that he is Thoth—the inventor and sustainer of this entire tarot universe.[315]

As if to attract Mercury's attention so that he may perform this most necessary magick, Harris painted this card as a veritable invocation of Mercury. All the sephiroth but one bear an image or word sacred to Mercury:

- Kether—we find the most common symbol of the planet Mercury;
- Chokmah—the symbol of Mercury as the Magus (Note that the right-angled positions of the arms are identical to the gesture made by the Magus in Atu I.);
- Binah—the symbol of alchemical Mercury;
- Chesed—the letter Pa, the Enochian equivalent of the letter "B" (Harris associated this with the Hebrew letter Beth which is assigned to Mercury);
- Geburah—the Hebrew letter Beth;
- Tiphareth—the name of Raphael (written in Hebrew), the ruling angel of Mercury;
- Netzach—the eight-pointed star of Mercury;
- Hod—the hexagram within the hexagon, symbol of the Sun (see below);
- Yesod—the Pythagorean Tetractys;
- Malkuth—the Mercurial caduceus made from the three mother letters of the Hebrew alphabet.

Why do all the sephiroth contain an image of Mercury except Hod, the sphere of Mercury itself? That is a very good question. Crowley mentions it as being the key to this remarkable regenerative process:

> These disks are inscribed with various symbols of mercurial character, except that the coin in the place of Hod (Mercury) on the Tree is marked with the cipher of the Sun. This indicates the only possibility of issue from the impasse produced by the exhaustion of all the elemental forces.[316]

I take this to mean that, at this stage of the game, Mercury needs inspiration and direction. Crowley said it most succinctly:

> When wealth accumulates beyond a certain point, it must either become completely inert and cease to be wealth, or call in the aid of intelligence to use it rightly. . . . In this way, Carnegie establishes a Library, Rockefeller endows Research, simply because there is nothing else to do.[317]

By plugging in the Sun in the sphere of Mercury, in a Tree of Life otherwise loaded with Mercury, Harris is calling in the aid of intelligence to give this card the spiritual integrity necessary to regenerate the world and become the ultimate cosmic philanthropist.

See chapter 20 for the general divinatory meanings of this card.

How I should like to do them all again.[318]
—Harris to Crowley, date uncertain.

CHAPTER TWENTY

✺

METHOD OF DIVINATION AND THE MEANINGS OF THE CARDS

All divination resembles an attempt by a man born blind to obtain sight by getting blind drunk.[319]

The cards are not to be sold without the book. If the book can be printed without illustrations it need not cost more than £300. If Lady Harris likes, she can give it away with the cards, I do not want any money out of it: and she can say she wrote it, I don't care. But I will not allow the cards to be issued so that they can be used only for gambling or fortune-telling.[320]
  —Crowley, Legal memorandum regarding "Stipend," date uncertain.

You may think it odd (after I have written so much about things like projective geometry, the Golden Dawn, changing Aeons, desert visions, the Hermetic Rose Cross, the Tree of Life, color scales, guardian angels, and the magical, alchemical, and Qabalistic intricacies of the Thoth Tarot) that I appear to have such precious little to say about the use of the cards in divination. I assure you this is not because I wish to denigrate the tarot's potential as a divinatory device or discourage its use as such. On the contrary, I use the cards for divination, Crowley used the cards for divination, and many of the most gifted tarot readers in the world use the Thoth Tarot for divination.

Throughout this book, I have tried to remain true to the promise of its title. I know. I probably slipped in a few places here and there and stuck in a little too much DuQuette. But, for the most part, I believe I've been a faithful Crowley delivery system, and I do not intend to spoil that now by introducing Lon Milo DuQuette's subjective thoughts on tarot spreads and the divinatory meanings of the Thoth Tarot.

Any adept reader of tarot cards will tell you that if you wish to use the tarot as a divinatory tool, it is best to choose a spread and to develop a personal glossary of meanings based upon your own familiarity with the qualities and characteristics of each card and the knowledge and experience you gather in actually working with the cards.

To develop that experience, you need to start somewhere—and for most people that somewhere usually entails reading the cards for yourself or others and looking up the meaning of the cards in a book. If that is what you intend to do with this book, then I am going to stay completely out of the way. The method of divination and meanings you will find in this chapter have been culled exclusively from Crowley's own writings and from the tarot material found in *The Equinox*, Volume I.[321]

You will see that Crowley's method of divination is extremely complex and incorporates many of the astrological and Qabalistic principles I've discussed throughout the book. If you are just beginning your tarot career, you will most likely want to start with a simpler method, such as the three-card Past-Present-Future spread, or others you can find in other tarot texts.

A METHOD OF DIVINATION BY THE TAROT
O.M. (Aleister Crowley)[322]

[This method is that given to students of the grade Adept Adeptus Minor in the R. R. et A. C. But it has been revised and improved, while certain safeguards have been introduced in order to make its abuse impossible.—O.M.]

1. THE SIGNIFICATOR.
   Choose a card to represent the Querent, using your knowledge or judgment of his character rather than dwelling on his physical characteristics.
2. Take the cards in your left hand. In the right hand hold the wand over them, and say: I invoke thee, I A O, that thou wilt send H R U, the great Angel that is set over the operations of this Secret Wisdom, to lay his hand invisibly upon these consecrated cards of art, that thereby we may obtain true knowledge of hidden things, to the glory of thine ineffable Name. Amen.
3. Hand the cards to Querent, and bid him think of the question attentively, and cut.
4. Take the cards as cut, and hold as for dealing.

First Operation

This shows the situation of the Querent at the time when he consults you.

1. The pack being in front of you, cut, and place the top half to the left.

2. Cut each pack again to the left.
3. These four stacks represent I H V H, from right to left.
4. Find the Significator. If it be in the Yod pack, the question refers to work, business, etc.; if in the Hé pack, to love, marriage, or pleasure; if in the Vau pack, to trouble, loss, scandal, quarrelling, etc.; if in the Hé final pack, to money, goods, and such purely material matters.
5. Tell the Querent what he has come for: if wrong, abandon the divination.
6. If right, spread out the pack containing the Significator, face upwards. Count the cards from him, in the direction in which he faces.[323]

The counting should include the card from which you count.
For Knights, Queens and Princes, count 4.
For Princesses, count 7.
For Aces, count 11.
For small cards, count according to the number.
For trumps, count 3 for the elemental trumps; 9 for the planetary trumps; 12 for the Zodiacal trumps.
Make a "story" of these cards. This story is that of the beginning of the affair.

7. Pair the cards on either side of the Significator, then those outside them, and so on. Make another "story," which should fill in the details omitted in the first.
8. If this story is not quite accurate, do not be discouraged. Perhaps the Querent himself does not know everything. But the main lines ought to be laid down firmly, with correctness, or the divination should be abandoned.

Second Operation

DEVELOPMENT OF THE QUESTION

1. Shuffle, invoke suitably, and let Querent cut as before.
2. Deal cards into twelve stacks, for the twelve astrological houses of heaven.
3. Make up your mind in which stack you ought to find the Significator, "e.g." in the seventh house if the question concerns marriage, and so on.
4. Examine this chosen stack. If the Significator is not there, try some cognate house. On a second failure, abandon the divination.
5. Read the stack counting and pairing as before.

Third Operation

FURTHER DEVELOPMENT OF THE QUESTION

1. Shuffle, etc., as before.
2. Deal cards into twelve stacks for the twelve signs of the Zodiac.
3. Divine the proper stack and proceed as before.

Fourth Operation

PENULTIMATE ASPECTS OF THE QUESTIONS

1. Shuffle, etc., as before.
2. Find the Significator: set him upon the table; let the thirty-six cards following form a ring round him.
3. Count and pair as before.

[Note that the nature of each Decan is shewn by the small card attributed to it, and by the symbols given in Liber DCCLXXVII, cols. 149–151.]

Fifth Operation

FINAL RESULT

1. Shuffle, etc., as before.
2. Deal into ten packs in the form of the Tree of Life.
3. Make up your mind where the Significator should be, as before; but failure does not here necessarily imply that the divination has gone astray.
4. Count and pair as before.

[Note that one cannot tell at what part of the divination the present time occurs. Usually Op. 1 seems to indicate the past history of the question; but not always so. Experience will teach. Sometimes a new current of high help may show the moment of consultation.

I may add that in material matters this method is extremely valuable. I have been able to work out the most complex problems in minute detail. O.M.]

It is quite impossible to obtain satisfactory results from this or any other system of divination unless the Art is perfectly required. It is the most sensitive, difficult and perilous branch of Magick. The necessary conditions, with a comprehensive comparative review of all important methods in use, are fully described and discussed in "Magick," Chapter XVII.

The abuse of divination has been responsible, more than any other cause, for the discredit into which the whole subject of Magick had fallen when the Master Therion undertook the task of its rehabilitation. Those who neglect his warnings and profane the Sanctuary of Transcendental Art have no other than themselves to blame for the formidable and irremediable disasters which infallibly will destroy them. Prospero is Shakespeare's reply to Dr. Faustus.

DIVINATORY MEANINGS OF THE TWENTY-TWO ATUS OF THE MAJOR ARCANA[324]

THE FOOL
In spiritual matters, the Fool means idea, thought, spirituality, that which endeavours to transcend earth. In material matters, it may, if badly dignified, mean folly, eccentricity, or even mania. But the essential of this card is that it represents an original, subtle, sudden impulse or impact, coming from a completely strange quarter. All such impulses are right, if rightly received; and the good or ill interpretation of the card depends entirely on the right attitude of the Querent.

THE MAGUS
Skill, wisdom, adroitness, elasticity, craft, cunning, deceit, theft. Sometimes occult wisdom or power, sometimes a quick impulse, "a brain-wave." It may imply messages, business transactions, the interference of learning or intelligence with the matter in hand.

THE HIGH PRIESTESS
Pure, exalted and gracious influence enters the matter. Hence, change, alternation, increase and decrease, fluctuation. There is, however, a liability to be led away by enthusiasm; one may become "moon-struck" unless careful balance is maintained.

THE EMPRESS
Love, beauty, happiness, pleasure, success, completion, good fortune, graciousness, elegance, luxury, idleness, dissipation, debauchery, friendship, gentleness, delight.

THE EMPEROR
War, conquest, victory, strife, ambition, originality, over-weening confidence and megalomania, quarrelsomeness, energy, vigour, stubbornness, impracticability, rashness, ill-temper.

THE HIEROPHANT
Stubborn strength, toil, endurance, placidity, manifestation, explanation, teaching, goodness of heart, help from superiors, patience, organization, peace.

THE LOVERS
Openness to inspiration, intuition, intelligence, second sight, childishness, frivolity, thoughtfulness divorced from practical consideration, indecision, self-contradiction, triviality, the "high-brow."

THE CHARIOT
Triumph, victory, hope, memory, digestion, violence in maintaining traditional ideas, the "die-hard," ruthlessness, lust of destruction, obedience, faithfulness, authority under authority.

ADJUSTMENT
Justice, or rather *justesse*, the act of adjustment, suspension of all action pending decision; in material matters, may refer to law suits or prosecutions. Socially, marriage or marriage agreements; politically, treaties.

THE HERMIT
Illumination from within, secret impulse from within; practical plans derived accordingly. Retirement from participation in current events.

FORTUNE
Change of fortune. (This generally means good fortune because of the fact of consultation implies anxiety or discontent.)

LUST
Courage, strength, energy and action, *une grand passion*; resort to magick, the use of magical power.

THE HANGED MAN
Enforced sacrifice, punishment, loss, fatal or voluntary, suffering, defeat, failure, death.

DEATH
Transformation, change, voluntary or involuntary, in either case logical development of existing conditions, yet perhaps sudden and unexpected. Apparent death or destruction, but such interpretation is illusion.

ART

Combination of forces, realization, action based on accurate calculation; the way of escape, success after elaborate maneuvers.

THE DEVIL

Blind impulse, irresistibly strong and unscrupulous, ambition, temptation, obsession, secret plan about to be executed; hard work, obstinacy, rigidity, aching discontent, endurance.

THE TOWER

Quarrel, combat, danger, ruin, destruction of plans, sudden death, escape from prison.

THE STAR

Hope, unexpected help, clearness of vision, realization of possibilities, spiritual insight, with bad aspects, error of judgement, dreaminess, disappointment.

THE MOON

Illusion deception, bewilderment, hysteria, even madness, dreaminess, falsehood, error, crisis, "the darkest hour before the dawn," the brink of important change.

THE SUN

Glory, gain riches, triumph, pleasure, frankness, truth, shamelessness, arrogance, vanity, manifestation, recovery from sickness, but sometimes sudden death.

THE AEON

Final decision in respect of the past, new current in respect of the future; always represents the taking of a definite step.

THE UNIVERSE

The matter of the question itself, synthesis, the end of the matter, may mean delay, opposition, obstinacy, inertia, patience, perseverance, persistent stubbornness in difficulty. The crystallization of the whole matter involved.

DIVINATORY MEANINGS OF THE FIFTY-SIX CARDS OF THE MINOR ARCANA[325]

ACE OF WANDS

It symbolizes Force—strength, rush, vigour, energy, and it governs, according to its nature, various works and questions. It implies Natural, as opposed to Invoked, Force.

Knight of Wands

He is active, generous, fierce, sudden, impetuous. If ill dignified, he is evil-minded, cruel, bigoted, brutal.

Queen of Wands

Adaptability, steady force applied to an object, steady rule, great attractive power, power of command, yet liked notwithstanding. Kind and generous when not opposed. If ill dignified, obstinate, revengeful, domineering, tyrannical, and apt to turn against another without a cause.

Prince of Wands

Swift, strong, hasty; rather violent, yet just and generous; noble and scorning meanness. If ill dignified—cruel, intolerant, prejudiced and ill natured.

Princess of Wands

Brilliance, courage, beauty, force, sudden in anger or love, desire of power, enthusiasm, revenge. If ill dignified, she is superficial, theatrical, cruel, unstable, domineering.

Two of Wands

Influence over others, authority, power, dominion.
Strength, domination, harmony of rule and of justice. Boldness, courage, fierceness, shamelessness, revenge, resolution, generous, proud, sensitive, ambitious, refined, restless, turbulent, sagacious withal, yet unforgiving and obstinate.

Three of Wands

Pride, arrogance, self-assertion.
Established force, strength, realization of hope. Completion of labour. Success after struggle. Pride, nobility, wealth, power, conceit. Rude self-assumption and insolence. Generosity, obstinacy, etc.

Four of Wands

Settlement, arrangement, completion.
Perfection or completion of a thing built up with trouble and labour. Rest after labour, subtlety, cleverness, beauty, mirth, success in completion. Reasoning faculty, conclusions drawn from previous knowledge. Unreadiness, unreliable and unsteady through over-anxiety and hurriedness of action. Graceful in manner, at times insincere, etc.

FIVE OF WANDS
Quarrelling and fighting.
Violent strife and boldness, rashness, cruelty, violence, lust, desire, prodigality and generosity; depending on whether the card is well or ill dignified.

SIX OF WANDS
Gain.
Victory after strife: Love: pleasure gained by labour: carefulness, sociability and avoiding of strife, yet victory therein: also insolence, and pride of riches and success, etc. The whole dependent on the dignity.

SEVEN OF WANDS
Opposition, yet courage.
Possible victory, depending on the energy and courage exercised; valour; opposition, obstacles and difficulties, yet courage to meet them; quarrelling, ignorance, pretence, and wrangling, and threatening; also victory in small and unimportant things: and influence upon subordinates.

EIGHT OF WANDS
Hasty communications and messages; swiftness.
Too much force applied too suddenly. Very rapid rush, but quickly passed and expended. Violent, but not lasting. Swiftness, rapidity, courage, boldness, confidence, freedom, warfare, violence; love of open air, field-sports, gardens and meadows. Generous, subtle, eloquent, yet somewhat untrustworthy; rapacious, insolent, oppressive. Theft and robbery. According to dignity.

NINE OF WANDS
Strength, power, health, recovery from sickness.
Tremendous and steady force that cannot be shaken. Herculean strength, yet sometimes scientifically applied. Great success, but with strife and energy. Victory, preceded by apprehension and fear. Health good, and recovery not in doubt. Generous, questioning and curious; fond of external appearances: intractable, obstinate.

TEN OF WANDS
Cruelty, malice, revenge, injustice.
Cruel and overbearing force and energy, but applied only to material and selfish ends. Sometimes shows failure in a matter, and the opposition too strong to be controlled; arising from the person's too great selfishness at the beginning. Ill-will, levity, lying, malice, slander, envy, obstinacy; swiftness in evil and deceit, if ill dignified. Also generosity, disinterestedness and self-sacrifice, when well dignified.

ACE OF CUPS
It symbolizes Fertility—productiveness, beauty, pleasure, happiness, etc.

KNIGHT OF CUPS
Graceful, poetic, Venusian, indolent, but enthusiastic if roused. Ill dignified, he is sensual, idle and untruthful.

QUEEN OF CUPS
She is imaginative, poetic, kind, yet not willing to take much trouble for another. Coquettish, good-natured and underneath a dreamy appearance. Imagination stronger than feeling. Very much affected by other influences, and therefore more dependent upon dignity than most symbols.

PRINCE OF CUPS
He is subtle, violent, crafty and artistic; a fierce nature with calm exterior. Powerful for good or evil but more attracted by the evil if allied with apparent Power or Wisdom. If ill dignified, he is intensely evil and merciless.

PRINCESS OF CUPS
Sweetness, poetry, gentleness and kindness. Imaginative, dreamy, at times indolent, yet courageous if roused. When ill dignified she is selfish and luxurious.

TWO OF CUPS
Marriage, love, pleasure.
Harmony of masculine and feminine united. Harmony, pleasure, mirth, subtlety: but if ill dignified—folly, dissipation, waste, silly actions.

THREE OF CUPS
Plenty, hospitality, eating and drinking, pleasure, dancing, new clothes, merriment.
Abundance, plenty, success, pleasure, sensuality, passive success, good luck and fortune; love, gladness, kindness, liberality.

FOUR OF CUPS
Receiving pleasure or kindness from others, but some discomfort therewith.
Success or pleasure approaching their end. A stationary period in happiness, which may, or may not, continue. It does not mean love and marriage so much as the previous symbol. It is too passive a symbol to represent perfectly complete happiness. Swiftness, hunting and pursuing. Acquisition by contention: injustice sometimes; some drawbacks to pleasure implied.

FIVE OF CUPS
Disappointment in love, marriage broken off, unkindness of a friend; loss of friendship.
Death, or end of pleasure: disappointment, sorrow and loss in those things from
which pleasure is expected. Sadness, treachery, deceit; ill-will, detraction; charity
and kindness ill requited; all kinds of anxieties and troubles from unsuspected and
unexpected sources.

SIX OF CUPS
Beginning of wish, happiness, success, or enjoyment.
Commencement of steady increase, gain and pleasure; but commencement only.
Also affront, detection, knowledge, and in some instances contention and strife
arising from unwarranted self-assertion and vanity. Sometimes thankless and pre-
sumptuous; sometimes amiable and patient. According to dignity as usual.

SEVEN OF CUPS
*Lying, promises unfulfilled; illusion, deception, error; slight success at outset, not
retained.*
Possible victory, but neutralized by the supineness of the person: illusionary success, deception in the moment of apparent victory. Lying, error, promises unfulfilled. Drunkenness, wrath, vanity. Lust, fornication, violence against women,
selfish dissipation, deception in love and friendship. Often success gained, but not
followed up. Modified as usual by dignity.

EIGHT OF CUPS
Success abandoned; decline of interest.
Temporary success, but without further results. Thing thrown aside as soon as
gained. Not lasting, even in the matter in hand. Indolence in success. Journeying
from place to place. Misery and repining without cause. Seeking after riches.
Instability.

NINE OF CUPS
Complete success, pleasure and happiness, wishes fulfilled.
Complete and perfect realization of pleasure and happiness, almost perfect; self-
praise, vanity, conceit, much talking of self, yet kind and lovable, and may be self-
denying therewith. High-minded, not easily satisfied with small and limited
ideas. Apt to be maligned through too much self-assumption. A good and generous, but sometimes foolish nature.

TEN OF CUPS
Matter settled: complete good fortune.
Permanent and lasting success and happiness, because inspired from above. Not so sensual as "Lord of Material Happiness," yet almost more truly happy. Pleasure, dissipation, debauchery, quietness, peacemaking. Kindness, pity, generosity, wantonness, waste, etc., according to dignity.

ACE OF SWORDS
It symbolizes "Invoked," as contrasted with Natural Force: for it is the Invocation of the Sword. Raised upward, it invokes the Divine crown of Spiritual Brightness, but reversed it is the Invocation of Demonic Force; and becomes a fearfully evil symbol. It represents, therefore, very great power for good or evil, but invoked; and it also represents whirling Force, and strength through trouble. It is the affirmation of Justice upholding Divine Authority; and it may become the Sword of Wrath, Punishment, and Affliction.

KNIGHT OF SWORDS
He is active, clever, subtle, fierce, delicate, courageous, skilful, but inclined to domineer. Also to overvalue small things, unless well dignified. If ill dignified, deceitful, tyrannical and crafty.

QUEEN OF SWORDS
Intensely perceptive, keen observation, subtle, quick and confident: often persevering, accurate in superficial things, graceful, fond of dancing and balancing. If ill dignified, cruel, sly, deceitful, unreliable, though with a good exterior.

PRINCE OF SWORDS
Full of ideas and thoughts and designs, distrustful, suspicious, firm in friendship and enmity; careful, observant, slow, over-cautious, symbolizes Alpha and Omega; he slays as fast as he creates. If ill dignified: harsh, malicious, plotting; obstinate, yet hesitating; unreliable.

PRINCESS OF SWORDS
Wisdom, strength, acuteness; subtlety in material things: grace and dexterity. If ill dignified, she is frivolous and cunning.

TWO OF SWORDS

Quarrel made up, yet still some tension in relations: actions sometimes selfish, sometimes unselfish.

Contradictory characters in the same nature, strength through suffering; pleasure after pain. Sacrifice and trouble, yet strength arising therefrom, symbolized by the position of the rose, as though the pain itself had brought forth beauty. Arrangement, peace restored; truce; truth and untruth; sorrow and sympathy. Aid to the weak; arrangement; justice, unselfishness; also a tendency to repetition of affronts on being pardoned; injury when meaning well; given to petitions; also a want of tact, and asking question of little moment; talkative.

THREE OF SWORDS

Unhappiness, sorrow, and tears.

Disruption, interruption, separation, quarrelling; sowing of discord and strife, mischief-making, sorrow and tears; yet mirth in Platonic pleasures; singing, faithfulness in promises, honesty in money transactions, selfish and dissipated, yet sometimes generous: deceitful in words and repetitions; the whole according to dignity.

FOUR OF SWORDS

Convalescence, recovery from sickness; change for the better.

Rest from sorrow; yet after and through it. Peace from and after war. Relaxation of anxiety. Quietness, rest, ease and plenty, yet after struggle. Goods of this life; abundance; modified by dignity as is usual.

FIVE OF SWORDS

Defeat, loss, malice, spite, slander, evil-speaking.

Contest finished and decided against the person; failure, defeat, anxiety, trouble, poverty, avarice, grieving after gain, laborious, unresting; loss and vileness of nature; malicious, slanderous, lying, spiteful and tale-bearing. A busybody and separator of friends, hating to see peace and love between others. Cruel, yet cowardly, thankless and unreliable. Clever and quick in thought and speech. Feelings of pity easily roused, but unenduring.

SIX OF SWORDS

Labour, work, journey by water.

Success after anxiety and trouble; self-esteem, beauty, conceit, but sometimes modesty therewith; dominance, patience, labour, etc.

SEVEN OF SWORDS

Journey by land: in character untrustworthy.

Partial success. Yielding when victory is within grasp, as if the last reserves of strength were used up. Inclination to lose when on the point of gaining, through not continuing the effort. Love of abundance, fascinated by display, given to compliments, affronts and insolences, and to spy upon others. Inclined to betray confidences, not always intentionally. Rather vacillatory and unreliable.

EIGHT OF SWORDS

Narrow, restricted, petty, a prison.

Too much force applied to small things: too much attention to detail at the expense of the principal and more important points. When ill dignified, these qualities produce malice, pettiness, and domineering characteristics. Patience in detail of study; great care in some things, counterbalanced by equal disorder in others. Impulsive; equally fond of giving or receiving money or presents; generous, clever, acute, selfish and without strong feeling of affection. Admires wisdom, yet applies it to small and unworthy objects.

NINE OF SWORDS

Illness, suffering, malice, cruelty, pain.

Despair, cruelty, pitilessness, malice, suffering, want, loss, misery. Burden, oppression, labour, subtlety and craft, dishonesty, lying and slander. Yet also obedience, faithfulness, patience, unselfishness, etc. According to dignity.

TEN OF SWORDS

Ruin, death, defeat, disruption.

Almost a worse symbol than the Nine of Swords. Undisciplined, warring force, complete disruption and failure. Ruin of all plans and projects. Disdain, insolence and impertinence, yet mirth and jollity therewith. A marplot, loving to overthrow the happiness of others; a repeater of things; given to much unprofitable speech, and of many words. Yet clever, eloquent, etc., according to dignity.

ACE OF DISKS

It represents materiality in all senses, good and evil: and is, therefore, in a sense, illusionary: it shows material gain, labour, power, wealth, etc.

KNIGHT OF DISKS

Unless very well dignified he is heavy, dull, and material. Laborious, clever, and patient in material matters. If ill dignified, he is avaricious, grasping, dull, jealous; not very courageous, unless assisted by other symbols.

Queen of Disks

She is impetuous, kind; timid, rather charming; great-hearted; intelligent, melancholy; truthful, yet of many moods. If ill dignified she is undecided, capricious, changeable, foolish.

Prince of Disks

Increase of matter. Increases good or evil, solidifies; practically applies things. Steady; reliable. If ill dignified he is selfish, animal and material: stupid. In either case slow to anger, but furious if roused.

Princess of Disks

She is generous, kind, diligent, benevolent, careful, courageous, persevering, pitiful. If ill dignified she is wasteful and prodigal.

Two of Disks

Pleasant change, visit to friends.
The harmony of change, alternation of gain and loss; weakness and strength; everchanging occupation; wandering, discontented with any fixed condition of things; now elated, then melancholy; industrious, yet unreliable; fortunate through prudence of management, yet sometimes unaccountably foolish; alternatively talkative and suspicious. Kind, yet wavering and inconsistent. Fortunate in journeying. Argumentative.

Three of Disks

Business, paid employment, commercial transaction.
Working and constructive force, building up, creation, erection; realization and increase of material things; gain in commercial transactions, rank; increase of substance, influence, cleverness in business, selfishness. Commencement of matters to be established later. Narrow and prejudiced. Keen in matters of gain; sometimes given to seeking after impossibilities.

Four of Disks

Gain of money or influence: a present.
Assured material gain: success, rank, dominion, earthy power, completed but leading to nothing beyond. Prejudicial, covetous, suspicious, careful and orderly, but discontented. Little enterprise or originality. According to dignity as usual.

Five of Disks
Loss of profession, loss of money, monetary anxiety.
Loss of money or position. Trouble about material things. Labour, toil, land cultivation; building, knowledge and acuteness of earthly things, poverty, carefulness, kindness; sometimes money regained after severe toil and labour. Unimaginative, harsh, stern, determined, obstinate.

Six of Disks
Success in material things, prosperity in business.
Success and gain in material undertakings. Power, influence, rank, nobility, rule over the people. Fortunate, successful, liberal and just. If ill dignified, may be purse-proud, insolent from excess, or prodigal.

Seven of Disks
Unprofitable speculations and employments; little gain for much labour.
Promises of success unfulfilled. (Shewn, as it were, by the fact that the rosebuds do not come to anything.)[326] Loss of apparently promising fortune. Hopes deceived and crushed. Disappointment, misery, slavery, necessity and baseness. A cultivator of land, and yet a loser thereby. Sometimes it denotes slight and isolated gains with no fruits resulting therefrom, and of no further account, though seeming to promise well.

Eight of Disks
Skill: prudence: cunning.
Over-careful in small things at the expense of great: "Penny wise and pound foolish": gain of ready money in small sums; mean; avaricious; industrious; cultivation of land; hoarding, lacking in enterprise.

Nine of Disks
Inheritance, much increase of goods.
Complete realization of material gain, goods, riches; inheritance; covetous; treasuring of goods; and sometimes theft and knavery. The whole according to dignity.

Ten of Disks
Riches and wealth.
Completion of material gain and fortune; but nothing beyond: as it were, at the very pinnacle of success. Old age, slothfulness; great wealth, yet sometimes loss in part; heaviness; dullness of mind, yet clever and prosperous in money transactions.

CHAPTER TWENTY-ONE

GLOSSARY OF THELEMIC AND TAROT TERMS

A∴A∴ "It is commonly believed that A∴A∴ stands for Argenteum Astrum (Silver Star). I have been informed in no uncertain terms that this is not the case. The A∴A∴ was founded in 1907 by Crowley and George Cecil Jones. Based upon the classic Rosicrucian grade system of the Golden Dawn, the A∴A∴ requires the Magician to actually achieve the states of consciousness and magical powers embodied in each of the ten sephiroth (i.e., the Magician is only an Adeptus Minor when he or she has actually achieved the Knowledge and Conversation of the Holy Guardian Angel). The A∴A∴ is not a lodge system, and is entirely secret."[327]

Abrahadabra: "The word of the Aeon . . . the cypher of the Great Work."[328]

Abyss: On the diagram of the Tree of Life the Abyss is the area (or rather, non-area) that separates the first three sephiroth (the supernal triad—the Ideal) from the seven remaining sephiroth (the Actual).

Adeptus Exemptus: A∴A∴ Grade of an initiate who has achieved the level of consciousness represented by Chesed, the fourth sephira of the Tree of Life. Attainment of the next grade, that of Master of the Temple, entails crossing the Abyss.

Adeptus Minor: A∴A∴ Grade of an initiate who has achieved the level of consciousness represented by Tiphareth the sixth sephira of the Tree of Life. In this grade, one attains the knowledge and conversation of the Holy Guardian Angel.

Adjustment: Atu VIII of the Thoth Tarot. The traditional name of this card is Justice. See Lamed.

Aeon: Atu XX of the Thoth Tarot. The traditional name of this card is Judgment or The Last Judgment. The Aeon represents the birth of the Aeon of Horus, which signaled the last judgment (end of the world) of the previous Age, the Aeon of Osiris. See Aeon of Horus; Aeon of Isis; Aeon of Osiris; Shin; Fire; Spirit.

Aeon of Horus: The present magical age of human development. According to Crowley, it began at the Equinox of the Gods, March 20, 1904. Inspired by the knowledge that the Sun is perpetually shining (and not killed and reborn with each daily and yearly cycle), enlightened worshipers of the Aeon of Horus view life as a process of continual growth and strife by which one eventually develops the death-conquering consciousness of the continuity of existence. In the Aeon of Horus, it is the individual, not the tribe, family or nation, that is the basic unit of society.

Aeon of Isis: Magical age of human development at which time the pursuit of basic nourishment was the dominant theme in human consciousness and endeavor. The Earth and the powers of woman were deified as the source of all life and nourishment. This matriarchal age was characterized by the mysteries of the hunt, goddess worship, and cannibalism.

Aeon of Osiris: Magical age of human development at which time the mysteries of life and death were the dominant theme in human consciousness and endeavor. The Sun and powers of man were deified as the supreme source of all life. This patriarchal age was obsessed with overcoming death and was characterized by the mysteries of agriculture, human sacrifice, and the worship of male gods who are murdered and resurrected.

Ain—Nothing: Profound negativity, precluding even the concept of negative existence. First of the three negative veils from which Kether (One) emerges. See Fool.

Ain-Soph—Nothing without Limit: Second of the three negative veils from which Kether (One) emerges. See Fool.

Ain-Soph-Aur—Limitless Light: Third and last of the three negative veils from which Kether (One) emerges. See Fool.

Aleph—א: Ox. Hebrew equivalent to English letter A and the number 1. On the Tree of Life, it is path 11, joining the first sephira, Kether, with the second sephira, Chokmah. Represents the element air. Tarot trump—the Fool.

Angel: Traditionally, the man or angel is the Kerubic emblem of Aquarius. However, in the New Aeon (and as represented in the Thoth Tarot), the angel is the Kerubic emblem of Scorpio. See Kerubic Emblems.

Ankh-af-na Khonsu: Twenty-fifth *dynasty* Egyptian priest of Mentu and political figure. His self-painted funeral stèle was on display at Cairo's Boulak museum in the spring of 1904 and served as the magical talisman that triggered the psychic events leading up to the Equinox of the Gods and Crowley's reception of *The Book of the Law.*

Art: Atu XIV of the Thoth Tarot. The traditional name of this card is Temperance. See Samekh, Sagittarius.

Assiah: See Qabalistic Worlds.

Astrological Age: By observing the relative position of the Sun against the backdrop of the zodiacal band at the vernal equinox, ancient observers discovered that the Sun seemed to fall a bit short of its starting position of the previous year, resulting in the loss of approximately one full degree every seventy-two years. This makes the Sun appear to move backward across the belt of the zodiac at the approximate rate of one zodiac sign every two thousand one hundred sixty years. The ancients called this process the precession of the equinoxes. The time it takes to move from one sign to another is known as an astrological age. This phenomenon is actually caused by an extremely slow wobble of Earth's axis, which, like a spinning top, traces circles in space with its north and south poles. Astrologers generally agree we have recently entered or are about to enter the astrological Age of Aquarius.

Atu: The trumps of the Thoth Tarot are numbered by roman numerals and designated Atus. "Some Etymologists of a singularly idle disposition have tried to derive the French word "atout" from the ATU meaning House. It may seem simpler to suggest that 'atout' is short for 'bon a tout', meaning 'good for anything', because a trump will take any card of any suit."[329]

Atziluth: See Qabalistic Worlds

Ayin—ע: Eye. Hebrew equivalent to English letters A, Au, or O, and the number seventy. On the Tree of Life, it is path 26, joining the sixth sephira, Tiphareth, with the eighth sephira, Hod. Represents the zodiac sign Capricorn. tarot trump—the Devil.

Babalon: In the Thelemic pantheon, Babalon is one of two major aspects of female deity, Nuit being the other. Just as Nuit is paired with Hadit, her male counterpart, Babalon, joins with the Therion, the Beast. The following is excerpted from *The Magick of Thelema.*

> Therion/Babalon as Chokmah/Binah—To the student of the Qabalah the easiest way to begin to understand Therion and Babalon is to conceptualize them as personifications of the second and third Sephiroth of the Tree of Life, Chokmah and Binah, respectively.
>
> The second Sephira, Chokmah represents the original concept of duality, and as such is the chaotic despoiler of the perfect unity of the first Sephira, Kether. Chaos is another title of Chokmah and in certain Thelemic rituals is identified with Therion. Chokmah is also the Divine Will, the Logos, the Word whose vibration is the creative essence of the universe. As the supernal Father, Chokmah/Therion is the archetype of the lingam, the universal Male.
>
> The third Sephira, Binah represents the original reconciliation and balance of the Divine Self (Kether) and the reflected Not Self (Chokmah). She is viewed as the all-receptive mate of Chokmah and when they are united the primal unity of Kether is realized. As Binah/Babalon resides just above the Abyss, She eventually receives unto Herself the totality of the life of the evolving universe. This universal life is symbolized as the "blood of the Saints" which She gathers up into her great cup (the Holy Grail). This she shares with the Beast, and they unite in drunken ecstasy. Thus she is called the Great Whore for in her "shamelessness" she receives all and refuses none."[330]

Beast: In the Thelemic pantheon, the Beast is one of two major aspects of male deity, Hadit being the other. On the Tree of Life, the Beast is associated with the second sephira, Chokmah. See Babalon.

Beth—ב: House. Hebrew equivalent to English letter B and the number two. *On the Tree of Life, it is path 12, joining the first sephira, Kether, with the third sephira, Binah. Represents the planet Mercury; Tarot trump—the Magus.

Binah—Understanding: The third sephira of the Tree of Life; the sphere of Saturn. Binah is also sephirotic home to the great mother, Babalon, and Nuit. In tarot, it is the home of the four court-card Queens, and the small-card threes.

Blood of the Martyrs (Saints): The consciousness and the essence of all evolving life. See the Chariot, Holy Grail, Babalon.

The Book of the Law: Liber AL vel Legis, The Book of the Law, was dictated to Crowley on April 8, 9, and 10, 1904, in Cairo by a præter human intelligence calling itself Aiwass. It is the primary holy book of Thelema and the source of doctrines relating to the Thoth Tarot, especially the concept of the Hebrew letter Tzaddi not being attributed to the Star trump.

Briah: See Qabalistic Worlds.

Bull—Taurus: See Kerubic Emblems.

Chariot: Atu VII of the Thoth Tarot. See Cheth.

Charioteer: Conveyor of the Holy Grail. Alternate title for Atu VII, the Chariot.

Chesed—Mercy: The fourth sephira on the Tree of Life; the sphere of Jupiter. As the first sephira below the Abyss, Chesed is the highest manifestation of the universe in actuality (the supernal triad above it being the inscrutable and unmanifest ideal). Consequently, Chesed is the perfect environment for the Demiurge (Demiourgos), the creator god who, because it seemingly created the universe, mistakenly thinks and acts as if it were the supreme being. Because it is not really the supreme being, the Demiurge has a real blind spot concerning its omnipotence, and, like a spoiled child, is constantly trying to prove its divinity. This leaves us with a creator who is violently insecure and paranoid. The jealous and psychotic behavior of the mythological composite gods associated with Chesed—Zeus/Jupiter/Jove/Jehovah—are frightfully consistent with this syndrome. In tarot, Chesed is the home of the small-card fours.

Cheth—ח: Fence. Hebrew equivalent to English letters Ch and the number eight. On the Tree of Life, it is path 18, joining the third sephira, Binah, with the fifth sephira, Geburah. Represents the zodiac sign Cancer. Tarot trump—the Chariot.

Chiah: See Parts of the Soul.

Chokmah—Wisdom: The second sephira of the Tree of Life; the sphere of the zodiac. Chokmah is also sephirotic home to the All-Father, the Beast, and Hadit. In tarot, Chokmah is the home of the four court-card Knights and the small-card twos.

Choronzon: See Daath.

Color Scales: The pure divine consciousness becomes obscured as it descends the ten sephiroth of each of the four Qabalistic worlds. The Qabalists imagine this descent of spirit into matter as a pure light broken into progressively lower vibrations. The four scales of color are, in descending order: The King, Queen, Prince, and Princess scales. See chapter 10.

Crowley, Edward Alexander (Aleister): 1875–1947. A very interesting and controversial person.

Crowley, Rose Edith: 1874–1932. Aleister Crowley's first wife. Older sister of Sir Gerald Festus Kelly (1879–1972), later president of the Royal Art Academy in England. Rose was very instrumental in the psychic events leading up to and including the reception of *The Book of the Law*. Crowley considered her his first Scarlet Woman (Shakti).

Cup: Magical weapon representing the magician's understanding. The cup represents the Neshamah (soul intuition) part of the soul, and the Qabalistic world of Briah (creative world).

Cup of Babalon: Binah personified as the vessel that receives the totality of the essence of all evolving life (blood of the Saints) and receives the Master of the Temple ($8° = 3^\square$) after he or she has crossed the Abyss (the pathless area on the Tree of Life between the fourth sephira, Chesed, and the third sephira, Binah). See Atu XI, Lust; Atu VII, the Chariot; Atu XII, the Universe; Babalon; Binah; Master of the Temple; Nuit; and Holy Grail.

Cup of Fornication: See Holy Grail.

Cups: See Suits. In tarot readings, Cups often indicate matters of the heart, romance, love, creativity, art, and emotions.

Daath—Knowledge: A phantom or false sephira of the Tree of Life positioned in the Abyss separating the supernal triad from the rest of the Tree. While knowledge is a vital and necessary tool in one's initiatory journey, the reasoning faculties have their limits and must eventually be overcome before the highest levels of consciousness can be achieved. Daath is the false crown of reason, and the Abyss is the abode of Choronzon, archdemon of dispersion. It is this great devil's duty to engage the initiate in conversation—endless loops of rationalizations that prevent him or her from finally surrendering to transcendent consciousness.

Daleth—ד: Door. Hebrew equivalent to English letter D and the number four. On the Tree of Life, it is path 14, joining the second sephira, Chokmah, with the third sephira, Binah. Represents the planet Venus; Tarot trump III—the Empress.

Death: Atu XIII of the Thoth Tarot. See Nun.

Decan: Period of ten degrees in the zodiacal year. Each of the thirty-six small cards of the Thoth Tarot represents one of the thirty-six decans of the year. See Planets.

Demiurge (Demiourgos): See Chesed. In the Thoth Tarot, the behavior of the Demiurge is expressed in Atu X, Fortune, and the small-card fours.

Devil: Atu XV of the Thoth Tarot. See Ayin.

Disk: Magical weapon representing the magician's body and material environment. The disk represents the Nephesh (animal soul) part of the soul and the Qabalistic world of Assiah (material world).

Disks: See Suits. In tarot readings, disks often indicate practical and material matters, money, labor, home, investment, and the physical body.

Double Letters (Hebrew): The seven double letters of the Hebrew alphabet originally could be pronounced in two distinct ways. The Sephir Yetzirah attributes them to the seven planets of the ancients. Translations vary as to the planetary assignments. The Adepts of the Golden Dawn chose the following, as did Crowley for the Thoth Tarot:

ב Beth: Mercury (The Magus)
ג Gimel: Moon (The Priestess)
ד Daleth: Venus (The Empress)

כ Kaph: Jupiter (Fortune)
פ Pé: Mars (The Tower)
ר Resh: Sun (The Sun)
ת Tau: Saturn (The Universe)

Eagle: Traditionally, the eagle is the Kerubic emblem of Scorpio. However, in the New Aeon (and as represented in the Thoth Tarot), the eagle is the Kerubic emblem of Aquarius. See Kerubic Emblems. In alchemy, the eagle can relate to the Moon and to fundamental forces and organic substances of female sexuality.

Emperor: Atu IV of the Thoth Tarot. See Tzaddi.

Empress: Atu III of the Thoth Tarot. See Daleth.

Enochian Aethyrs: Just as the Tree of Life classifies the heavens of human consciousness into ten major divisions (sephiroth), the Enochian magick of Dr. John Dee divides the heavens into thirty Aires, or Aethyrs. By ceremonially intoning various "calls" in the angelic language, one can systematically penetrate these Aethyrs and experience a vision unique to that level of consciousness. Crowley's visions of the thrity Aethyrs are chronicled in *The Vision and The Voice*,[331] and directly influence the imagery found on several trumps, especially the Magus, the Lovers, the Chariot, Lust, Art, and the Universe.

Equinox of the Gods: See Aeon of Horus.

Etz Ha-Chayim : See Tree of Life.

Fool: Atu 0 of the Thoth Tarot. See Aleph.

Fortune: Atu X of the Thoth Tarot. Traditional name of this card is the Wheel of Fortune. See Kaph.

Geburah—Severity: The fifth sephira of the Tree Life; the sphere of Mars. In tarot, Geburah is home to the small-card fives.

Geomancy: The Earth Oracle—a technique of divination traditionally associated with the Earth and the elemental spirits of the Earth (gnomes). See Geomantic Figures.

Geomantic Figures: There are sixteen geomantic figures which, in a divinatory operation, are randomly generated. Each figure is a column of four levels. Each level either contains a single dot or two dots. The sixteen figures represent the twelve signs of the zodiac and the Moon's north and south nodes. There are two cards in the Thoth Tarot, the Seven and Eight of Disks, that use geomantic figures in their imagery.

Gimel—ג: Camel. Hebrew equivalent to English letter G and the number three. On the Tree of Life, it is path 13, joining the first sephira, Kether, with the sixth sephira, Tiphareth. Represents the planet Luna; Tarot trump II—the High Priestess.

Golden Dawn: Founded in 1888, the Order of the Golden Dawn was arguably the most influential magical society of the nineteenth and twentieth centuries. Members of the Grade of Adeptus Minor were encouraged to paint their own deck of tarot cards based upon esoteric designs and principles. Many of the cards of the Thoth Tarot are based on the Golden Dawn model. Aleister Crowley joined in 1898 and would later become the catalyst in the events that would bring about the Order's destruction. Nevertheless, the basic degree structure of the Golden Dawn would serve as the model for Crowley's Order of A∴A∴.

Gunas: "All the qualities that can be predicated of anything may be ascribed to one or more of these Gunas: Tamas is darkness, inertia, sloth, ignorance, death and the like; Rajas is energy, excitement, fire, brilliance, restlessness; Sattvas is calm, intelligence, lucidity and balance."[332]

Hadit (alternate spelling "Hadith"): "The Second Deity of the Thelemic Trinity. Lover of Nuit. He is depicted on the Stèle of Revealing as a winged globe at the heart of Nuit. He is conceptualized as the infinity of an ultimately contracted universe; the point in the center of the circle. He is 'the ubiquitous point of view, the only philosophically tenable conception of Reality.'[333] [Perhaps the concept of the pre-'Big-Bang' negative singularity postulated by modern physics.] Qabalists may wish to consider the similarities to the First Veil of the Negative proceeding Kether, AIN (Nothing)."[334]

Hanged Man: Atu XII of the Thoth Tarot. See Mem.

Hé—ה: Window. Hebrew equivalent to English letters H or E and the number five. On the Tree of Life, it is path 15, joining the second sephira, Chokmah, with the sixth sephira, Tiphareth. Represents the zodiac sign Aquarius. Tarot trump—the Star.

Hermit: Atu IX of the Thoth Tarot. See Yod.

Heru-ra-ha: The single name for the twin forms of the Egyptian god Horus. Hoor-pa-kraat is the passive form, and Ra-Hoor Khut is the active form. As far as we know, Heru-ra-ha is a name found only in *The Book of the Law,* chapter II, verse 35: "The half of the word of Heru-ra-ha, called Hoor-pa-kraat and Ra-Hoor-Khut." In the Thoth Tarot, Heru-ra-ha is found in his double form on Atu XX, the Aeon.

Hierophant: Atu V of the Thoth Tarot. See Vau.

High Priestess: Atu II of the Thoth Tarot. See Gimel.

Hod—Splendor: The eighth sephira of the Tree of Life; the sphere of Mercury. In tarot, Hod is home to the small-card eights.

Holy Grail (Crowley spelled it Graal): See Cup of Babalon.

Holy Guardian Angel: Angelic being, or level of human consciousness personified as an angel, representing supreme spiritual realization of one's personal and devotional ideal. On the Tree of Life, this experience and level of consciousness is represented by the sixth sephira, Tiphareth. In the Thoth Tarot, the concept is echoed in the court-card Princes and the small-card sixes. See Adeptus Minor.

Hoor-pa-kraat: The passive form of the God Horus. Together with his twin brother, Ra-Hoor Khut, he becomes the composite deity Heru-ra-ha. In the Thoth Tarot, Hoor-pa-kraat is found on Atu XX, the Aeon. He is the large, transparent child-god standing in front of his brother, the enthroned Ra-Hoor Khut.

Horus: Egyptian god, son of Isis and Osiris. In Egyptian mythology, Horus avenges the murder of his father. See Aeon of Horus, Hoor-pa-kraat, and Ra-Hoor-Khut.

Isis: Egyptian goddess, sister-wife of Osiris and mother of Horus. In the Thoth Tarot, Isis is portrayed in various aspects in trumps the Priestess, the Empress, the Lovers, Lust, and the Star. See Aeon of Isis.

Kaph—כ: Palm of hand. Hebrew equivalent to English letter K and the number twenty. On the Tree of Life, it is path 21, joining the fourth sephira, Chesed, with the seventh sephira, Netzach. Represents the planet Jupiter. Tarot trump—Fortune.

Kerubic Emblems: In the Thoth Tarot, the Kerubs, or Angels of the Elements, can be found in the corners of the Hierophant and the Universe trumps and represent the fixed signs of the zodiac. Because of a revelation in Crowley's vision of the twenty-third Aethyr of *The Vision and the Voice*, the Kerubs of the New Aeon (and the Thoth Tarot) are as follows: lion (Leo), eagle (Aquarius), angel (Scorpio), and bull (Taurus).

Kether—The Crown: The first and highest sephira of the Tree of Life; the *primum mobile*. In tarot, Kether is the home of the small-card aces.

King Scale of Color: The King scale is the highest and represents the essence—the invisible foundation—of color.

Knight: In the Thoth Tarot, the Knight is the primary male figure of the court cards. He is the Yod of the Tetragrammaton and represents aspects of God the Father. He is the husband of the Queen and father of the Prince and Princess. (In most traditional decks he is called the King. He is the fiery aspect of his suit and is shown seated on a horse. His position on the Tree of Life is in the second sephira, Chokmah.) See Yod Hé Vau Hé.

Lamed—ל: Ox goad. Hebrew equivalent to English letter L and the number thirty. On the Tree of Life, it is path 22, joining the fifth sephira, Geburah, with the sixth sephira, Tiphareth. Represents the zodiac sign Libra. Tarot trump—Adjustment.

Liber AL vel Legis: See *The Book of the Law*.

Lion: Symbol of the zodiac sign of Leo. In alchemy, the lion can relate to the Sun and to fundamental forces and organic substances of male sexuality. See Kerubic Emblems.

Lovers: Atu VI of the Thoth Tarot. See Zain.

Lust: Atu XI of the Thoth Tarot. See Teth.

Magus: Atu I of the Thoth Tarot. See Beth.

Magus: A∴A∴ Grade of an initiate who has achieved the level of consciousness represented by Chokmah, the second sephira on the Tree of Life.

Malkuth—Kingdom: The tenth and lowest sephira of the Tree Life; the sphere of the Earth and material existence. In tarot, the home of the court-card Princesses, and the small-card tens.

Master of the Temple: A∴A∴ Grade of an initiate who has crossed the Abyss and achieved the level of consciousness represented by Binah, the third sephira on the Tree of Life.

Mem—מ: Water. Hebrew equivalent to English letter M and the number forty. On the Tree of Life, it is path 23, joining the fifth sephira, Geburah, with the eighth sephira, Hod. Represents the element water. Tarot trump—the Hanged Man. See Mother Letters.

Mercury (alchemical): "Represents action all forms and phases. His is the fluidic basis of all transmission of activity: and, on the dynamic theory of the Universe, he is himself the substance thereof."[335]

Möbius Strip (or Möbius Band): Named for the astronomer and mathematician August Ferdinand Möbius (1790–1868), a professor at the University of Leipzig, a Möbius strip is a nonorientable surface. One can make one by attaching the two ends of a long strip of paper after twisting one end 180 degrees.

Modes: In astrology, the signs of the zodiac are divided into four elemental categories (fire, water, air, and earth). Each of these four elemental categories is in turn divided into three modes (cardinal, fixed, and mutable) that represent three fundamental ways the energy of the element develops and manifests. The three modes are as follows:

> *Cardinal* represents "the first keen onrush of that element."[336] Cardinal signs burst into their element at the equinoxes and solstices and say, "Here I am!"

> *Fixed* signs define and concentrate the element. The energy of the element is focused upon being what it is. Fixed signs don't say, "Here I am," they say, "This is what I am." The fixed signs are represented in the Thoth Tarot by the Kerubic emblems found on the Hierophant and the Universe.

> *Mutable* signs are more subtle. They do not express the energy of the cardinal or the stability of the fixed, and by comparison seem weak. But the mutable signs are not weak; they're just sensitive and willing to give of themselves. They are flexible and can adapt the element to the adventures of an ever-changing universe.

Moon: Atu XVIII of the Thoth Tarot. See Qoph.

Mother Letters (Hebrew): There are three primary or mother letters in the Hebrew alphabet. The sephir Yetzirah attributes them to the three primitive elements.

א Aleph: Air (The Fool)

מ Mem: Water (The Hanged Man)

ש Shin: Fire (The Aeon)

Neophyte: A∴A∴ Grade of an initiate who has achieved the level of consciousness represented by Malkuth, the tenth sephira on the Tree of Life.

Nephesh: See Parts of the Soul.

Neshamah: See Parts of the Soul.

Netzach—Victory: The seventh sephira on the Tree Life; the sphere of Venus. In tarot, Netzach is home to the small-card sevens.

Notariqon: One of several Qabalistic techniques of manipulating letters and words in order to discover additional esoteric meanings. There are two kinds of Notariqon. The first condenses a word, sentence, or phrase into a simpler one by reading only the initial letters in an attempt to retrieve a more fundamental truth. The second expands a word into a sentence whose component words are the initials of the original word.

Nuit (alternate spelling "Nuith," "Nut"): "The First Deity of the Thelemic Trinity; traditionally the Egyptian Goddess of the night sky. She is the 'star goddess who is the category of unlimited possibility.'[337] Upon the Stélé of Revealing, and in Egyptian art, she is depicted as an azure goddess, tall and slender, arching of the earth (similar in appearance to the Greek letter Omega). She is conceptualized as the infinity of an ultimately expanded universe (the circumference of the circle). All things, therefore, are contained within her body. Qabalists may wish to consider the similarities to the Second Veil of the Negative proceeding Kether, AIN SOPH (No Limit)."[338]

Nun—נ: Fish. Hebrew equivalent to English letter N and the number fifty. On the Tree of Life, it is path 24, joining the sixth sephira, Tiphareth, with the seventh sephira, Netzach. Represents the zodiac sign Scorpio. Tarot trump—Death.

Orphic Egg: Alchemical symbol showing an egg (sometimes winged) entwined with a serpent. Fertilization and the subsequent care of the Orphic egg is the subject of an alchemical allegory of the great work. In the Thoth Tarot, the trumps Magus, Lovers, Hermit, Death, and Art, either display the Orphic egg or are concerned with its care.

Osiris: Egyptian god of the dead, brother/husband of Isis, and father of Horus. In the Thoth Tarot, Osiris is portrayed in various aspects in trumps the Hierophant and Death. See Aeon of Osiris.

Parts of the Soul: The Hebrew Qabalah divides the human soul into various levels that reflect, on a microcosmic level, universal levels of consciousness and being. One very simple mode of division is by four (corresponding to the four letters of the Tetragrammaton, יהוה, Yod Hé Vau Hé). The tarot is, in many ways, an expression of this fourfold division. The four parts of the soul and some of their correspondences are as follows:

Nephesh—The Animal Soul: The first and lowest of the four parts of the soul; corresponds to the final Hé of the Tetragrammaton, the element of earth, the suit of Disks in the tarot, and to Assiah, the material world, the first and lowest of the four Qabalistic worlds.

Ruach—The Intellect
The second of the four parts of the soul; corresponds to the Vau of the Tetragrammaton, the element of air, the suit of Swords in the tarot, and to Yetzirah, the formative world.

Neshamah—The Soul Intuition
The third and second highest of the four parts of the soul; corresponds to the first Hé of the Tetragrammaton, the element of water, the suit of Cups in the tarot, and to Briah, the creative world.

Chiah—The Life Force
The fourth and highest of the four parts of the soul; corresponds to the Yod of the Tetragrammaton, the element of fire, the suit of Wands in the tarot, and to Atziluth, the archetypal world.

Pé—פ: Mouth. Hebrew equivalent to English letter P or F and the number eighty. On the Tree of Life, it is path 27, joining the seventh sephira, Netzach, with the eighth sephira, Hod. Represents the planet Mars. Tarot trump—the Tower.

Pentacles: Another name for Disks. See Suits.

Planets: The Thoth Tarot deals primarily with the seven planets of the ancients: Saturn (the Universe), Jupiter (Fortune), Mars (the Tower), Sol (the Sun), Venus (the Empress), Mercury (the Magus), and Luna (the Priestess). This is the order in which the planetary spheres (sephiroth 3 through 9) are arranged on the Tree of Life. These seven planets are also allotted (in this same repeating order) to the thirty-six small cards of the Thoth Tarot, starting with Saturn on the Five of Wands (at 0° Leo) and changing every decan (10°), until every decan of the year has been assigned a planet. (The last decan of Pisces and the first decan of Aries are both assigned the planet Mars.)

Precession of the Equinox: See Astrological Age.

Prince: In the Thoth Tarot, the Prince is the secondary male figure of the court cards. He is the Vau of the Tetragrammaton and represents aspects of God the Son and the Holy Guardian Angel of each human being. He is the son of the Knight and Queen and brother/lover (and in certain ways, the father) of the Princess. In some traditional decks, he is called the Knight. He is the airy aspect of his suit and is shown standing in a chariot. His position on the Tree of Life is in the sixth sephira, Tiphareth. See Yod Hé Vau Hé.

Prince Scale of Color: The Prince scale combines the colors of the King and Queen scales.

Princess: In the Thoth Tarot, the Princess is the secondary female figure of the court cards. In some traditional decks, she is called the Page. She is the final Hé of the Tetragrammaton and represents aspects of the unredeemed soul of each of us. Her position on the Tree of Life is the tenth sephira, Malkuth. (See Yod Hé Vau Hé.) She is the daughter of the Knight and Queen and sister/lover of the Prince. (In certain ways, she is also viewed as the daughter of the Prince.) She is the earthy aspect of her suit and is shown standing. In the Western Mysteries, the quest for spiritual liberation is characterized in the story of a sleeping Princess (each of us) who is awakened by a Prince (our Holy Guardian Angel), who marries the Princess and makes her Queen (God the Mother), which at the same time makes him the King (God the Father). Unlike the Knight, Queen, and Prince, the Princess does not rule a 30° period of the year. Instead, she is considered the throne of the aces and rules, with her ace, one quarter of the surface of the Earth. See chapter 11.

Princess Scale of Color: The Princess scale represents the lowest, most mixed and polluted levels of light. See chapter 10.

Qabalah (alternate spellings, Cabala, Kabbalah): Known as the Holy Kabbalah in esoteric Judaism, Cabala in mystic Christianity, and Qabalah in Western Hermeticism, the Qabalah is the foundation of nearly all the mystical systems of the West, including astrology, magick, and tarot.

Qabalistic Worlds: The Qabalah divides the one cosmic reality into four descending levels of divine consciousness or worlds (corresponding to the four letters of the Tetragrammaton, יהוה, Yod Hé Vau Hé). These four worlds reflect on a macrocosmic level the four microcosmic aspects of the human soul. The tarot is, in many ways, an expression of this four-fold division. The four Qabalistic worlds and some of their correspondences are as follows:

Assiah—The Material World

The lowest of the four Qabalistic worlds; corresponds to the final Hé of the Tetragrammaton, the element of earth, and the suit of Disks in the tarot. In Assiah, the impurities produced by the degeneration of the light as it passes through the worlds above it (Atziluth, Briah, and Yetzirah) are crystallized to form the material world and human existence. Assiah's corresponding part in the human soul is the Nephesh—the animal soul.

Yetzirah—The Formative World

The second to the lowest of the four Qabalistic worlds; corresponds to the Vau of the Tetragrammaton, the element of air, and the suit of Swords in the tarot. In Yetzirah, the universal organization of Briah becomes specific, and a hierarchy of angels with individual duties is established. This world is the mind and the mind's eye of the deity. Yetzirah's corresponding part in the human soul is the Ruach—the intellect.

Briah—The Creative World

The third and second highest of the four Qabalistic worlds; corresponds to the first Hé of the Tetragrammaton, the element water; and the suit of Cups in the tarot. In Briah, the pure light of Atziluth begins to become organized. This is the throne and abode of the highest archangels and could be viewed as the heart of the deity. Briah's corresponding part in the human soul is the Neshamah—the divine soul intuition.

Atziluth—The Archetypal World

The highest of the four Qabalistic worlds; corresponds to the Yod in the Tetragrammaton, the element fire, and the suit of Wands in the tarot. In Atziluth, the male and female aspects of the deity are united in bliss. The remaining three worlds (Briah, Yetzirah, and Assiah) are the product of this union, and continue to diminish in purity. Atziluth could be considered the will of the deity in its purest aspect. Atzuluth's corresponding part in the human soul it is the Chiah—the life force.

Qoph—ק: Back of Head. Hebrew equivalent to English letter Q and the number 100. On the Tree of Life, it is path 29, joining the seventh sephira, Netzach, with the tenth sephira, Malkuth. Represents the zodiac sign Pisces. Tarot trump—the Moon.

Quadruplicities of the Zodiac: The twelve signs of the zodiac are categorized, according to element, into four groups of three signs. The four Quadruplicities are as follows:

> Fire Signs: Aries, Leo, Sagittarius
> Water Signs: Cancer, Scorpio, Pisces
> Air Signs: Libra, Aquarius, Gemini
> Earth Signs: Capricorn, Taurus, Virgo

Queen: In the Thoth Tarot, the Queen is the primary female figure of the court cards. She is the first Hé of the Tetragrammaton and represents aspects of God the Mother. She is the wife of the Knight and mother of the Prince and Princess. She is the watery aspect of her suit and is shown enthroned. Her position on the Tree of Life is in the third sephira, Binah. See Yod Hé Vau Hé.

Queen Scale of Color: Queen scale of color actually manifests as the eye beholds them (shades, primary and secondary colors, etc.) See chapter 10.

Ra-Hoor-Khuit (alternate spellings, Ra-Hoor Khut, Ra-Hoor-Khuit, and Ra-Hoor-Khu-it): "The Third Deity of the Thelemic Trinity. The Crowned and Conquering Child of the union of Nuit and Hadit. As Nuit's expansion and Hadit's contraction are both infinite, so too must be their points of contact. This infinite contact creates a field of operation in which the universe can manifest. 'He is, however, known under his special name, Heru-ra-ha. A double god; his extroverted form is Ra-hoor-khuit; and his passive or introverted form Hoor-pa-kraat.'"[339]

"Qabalists may wish to consider the similarities to the Third Veil of the Negative proceeding Kether, AIN SOPH AUR (Limitless Light); also Kether itself. In one respect He is the fundamental archetype of the God-Man, and the Holy Guardian Angel."[340]

Rajas: See Gunas.

Resh—ר: Head or Face. Hebrew equivalent to English letter R and the number 200. On the Tree of Life, it is path 30, joining the eighth sephira, Hod, with the ninth sephira, Yesod. Represents the planet Sol. Tarot trump—the Sun.

Rose Cross: See chapter 8.

Ruach: See Parts of the Soul.

Salt (Alchemical): "The inactive principle of Nature; Salt is matter which must be energized by Sulfur to maintain the whirling equilibrium of the Universe."[341]

Samekh—ס: Tent peg. Hebrew equivalent to English letter S and the number sixty. On the Tree of Life, it is path 25, joining the sixth sephira, Tiphareth, with the ninth sephira, Yesod. Represents the zodiac sign Sagittarius. Tarot trump—Art.

Satvas: See Gunas.

Shemhamphorasch: The seventy-two-part Divided Name of God. Qabalistic tradition points out that three consecutive verses from the Book of Exodus are each composed of seventy-two Hebrew letters. These three verses, when arranged in three rows (the top row reading from right to left, the middle row reading from left to right, the bottom row reading from right to left), yield seventy-two columns of three letters that are designated Shemhamphorasch, the Divided Name of God. Each of these seventy-two aspects of deity is assigned an angel who is the executor of its will. The angel names are created by adding (to the end of each of the three letter names) the letters IH (for an angel of mercy) or the letters AL (for an angel of judgment). Each of these seventy-two angels is assigned five degrees of the zodiacal year. Because each of the thirty-six small cards of the tarot represents one decan (period of ten degrees), two angels of the Shemhamphorasch are resident in each small card.

Shin—ש: Tooth. Hebrew equivalent to English letters Sh and the number 300. On the Tree of Life, it is path 31, joining the eighth sephira, Hod, with the tenth sephira, Malkuth. Represents the element fire and the element spirit. Tarot trump—the Aeon.

Significator: Prior to using tarot in divination, one card (usually a court card) is chosen to represent the querent. This card is designated the Significator.

Simple Letters (Hebrew): Together with the three mother letters and the seven double letters of the Hebrew alphabet, there are twelve simple letters. The sephir Yetzirah attributes them to the twelve signs of the zodiac. Translations vary as to the zodiacal assignments. The Adepts of the Golden Dawn chose the following, with the exceptions of Tzaddi and Hé. This is the assignment of the Thoth Tarot.

צ Tzaddi: Aries (The Emperor)
ו Vau: Taurus (The Hierophant)
ז Zain: Gemini (The Lovers)
ח Cheth: Cancer (The Chariot)
ט Teth: Leo (Lust)
י Yod: Virgo (The Hermit)
ל Lamed: Libra (Adjustment)
נ Nun: Scorpio (Death)
ס Samekh: Sagittarius (Art)
ע Ayin: Capricorn (The Devil)
ה Hé: Aquarius (The Star)
ק Qoph: Pisces (The Moon)

Star: Atu XVII of the Thoth Tarot. See Hé, Aquarius.

Stèle of Revealing: Twenty-fifth dynasty Egyptian funeral marker of Ankh-af-na-khonsu, a notable political and religious figure of several royal administrations, which triggered a series of psychic and magical events that culminated with Crowley's reception of *The Book of the Law*.

Suits: The fifty-six cards of the Minor Arcana of the tarot are divided into four suits: Wands, Cups, Swords, and Disks. These suits represent, respectively, the elements of fire, water, air, and earth; the Qabalistic worlds of Atziluth, Briah, Yetzirah, and Assiah; and the four parts of the human soul of Chiah, Neshamah, Ruach, and Nephesh. The aces of each suit are the master cards of the suit, and can be thought of as containing within themselves the four court cards and the nine small cards of their respective suits.

Sulfur (Alchemical): "Sulfur is the male fiery energy of the Universe, the Rajas of Hindu philosophy. This is the swift creative energy, the initiative of all Being."[342]

Sun: Atu XIX of the Thoth Tarot. See Resh.

Supernal Triad—Kether-Chokmah-Binah: The three sephiroth existing above the Abyss. Even though each of the three sephiroth stand as separate emanations, they really comprise a trinity, each unit reflecting a different aspect of the supreme monad (Kether). In tarot, the supernal triad is home to court-card Knights (in Chokmah) and Queens (in Binah), and to small-card aces, twos, and threes in Kether, Chokmah, and Binah respectively.

Sword: Magical weapon representing the magician's mind. The sword represents the Ruach (intellect) part of the soul and the Qabalistic world of Yetzirah (formative world).

Swords: See Suits. In tarot readings, Swords often indicate matters of the mind, quarreling, lawsuits, anxiety, health, and science.

Tahuti: See Thoth.

Tamas: See Gunas.

Tau—ת: Mark or Cross. Hebrew equivalent to English letters Th and the number 400. On the Tree of Life, it is path 31, joining the ninth sephira, Yesod, with the tenth sephira, Malkuth. Represents the planet Saturn and element earth. Tarot trump—the Universe.

Teth—ט: Serpent. Hebrew equivalent to English letter T and the number nine. On the Tree of Life, it is path 19, joining the fourth sephira, Chesed, with the fifth sephira, Geburah. Represents the zodiac sign Leo. Tarot trump—Lust.

Tetragrammaton: YHVH—יהוה. See Yod Hé Vau Hé.

Thelema: One of several words in Greek that mean "will." The word first received attention in 1535, when the French satirist Francois Rabelais wrote of the Abbey of Thelema in his colossal work, *Gargantua and Pantagruel.* Engraved above the entrance to the Abbey was the Abbey's motto, *Fay çe que vouldras,* "Do what thou wilt." In that work, it was the watchword of individual freedom. The word appears in chapter 1, Verse 39 of *The Book of the Law,* where Nuit tells the Scribe, "The word of the Law is θελημα" Among other things, Thelema has come to be known as the philosophy of life that presumes that each individual, like each star in the heavens, is possessed with a unique orbit and function in the universe. This, for lack of a better word, is our will. If each person properly understands and executes this will, his or her life will be in harmony with the forces and energies of the entire universe and we will fulfill our full potential as cosmic citizens.

Thelemite: One who attempts to discover, then execute, his or her will. See Thelema.

Thoth: Tahuti, the ibis-headed Egyptian god of wisdom. Patron deity of the tarot, Thoth is said to have taught humanity language and the written word. As messenger of the gods, he is identified with the Greek Hermes and the Roman Mercury.

Tiphareth—Beauty: The sixth sephira on the Tree Life; the sphere of the Sun. In tarot, Tiphareth is the home of the court-card Princes and the small-card sixes.

TO MEGA THERION: Greek for "The Great Beast," TO MEGA THE-RION was the motto Crowley took upon achieving the grade of Magus, $9° = 2^\square$ on October 12, 1915 e.v.

Tower: Atu XVI of the Thoth Tarot. See Pé.

Tree of Life—Etz ha-Chayim: Schematic representation of the fundamental statement of the Sepher Yetzirah, which states "Deity with the aid of numbers, letters, & words created the Universe in thirty-two mysterious paths of wisdom. They consist of Ten sephiroth out of nothing and of Twenty-two Letters."[343] The Tree of Life is usually represented as ten circular emanations (sephiroth) joined by twenty-two paths, to which the letters of the Hebrew alphabet are attributed.

Triplicities of the Zodiac: The twelve signs of the zodiac are categorized, according to modes, into three groups of four signs. The Triplicities are as follows:

> Cardinal Signs: Aries, Cancer, Libra, Capricorn
> Fixed Signs: Leo, Scorpio, Aquarius, Taurus
> Mutable Signs: Sagittarius, Pisces, Gemini, Virgo

Trump: See Atu.

Typhon: Graeco-Egyptian reptilian deity associated with the active forces of destruction. In the Thoth Tarot, Typhon appears with Hermanubis and the Sphinx as one of the three beasts of Atu X, Fortune.

Tzaddi—צ: Fish Hook. Hebrew equivalent to English letters Tz or Z and the number ninety. On the Tree of Life, it is path 28, joining the seventh sephira, Netzach with the ninth sephira, Yesod. Represents the zodiac sign Aries. Tarot trump—the Emperor.

Universe: Atu XXI of the Thoth Tarot. See Tau, Saturn.

V.I.T.R.I.O.L.: The universal solvent of alchemy created by the proper combination and balancing of the alchemical elements of mercury, salt, and sulfur. Its letters are the initials of the alchemical motto: Visita interiora terrae rectificando invenies occultam lapidem—"Visit the interior parts of the earth: by rectification thou shalt find the hidden stone." In the Thoth Tarot, this phrase appears on Atu XIV, Art.

Vau—ו: Nail. Hebrew equivalent to English letters V, W, U, and O and the number six. On the Tree of Life, it is path 16, joining the second sephira, Chokmah, with the fourth sephira, Chesed. Represents the zodiac sign Taurus. Tarot trump—the Hierophant.

Vision and the Voice: Liber XXX Aerum vel Saeculi sub figura CCCCXVII: being the Angels of the 30 Aethyrs of the Vision and the Voice (1911 E.V.).

Wand: Magical weapon representing the magician's will. The wand represents the Chiah (life force) part of the soul, and the Qabalistic world of Atziluth (archetypal world).

Wands: See Suits. In tarot readings, Wands often indicate matters of power, endeavor, struggle, business, character, career.

Yesod—Foundation: The ninth sephira on the Tree of Life; the sphere of the Moon. In tarot, Yesod is the home of the small-card nines.

Yetzirah: See Qabalistic Worlds

Yod Hé Vau Hé—הוהי—YHVH: The great Qabalistic Name of God, commonly pronounced Jehovah. Referred to as the Tetragrammaton. Qabalists categorize everything in creation, including the human soul, into four divisions, each corresponding to one of the four letters of the Great Name. In the tarot, the suit of Wands represents Yod; Cups, the first Hé; Vau, Swords; and the final Hé, Disks. See Parts of the Soul and Qabalistic Worlds.

Yod—י: Hand. Hebrew equivalent to English letters Y and I and the number ten. On the Tree of Life, it is path 20, joining the fourth sephira, Chesed, with sixth sephira, Tiphareth. Represents the zodiac sign Virgo. Tarot trump—the Hermit.

Zain—ז: Sword. Hebrew equivalent to English letter Z and the number seven.
On the Tree of Life, it is path 17, joining the third sephira, Binah, with the sixth
sephira, Tiphareth. Represents the zodiac sign Gemini. Tarot trump—the
Lovers.

NOTES

TITLE PAGE

1. From "The Rites of Eleusis, The Rite of Mercury," *The Equinox* I (6), (reprint, York Beach, ME: Weiser Books, 1992). Supplement, p. 103.

PART I

1. Aleister Crowley, *The Book of Thoth by The Master Therion: A Short Essay on the Tarot of the Egyptians* (London: O.T.O., 1944); *The Equinox* III (5), (reprint, York Beach, ME: Samuel Weiser, 1992), p. 3. All quotes from *The Book of Thoth* that follow are from this edition.
2. A nonprofit corporation based on the mystical-occult teachings and practice of the Holy Qabalah and Sacred Tarot, founded by Dr. Paul Foster Case, extended by Dr. Ann Davies. International Headquarters: 5101 North Figueroa Street, Los Angeles, CA 90042.
3. Lon Milo DuQuette, *My Life with the Spirits* (York Beach, ME: Weiser Books, Inc., 1999), pp. 68–70.
4. *The Confessions of Aleister Crowley* (London, 1929; abridged one-volume edition, ed. John Symonds and Kenneth Grant, London, 1969; reprint, London and New York: Arkana, 1989).
5. Judith Hawkins-Tillirson is a senior buyer for a major book distribution company and one of the most knowledgeable and respected professionals in the field of esoteric literature. She is a dear friend of the family, and was kind enough to pen the Introduction to my *Tarot of Ceremonial Magick* (York Beach, ME: Weiser Books, 1995).
6. Aleister Crowley to Mr. Pearson, photoengraver, May 29, 1942.
7. *Nee* Marguerite Frieda Bloxam, 1877–1962.

8. Harris first exhibited some of the paintings in 1941 and 1942. However, it is clear that she continued working for nearly a year after that on one or more versions that would eventually be included in the Thoth Tarot.

9. 1875–1947.

10. By 1920, Crowley still held the world's record for a number of mountaineering feats, including the greatest pace uphill (4, 000 feet in 83 minutes) at over 16, 000 feet on Mexico's Iztaccihuatl in 1900; the first ascent of the Nevado de Toluca by a solitary climber 1901; and his 1902 assault on K2, where he spent 65 days on the Baltoro glacier.

11. Ghostwriting for Evangeline Adams, Crowley wrote the bulk of the material first published under her name, including her classic texts, *Astrology: Your Place in the Sun* (1927) and *Astrology: Your Place Among the Stars* (1930). These works made astrology a household word in America and Europe and catapulted Adams to celebrated status as "Astrologer to Wall Street and Washington." Recently, Crowley's co-authorship has been graciously acknowledged by the Adams estate and has resulted in the release of Aleister Crowley and Evangeline Adams, *The General Principles of Astrology* (York Beach, ME: Red Wheel / Weiser, 2001).

12. It is often forgotten that the United States was very close to entering the First World War on Germany's side. Much to the horror of the German Foreign Ministry, Crowley's editorials made it appear that it was Germany's intention (in fact, its foreign policy) to engage in unrestricted submarine warfare against civilian shipping. Even though this was, at the time, an outrageous falsehood, Crowley's editorials were used to create an anti-German hysteria that would eventually sweep the United States into the conflict on England's side. In a very real way, Aleister Crowley saved his beloved England using only his pen as a magical wand.

13. Ian (Lancaster) Fleming (1908–1964)—pseudonym, Atticus—British journalist, secret service agent, writer, whose most famous creation was superhero James Bond, Agent 007. Crowley and Fleming were indeed friends. Copies of their correspondence still exists, some of which discuss matters of occult propaganda and the interrogation of Rudolf Hess.

14. He called his system "Scientific Illuminism." Its motto: "The Method of Science—The Aim of Religion."

15. Michele Jackson of the American Tarot Association writes, "My observations would lead me to believe that *[among professional Tarot readers]* the *Thoth* deck is second only to Rider-Waite as the most popular."

16. Originally published in an edition limited to 200 numbered and signed copies, 1944. Reprinted by Samuel Weiser, Inc., 1969, 1974, 1986, 1991.

17. *The Book of Thoth*, p. 4.

18. Crowley responded to this on December 19, 1939, by writing, "You can't get out of it like that. I believe the basis of the feeling is that there should be a special prerogative to understand spiritual matters, a feeling of heirship. The fact remains that you do not employ such arrogant impertinence with regard to such subjects as logic and mathematics. Bertrand Russell is certainly a thousand times more difficult than ever I am, but you understand him better because you accept the postulate, that subjects like these must be worked at, as with you are annoyed."

19. Israel Regardie, *The Eye in the Triangle* (Scottsdale, AZ: New Falcon Press, 1989), p. 59.

20. Regardie, *The Eye in the Triangle;* Lawrence Sutin, *Do What Thou Wilt: A Life of Aleister Crowley* (New York: St. Martin's Press, 2000); Roger Hutchinson, *Aleister Crowley: The Beast Demystified* (Edinburgh: Mainstream Publishing, 1998); and especially Richard Kaczynski, *Perdurabo: The Life of Aleister Crowley* (Scottsdale, AZ. New Falcon Press, 2002).

21. From George M. Lamsa, trans., *The Holy Bible from Ancient Eastern Manuscripts* (Philadelphia, PA: A. J. Holman Company, 1967), p. 961.

22. Sephiroth is the plural form; sephira is the singular form.

23. Harris to Aleister Crowley—January 28, 1940.

24. This letter is from the personal correspondence of the author.

25. On May 11, 1938, she was formally initiated by Crowley and took as her magical name Soror TZBA, a Hebrew word meaning "hosts" (also "army," "arduous," and "busy"). TZBA in Hebrew enumerates to the sacred Thelemic number 93.

26. Susan Roberts, *Magician of the Golden Dawn* (Chicago, IL: Contemporary Books, Inc., 1978). p. 309.

27. Co-Masonry, under the sponsorship of the Theosophical Society, operates the three Blue Lodge degrees of Freemasonry, and allows both men and women as members.

28. The concept of the Holy Guardian Angel is a key element in the Western magical tradition in general and Crowley's *Scientific Illuminism* in particular. See chapter 11.

29. *The Equinox* I (8), ed. Soror Virakam, (reprint, York Beach, ME: Samuel Weiser, 1992).

30. Crowley to Harris, December 19, 1939.

31. Two program essays are known to exist. The first, obviously an edited version of Crowley's notes, carried the ponderous title *Exhibition of Playing Cards: The Tarot (Book of Thoth) 78 Paintings According to the Initiated Tradition and Modern Scientific Thought with Other Occult and Alchemical Designs.* The second, written for the Berkeley exhibition, was written by Harris's friend Robert Cecil and was simply titled *Exhibition of 78 Paintings of the Tarot Cards by Frieda Harris.*

32. 1918–1985. Major Grady Louis McMurtry would also be instrumental in rescuing Crowley's magical society, Ordo Templi Orientis, from certain extinction. In the 1970s, my wife, Constance, and I had the great privilege to receive our early O.T.O. degree initiations from this remarkable and extremely colorful man.

33. In 1977, through the kind efforts of Mr. Gerald Yorke and Mr. Stephen Skinner, the paintings were again photographed and the new prints used to greatly enhance the quality of subsequent editions of the Thoth Tarot.

34. A handful of atrociously reproduced prototype decks were manufactured in 1944. Neither Crowley nor Harris appears to have profited by this venture.

35. July 23, 1958, letter to Edward Bryant from the collection of Mr. Clive Harper.

36. *The Book of Thoth,* p. xii.

37. Harris to Crowley, date uncertain.

38. Or Projective Synthetic Geometry.

39. 1861–1925.

40. Aleister Crowley, *The Book of the Law,* II: 64 (York Beach, ME: Weiser Books, 1976).

41. Aleister Crowley, *The Equinox of the Gods* (London: O.T.O., 1936; *The Equinox* III

(3), corrected facsimile editions (Scottsdale, AZ: New Falcon Publications, 1991) and (New York: 93 Publishing, 1992).

42. On the Stèle, Nuit, the goddess of the night sky, is seen stretching herself over the top and sides of the Stèle. As the personification of an infinitely expanded universe, we could symbolize her as the circumference of an ever-expanding circle.

43. On the Stèle, Hadit is the god pictured as a winged solar disk directly beneath the heart of Nuit. As the personification of an infinitely contracted point we could symbolize him as an ever-present point at the very center of an ever-expanding circle.

44. He did no such thing, but the story of why he chose to say that he did must be read in its entirety to appreciate Crowley's outrageously twisted sense of humor. (See *The Confessions of Aleister Crowley*.)

45. Lamsa, *The Holy Bible from Ancient Eastern Manuscripts*, 2 Kings II: 23–25.

46. *The Book of the Law*, I: 49.

47. Ra-Hoor-Khuit is the active aspect of the god Horus. His passive aspect is represented by his twin brother, Hoor-pa-kraat (whom the Greeks called Harpocrates).

48. In most traditional tarot decks, the four Kerubic beasts appear in the corners of the trumps Fortune and the Universe.

49. As tarot scholar Bob O'Neal points out, the sequence of trumps 13 through 21 could easily serve as flash cards illustrating the events of The Book of the Revelation.

50. Biblical tradition holds that, after the great flood, God promised Noah he would never again destroy "all flesh" by water, but that the next great ethnic cleansing would be by fire.

51. For an expanded account of the mythical adventures of Egyptian archetypal Mother-Father-Child, see Lon Milo DuQuette, *The Magick of Thelema* (York Beach, ME: Samuel Weiser, Inc., 1993), p. 8.

52. These directions represent the situation in the Northern Hemisphere. For the Southern Hemisphere, the directions are, of course, reversed.

53. This section was first published as part of an article for the *Golden Dawn Journal* (St. Paul, MN: Llewellyn Publications, 1995.) It was later published in its entirety in *Angels, Demons and Gods of the New Millennium* (York Beach, ME: Weiser Books, and Lon Milo DuQuette, 1997).

54. Aleister Crowley, *Liber Cheth vel Vallum Abiegni*.

55. To induce the visions of *The Vision and The Voice* Crowley utilized Enochian magick, a powerful technique of ceremonial skrying (or traveling the spirit vision) first used by Edward Kelley and Dr. John Dee, the famous English mathematician and counselor to Elizabeth I. By reciting a series of Calls or Keys in the angelic language, Crowley systematically penetrated, in visions, the thirty Aethyrs or heavens of the Enochian celestial universe.

56. *The Equinox* I (5), London; (reprint, York Beach, ME: Weiser Books, 1992). Also see Aleister Crowley, *The Vision and The Voice with Commentary and Other Papers*, (York Beach, ME: Weiser Books, 1998), p. 67.

57. Even an hour or two of research will prove to the objective student that these terms (and many others in Crowley's writings) are merely very scary terms for very holy concepts.

58. The concept of personal guardian spirits that stand between humanity and the gods is ancient and universal. Zoroaster wrote of the Agathodaimon; the Platonic philosophers, Daemones; Socrates called his Genius.

59. "He will see annihilation where the perfected one finds immortality." The Buddha

60. DuQuette, *Angels, Demons, and Gods*, p. 24.

61. *The Equinox*, IV (2) (reprint, York Beach, ME: Red Wheel /Weiser, 1999).

62. Frater Achad (Charles Stanfield Jones), *De Mysteriis Rosae Rubeae et Aureae Crucis.* Privately published, date unknown.

63. At the time, I was an active member of Abdiel Lodge of the Rosicrucian Order, AMORC, in Long Beach, California.

64. *"Magister Iesus Christus—Deus est Homo—Benedictus Dominus Deus Noster qui dedit nobis Signum . . . "*—"beneath is written the Mystic Name of the owner of the cross."

65. "Kabbalah" is the preferred spelling among orthodox Jewish students. "Cabala" is the spelling variation most often used by Christian mystics. "Qabalah" is usually associated with the nonsectarian Hermetic applications of the art.

66. *The Book of Thoth*, p. 34.

67. The Sepher Yetzirah, see chapter 9.

68. The Sun (the God of our solar system) was viewed by the ancients as being surrounded by the six remaining "planets," a concept that consecrated the number six as the sacred symbol of the macrocosm and deity.

69. The fourth element, earth, is a combination of fire, water, and air. Earth will eventually manifest as a separate element when the arms of the Great Cross are formed.

70. Don't waste time worrying about the correct pronunciation of Hebrew words. There are several main dialects, and it is certain that any attempt you make will be ridiculed by someone. Pronounce them any way that is comfortable for you.

71. *The Book of Thoth*, p. 89.

72. DuQuette, *Magick of Thelema*, pp. 60–61.

73. *The Book of Thoth*, p. 18.

74. *The Book of Thoth*, p. 83.

75. *The Book of Thoth*, p. 90.

76. Recall from chapter 1, the two-fingered V for victory Crowley is said to have imparted to Winston Churchill to counteract the Nazi's solar symbol, the swastika.

77. In the Waite/Smith deck and many others, trump XX, the Last Judgment, shows a man, woman, and child arising from their tombs on judgment day. The woman is making the sign of the mourning of Isis, the child is making the sign of Apophis and Typhon, and the man is making the sign of Osiris risen.

78. *The Book of Thoth*, p. 30.

79. Rev. Dr. Isidor Kalisch, *Sepher Yezirah—A Book on Creation; or, The Jewish Metaphysics of Remote Antiquity* (New York: L. H. Frank & Co. 1877). Reprinted by The Supreme Council of The Ancient and Mystical Order Rosae Crucis, 1971. This passage is taken from chapter 1, section 1. By tradition, authorship of the Sepher Yetzirah is ascribed to the patriarch Abraham. This is highly doubtful, but the text is very ancient—perhaps the oldest philosophical treatise written in Hebrew.

80. The preexistent negativity is expressed as Ain (nothing), Ain Soph (without limit), and Ain Soph Aur (the limitless light).

81. DuQuette, *Angels, Demons and Gods*, p. 21.
82. *The Book of Thoth*, p. 180.
83. *The Book of Thoth*, p. 179.
84. *The Book of Thoth*, p. 182.
85. *The Book of Thoth*, p. 182.
86. *The Book of Thoth*, p. 182.
87. *The Book of Thoth*, p. 185.
88. *The Book of Thoth*, p. 187.
89. Yes, even the Three of Swords, Sorrow, is happy. See chapter 19.
90. Two of the tarot trumps, the Aeon (Fire) and the Universe (Saturn) serve also to represent respectively the elements of spirit and earth, and so, instead of 88 colors (4 x 22), the total number of colors for the trumps is 96 (4 x 24).
91. *The Book of Thoth*, pp. 278–281.
92. See chapter 13 regarding "Tzaddi is not the Star."
93. Two additional lines are added to the 1–32 Key scale to accommodate the dual attributes of the Aeon and the Universe. They are designated "32bis" for the earth attribute of the Universe (Tau), and "31bis" for the spirit attribute of the Aeon (Shin).
94. The curious capitalization styles that characterize the names of various colors are indicative of how they were originally commercially identified. I have done my best to reproduce the original references throughout the tables and text.
95. The aces are a category of their own.
96. Harris was also burdened with having to repeatedly redo each painting. Her letters refer to more than a few instances where her repeated striping of the delicate watercolors affected the ideal coloring of the finished painting.
97. DuQuette, *Angels, Demons and Gods*, p. 59.
98. Aleister Crowley, with Mary Desti and Leila Waddell, *Magick—Liber ABA—Book Four—Part III*, Second one-volume edition, revised and enlarged, (York Beach, ME: Weiser Books, 1997), p. 275.
99. *The Book of the Sacred Magic of Abra-Melin the Mage as Delivered by Abraham the Jew Unto His Son Lamech, a Grimoire of the Fifteenth Century* (London: Watkins, 1900); (reprinted NY: Dover Publications, Inc, 1975); most recent edition, Wellingborough, UK: Aquarian Press, 1983.
100. See Ruth Majereik, trans., *The Chaldean Oracles of Zoroaster*. (London and New York: Brill, 1989).
101. DuQuette, *Angels, Demons and Gods.*, p. 51.
102. *The Book of Thoth*, p. 89. As a reminder, "redintigration" is an archaic word meaning restoration to a former state.
103. *The Equinox* I (5), (reprint, York Beach, ME: Weiser Books, 1992), p. 76.
104. Lon Milo DuQuette, *The Chicken Qabalah of Rabbi Lamed Ben Clifford* (York Beach, ME: Weiser Books, 2001), pp. 171–172.
105. DuQuette, *The Magick of Thelema*, p. 124.
106. Donald Michael Kraig, *Modern Sex Magick* (St. Paul, MN: Llewellyn Publications, 1998), p. 361.

Part II

1. Lon Milo DuQuette.
2. First edition published in 1938 by Ordo Templi Orientis, London. Revised edition. (Scottsdale, AZ: New Falcon Publications, 1992.)
3. Titles vary among different decks. For example: King, Queen, Knight, Page; King, Queen, Prince, and Princess.
4. The theory I personally prefer holds that the Major Arcana expresses the dynamics of Briah, and the Minor Arcana that of Yetzirah. But, as each suit is an harmonic expression of one of the four Qabalistic worlds, the characterizations of any given card can become extremely difficult to follow.
5. *The Book of Thoth*, p. 44.
6. *The Book of Thoth*, p. 189.
7. Demiourgos or Demiurge, a creator god who mistakenly thinks it is the Supreme Deity. Tetragrammaton is Latin for הוהי YHVH the Hebrew Demiourgos.
8. *The Book of Thoth*, p. 189.
9. *The Book of the Law*, I: 57.
10. See Robert O'Neill, *Tarot Symbolism* (Lima, OH: Fairway Press, 1986), p. 293.
11. *The Book of the Law*, I: 57.
12. Harris to Crowley, September 18, 1939.
13. Aleister Crowley, *The Law Is for All* (Scottsdale, AZ: New Falcon Publications, 1991), p.142.
14. *The Book of the Law*, I: 57.
15. *The Book of the Law*, I: 57.
16. *The Book of Thoth*, p. 77.
17. *The Book of Thoth*, p. 75.
18. *The Book of Thoth*, p. 67.
19. Aleister Crowley, *777 and Other Qabalistic Writings* (York Beach, ME: Weiser Books, Inc. 1986), Column CLXXXI, p. 34.
20. Aleister Crowley, "General Characters of the Trumps as They Appear in Use," *The Book of Thoth*, pp. 253–254.
21. Harris to Crowley, date uncertain.
22. *The Book of Thoth*, p. 118.
23. See chapter 8.
24. See the Chariot.
25. *The Book of Thoth*, p. 69.
26. *The Book of Thoth*, p. 69.
27. Crowley, *777 and Other Qabalistic Writings*, Column CLXXXI, p. 34.
28. *The Book of Thoth*, p. 254.
29. Harris to Crowley, May 11, 1941.
30. See Aleister Crowley, *The Vision and The Voice*, p. 211.
31. *The Book of Thoth*, p. 69.
32. *The Book of Thoth*, p. 70.
33. *The Book of Thoth*, p. 72.
34. *Liber Magi*, vv. 7–10, and *The Book of Thoth*, p. 71.
35. I welcome this opportunity to disabuse whoever it was who suggested that, in this card, Mercury is standing tiptoe upon the tip of a surfboard-shaped altar.

36. Crowley, *777 and Other Qabalistic Writings,* Column CLXXXI, p. 34.
37. *The Book of Thoth,* p. 254.
38. *The Book of Thoth,* p. 112.
39. *The Book of Thoth,* p. 74.
40. *The Book of Thoth,* p. 73.
41. Olive Whicher, *Sunspace: Science at a Threshold of Spiritual Understanding* (London: Rudolf Steiner Press, 1989).
42. Compare with the Queen of Cups.
43. *The Book of Thoth,* p. 73.
44. Crowley, *777 and Other Qabalistic Writings,* Column CLXXXI, p. 34.
45. *The Book of Thoth,* p. 255.
46. *The Book of Thoth,* p. 75.
47. *The Book of Thoth,* p. 75.
48. *The Book of Thoth,* p. 77.
49. Aleister Crowley, *Orpheus, Liber Primus Vel Carminum* in Collected Works, vol. III (Foyers, Society for the Propagation of Religious Truth, 1907; reprint, Chicago, IL: Yogi Publications), p. 155.
50. Crowley, *777 and Other Qabalistic Writings,* Column CLXXXI, p. 34.
51. *The Book of Thoth,* p. 259.
52. Harris to Crowley, May 21, 1941.
53. *The Book of Thoth,* p. 78.
54. *The Book of the Law,* I: 57.
55. *The Book of Thoth,* p. 77.
56. *The Book of Thoth,* p. 77.
57. *The Book of Thoth,* p. 79.
58. Crowley *777 and Other Qabalistic Writings,* Column CLXXXI, p. 34.
59. *The Book of Thoth,* p. 255.
60. Harris to Crowley, January 28, 1940.
61. *The Book of the Law,* III:11.
62. *The Book of Thoth,* p. 79.
63. *The Book of Thoth,* p. 79.
64. Crowley, *Vision and the Voice,* p. 67.
65. Crowley *777 and Other Qabalistic Writings,* Column CLXXXI, p. 34.
66. *The Book of Thoth,* p. 256.
67. Harris to Crowley, date uncertain.
68. *The Book of Thoth,* p. 83.
69. *The Book of Thoth,* p. 82.
70. We will find the upward arrow in the Art card.
71. Crowley *Vision and The Voice,* p. 202.
72. Crowley, *777 and Other Qabalistic Writings,* Column CLXXXI, p. 34.
73. *The Book of Thoth,* p. 256.
74. Harris to Crowley, May 11, 1941.
75. Crowley, *Vision and The Voice,* pp. 148, 149.
76. *The Book of Thoth,* p. 256.
77. Crowley, *777 and Other Qabalistic Writings,* Column CLXXXI, p. 34.
78. *The Book of Thoth,* p. 256.
79. *The Book of Thoth,* p. 88.

80. Harris to Crowley sometime between November 3 and December 19, 1939.
81. Crowley to Harris, December 19, 1939.
82. Aubrey Beardsley (1872–1898), brilliant and controversial artist and illustrator.
83. Harris to Crowley, July 12, (1940?).
84. See comments on Atu XXI, the Universe.
85. *The Book of Thoth*, p. 86.
86. Crowley, *777 and Other Qabalistic Writings*, Column CLXXXI, p. 34.
87. *The Book of Thoth*, p. 257.
88. Harris to Crowley, November 30, 1939.
89. *The Book of Thoth*, p. 89.
90. *The Book of Thoth*, p. 89.
91. *The Book of Thoth*, p. 89.
92. The obsolete theory of preformationism posits that prior to conception, living beings exist microscopically fully formed.
93. Crowley, *777 and Other Qabalistic Writings*, Column CLXXXI, p. 34.
94. *The Book of Thoth*, pp. 253–260.
95. Harris to Crowley, May 10, 1939.
96. *The Book of Thoth*, p. 90.
97. See chapter 8.
98. In rough Latin, "That central thing in the middle of three other things."
99. Aleister Crowley et al., from "The Rite of Jupiter," and "The Rites of Eleusis," *The Equinox* I (6), Supplement, p. 25.
100. Crowley, *777 and Other Qabalistic Writings*, Column CLXXXI, p. 34.
101. *The Book of Thoth*, pp. 253–260.
102. Letter from Frieda Harris to Aleister Crowley, March 25, 1942.
103. Later in Crowley's visionary cycle the spelling of the goddess's name changes to "Babalon." See Crowley and *The Vision and The Voice*, p. 159.
104. Seven aspects of Crowley as the Beast. "The Head of an Angel: the head of a Saint: the head of a Poet: the head of an Adulterous Woman: the head of a Man of Valour: the head of a Satyr: and the head of a Lion-Serpent." See Aleister Crowley, *The Book of Lies* (York Beach, ME: Red Wheel / Weiser, 1981), p.108.
105. Crowley, *Vision and The Voice*, p. 150.
106. Crowley, *777 and Other Qabalistic Writings*, . Column CLXXXI, p. 34.
107. *The Book of Thoth*, pp. 253–260.
108. Harris to Crowley, November/December (date uncertain) 1939.
109. Crowley to Harris, December 19, 1939.
110. *The Book of Thoth*, p. 97.
111. *The Book of Thoth*, p. 96.
112. *The Book of Thoth*, p. 97.
113. *The Book of Thoth*, p. 96.
114. *The Book of Thoth*, p. 96.
115. Crowley, *777 and Other Qabalistic Writings*, Column CLXXXI, p. 34.
116. *The Book of Thoth*, pp. 253–260.
117. Harris to Crowley, November/December (date uncertain) 1939.
118. *The Book of Thoth*, p. 99.
119. *The Book of Thoth*, pp. 99, 100.
120. *The Book of Thoth*, p. 100.

121. *The Book of Thoth*, p. 100.
122. *The Book of Thoth*, p. 103.
123. *The Book of Thoth*, p. 100.
124. Crowley, *777 and Other Qabalistic Writings*, Column CLXXXI, p. 34.
125. *The Book of Thoth*, pp. 253–260.
126. Harris to Crowley, (date uncertain) 1939.
127. *The Book of Thoth*, p. 102.
128. *The Book of Thoth*, p. 103.
129. Crowley, *777 and Other Qabalistic Writings*, Column CLXXXI, p. 34.
130. *The Book of Thoth*, pp. 253–260.
131. Aleister Crowley, *Magick, Liber ABA*, Book Four. 2nd ed. rev., ed. Hymenaeus Beta, (York Beach, ME: Weiser Books, 1994), p. 277.
132. *The Book of Thoth*, p. 105.
133. *The Book of Thoth*, p. 107.
134. *The Book of Thoth*, p. 106.
135. From Aleister Crowley, *Konx Om Pax* (Chicago, IL: Teitan Press, 1990), p. 10.
136. Crowley, *777 and Other Qabalistic Writings*, Column CLXXXI, p. 34.
137. *The Book of Thoth*, pp. 253–260.
138. Harris to Crowley, date uncertain.
139. *The Book of Thoth*, p. 107.
140. *The Book of Thoth*, p. 108.
141. *The Book of Thoth*, p. 109.
142. *The Book of Thoth*, pp. 108–109.
143. Crowley, *777 and Other Qabalistic Writings*, Column CLXXXI, p. 34.
144. *The Book of Thoth*, pp. 253–260.
145. Harris to Crowley, date uncertain.
146. *The Book of Thoth*, p. 109.
147. *The Book of Thoth*, p. 109.
148. Aleister Crowley, *Liber LXV*, from *The Holy Books of Thelema* (York Beach, ME: Weiser Books, Inc., 1983), p. 83.
149. *The Book of the Law* I: 58.
150. Crowley, *777 and Other Qabalistic Writings*, Column CLXXXI, p. 34.
151. *The Book of Thoth*, pp. 253–260. The version from Crowley's *The Heart of the Master* (Scottsdale, AZ. New Falcon Publications, 1999) contains the additional line "[*Roll up the Excrement of the Earth, to create a Star!*]"
152. *The Book of Thoth*, p. 112.
153. *The Book of Thoth*, p. 112.
154. *The Book of Thoth*, p. 113.
155. Crowley, *777 and Other Qabalistic Writings*, Column CLXXXI, p. 34.
156. *The Book of Thoth*, pp. 253–260.
157. *The Book of the Law*, I: 3.
158. *The Book of Thoth*, p. 113.
159. *The Book of the Law*. The spelling varies in the texts.
160. *The Book of the Law* III: 35: "The half of the word of Heru-ra-ha, called Hoor-pa-kraat and Ra-Hoor-Khut."
161. *The Book of Thoth*, p. 114.
162. Crowley, *777 and Other Qabalistic Writings*, Column CLXXXI, p. 34.

163. *The Book of Thoth*, pp. 253–260.
164. *The Book of the Law*, I: 49.
165. *The Book of the Law*, II, 3, 4.
166. *The Book of Thoth*, p. 116.
167. Crowley, *777 and Other Qabalistic Writings*, Column CLXXXI, p. 34.
168. *The Book of Thoth*, p. 260.
169. Harris to Crowley, date uncertain.
170. *The Book of Thoth*, p. 118.
171. *The Book of Thoth*, pp. 116, 117.
172. The Canon was first published in 1897 by Elkin Matthews. The second edition was published by Research into Lost Knowledge Organisation in association with The Garnstone Press in 1974. Third edition published in 1981 by Research into Lost Knowledge Organisation, 8 The Drive, New Southgate, London N11 2DY. Distributed by Thorson's publishers Limited, Wellingborough, Northamptonshire.
173. Numbers 2:2.
174. The zodiacal year can be divided into seventy-two quinaries, or periods of five degrees. Each of the thirty-six small cards of the tarot represents two quinaries or one decan.
175. First edition, London: Ernest Benn LTD., 1928.
176. *The Book of Thoth*, p. 119.
177. See glossary, chapter 21.
178. *The Book of Thoth*, p. 118.
179. Or, if you prefer—elevated his initiatory consciousness from that represented by the fourth sephira, Chesed, to that of the third Sephira, Binah.
180. Crowley, *The Vision and The Voice* .
181. Crowley, *The Vision and The Voice*, pp. 174, 175.
182. Crowley, *Konx Om Pax*, p. 10.
183. Crowley, *Konx Om Pax*, p. 7.
184. Rabbi Lamed Ben Clifford.
185. *The Book of Thoth*, p. 177.
186. Matti Pitkänen. Department of Physics, Theoretical Physics Division, 2000.
187. *The Book of Thoth*, p. 177.
188. Harris to Crowley, date uncertain.
189. *The Book of Thoth*, p. 188.
190. This paraphrased from Crowley's comment on the Ace of Cups, *The Book of Thoth*, p.195.
191. *The Book of Thoth*, p. 195.
192. *The Book of Thoth*, p. 79.
193. *The Book of Thoth*, p. 202.
194. *The Book of Thoth*, p. 203.
195. Crowley, *Magick, Liber ABA*, Book Four, p. 86.
196. *The Book of Thoth*, p. 211.
197. *The Book of Thoth*, p. 149.
198. I believe, at the moment, her marvelous essay is only published on her website *http://members.cts.com/king/s/saoirse/TarotCards.html*, Copyright, © 1999.
199. Isabel Briggs Myers, *Gifts Differing*, (Consulting Psychologists Press, Palo Alto), 1995.

200. Arthur Rosengarten, *Psychology and Tarot: Spectrums of Possibility* (New York: Paragon House, 2000).
201. The entire zodiacal year is divided into 360 degrees, and each of the twelve signs of the zodiac is composed of thirty degrees. The thirty-degree period of a zodiac sign is divided into three ten-degree periods called decans.
202. *The Book of Thoth*, p. 151.
203. *The Book of Thoth*, p. 152.
204. *The Book of Thoth*, p. 153.
205. *The Book of Thoth*, p. 154.
206. See Leon Engers-Kennedy's famous painting of Crowley in *Equinox* III (1).
207. *The Book of Thoth*, p. 153, 154.
208. Harris to Crowley—date uncertain.
209. *The Book of Thoth*, p. 155.
210. *The Book of Thoth*, p. 155.
211. *The Book of Thoth*, p. 156.
212. *The Book of Thoth*, p. 156.
213. *The Book of Thoth*, p. 156.
214. *The Book of Thoth*, p. 157.
215. This is just the kind of comment one would expect from a Queen of Cups.
216. *The Book of Thoth*, p. 157.
217. *The Book of Thoth*, p. 158.
218. *The Book of Thoth*, p. 158.
219. *The Book of Thoth*, p. 158.
220. *The Book of Thoth*, p. 159.
221. Harris to Crowley, date uncertain.
222. *The Book of Thoth*, p. 160.
223 *The Book of Thoth*, p. 161.
224. *The Book of Thoth*, p. 161.
225. *The Book of Thoth*, p. 161.
226. *The Book of Thoth*, p. 163.
227. *The Book of Thoth*, p. 162.
228. *The Book of Thoth*, p. 162.
229. *The Book of Thoth*, p. 163.
230. *The Book of Thoth*, p. 163.
231. Harris to Crowley, November 3, 1939.
232. *The Book of Thoth*, p. 164.
233. *The Book of Thoth*, p. 166
234. *The Book of Thoth*, p. 166.
235. *The Book of Thoth*, p. 166.
236. *The Book of Thoth*, p. 166.
237. *The Book of Thoth*, p. 166.
238. Harris to Crowley—date uncertain.
239. *The Book of Thoth*, p. 167.
240. *The Book of Thoth*, p. 167.
241. Harris to Crowley, December 11, 1942.
242. *The Book of Thoth*, p. 169.
243. *The Book of Thoth*, p. 149.

244. *The Book of Thoth*, p. 169.

245. *The Book of Thoth*, p. 169.

246. *The Book of Thoth*, p. 171.

247. Lon Milo DuQuette, *Tarot of Ceremonial Magick*, (York Beach, ME: Red Wheel/Weiser, 1995), p. 121.

248. Obviously, because there are seven planets and thirty-six decans, we are left at the end of the year with one extra decan. This is remedied by having Mars repeat at the end of winter and the beginning of spring—to give, as it were, an extra dose of energy to overcome winter. Don't blame me. I didn't invent this system!

249. Joan Quigley, *Astrology for Adults* (New York: Holt, Rinehart and Winston, 1969), p. 131.

250. *The Book of Thoth*, p. 178.

251. *The Book of Thoth*, p. 189.

252. They are actually Phurbas or Kilas, the Tibetan triple-sided ritual dagger/nail/dart/spike.

253. *The Book of Thoth*, p. 189.

254. On the *Tree of Life*, the sixth sephira, Tiphareth, is by tradition the sphere of the Sun.

255. *The Book of Thoth*, p. 178.

256. *The Book of Thoth*, p. 190.

257. *The Book of Thoth*, p. 182.

258. *The Book of Thoth*, p. 182.

259. *The Book of Thoth*, p. 193.

260. *The Book of Thoth*, p. 193.

261. *The Book of Thoth*, p. 193.

262. *The Book of Thoth*, p. 186.

263. *The Book of Thoth*, p. 185.

264. *The Book of Thoth*, pp. 193, 194.

265. *The Book of Thoth*, p. 186.

266. *The Book of Thoth*, p. 194.

267. *The Book of Thoth*, p. 194.

268. *The Book of Thoth*, pp. 194, 195.

269. Harris to Crowley, March 25, 1942.

270. *The Book of Thoth*, p. 196.

271. *The Book of Thoth*, p. 196.

272. *The Book of Thoth*, p. 196.

273. *The Book of Thoth*, p. 197.

274. *The Book of Thoth*, p. 199.

275. *The Book of Thoth*, p. 182.

276. *The Book of Thoth*, p. 200.

277. *The Book of Thoth*, p. 184.

278. "Countin' Flowers On the Wall," written by Lew Dewitt. © Wallflower Music/Copyright Management.

279. *The Book of Thoth*, p. 184.

280. *The Book of Thoth*, p. 201.

281. Crowley to Harris, December 19, 1939.

282. DuQuette, *Tarot of Ceremonial Magick*, p. 166.

283. *The Book of Thoth*, p. 202.

284. Harris to Crowley, date uncertain.

285. Harris to Crowley, November 3, 1939.

286. *The Book of Thoth*, p. 205.

287. *The Book of Thoth*, p. 205.

288. *The Book of Thoth*, p. 205.

289. Harris to Crowley, November 3, 1939.

290. *The Book of Thoth*, p. 183.

291. *The Book of Thoth*, p. 207.

292. *The Book of Thoth*, p. 186.

293. *The Book of Thoth*, p. 208.

294. *The Book of Thoth*, pp. 208, 209.

295. Harris to Crowley, September 18, 1939.

296. *The Book of Thoth*, p. 209.

297. *The Book of Thoth*, p. 212.

298. *The Book of Thoth*, p. 178.

299. Aleister Crowley, *Liber LXV, Liber Cordis Cincti Sepente, sub figura* ` ﬥ ﬧ א *from The Holy Books of Thelema*, p. 66.

300. Harris to Crowley, January 7, 1940.

301. *The Book of Thoth*, pp. 212, 213.

302. See chapter 8, and Fortune.

303. *The Book of Thoth*, p. 213.

304. See "The Rites of Eleusis,"*The Equinox* I (6), Supplement p. 10.

305. See Five of Swords.

306. *The Book of Thoth*, p. 181.

307. *The Book of Thoth*, p. 215.

308. *The Book of Thoth*, p. 215.

309. *The Book of Thoth*, p. 215.

310. *The Book of Thoth*, p. 183.

311. *The Book of Thoth*, p. 216.

312. *The Book of Thoth*, p. 216.

313. *The Book of Thoth*, p. 187.

314. *The Book of Thoth*, p. 217.

315. I cannot resist mentioning that the Egyptian ibis, the long-beaked water bird sacred to Thoth, was known even in ancient times for its ability to use its beak to self-administer enemas.

316. *The Book of Thoth*, p. 217.

317. *The Book of Thoth*, p. 188.

318. Harris to Crowley, date uncertain.

319. *Frater Perdurabo (Aleister Crowley)*. Aleister Crowley, *Tarot Divination* (York Beach, ME: Red Wheel / Weiser, 1976), p. 300.

320. Aleister Crowley Memorandum regarding "Stipend"—date uncertain.

321. *The Equinox* vol. I. (reprint, York Beach, ME: Weiser Books 1992).

322. From "A Description of the Cards of the Tarot with their Attribution; Including a Method of Divination by Their Use,"*Equinox*, I (7), pp. 206–210).

323. Crowley is assuming that the Significator is a court card. The counting begins with

the Significator in the direction the figure in the card is facing. This is not always easy to determine in the Thoth Tarot.—Ed.

324. DuQuette, *The Book of Thoth*, pp. 253–260.
325. A Description of the Cards, *Equinox*, I (7), pp.143–210.
326. See description of original design, page 263.
327. *The Magick of Thelema*, p. 216.
328. *The Book of Thoth*, p. 85.
329. *The Book of Thoth*, p. 37.
330. *The Magick of Thelema*, p. 216.
331. *The Equinox* I (5).
332. *The Book of Thoth*, p. 90.
333. *The Book of Thoth*, p. 115.
334. *The Magick of Thelema*, p. 80.
335. *The Book of Thoth*, p. 70.
336. *The Book of Thoth*, p. 85.
337. *The Book of Thoth*, p. 85.
338. DuQuette, *The Magick of Thelema*, p. 80
339. *The Book of Thoth*, p. 85.
340. DuQuette, *The Magick of Thelema*, p. 81.
341. *The Book of Thoth*, p.75.
342. *The Book of Thoth*, p. 79.
343. Paraphrased from Kalisch, *Sepher Yezirah*, p. 14.

BIBLIOGRAPHY

Abraham the Jew. *The Book of the Sacred Magic of Abra-Melin the Mage as Delivered by Abraham the Jew Unto His Son Lamech, a Grimoire of the Fifteenth Century.* Translated by S.L. MacGregor Mathers. London: Watkins, 1900. Reprint, New York: Dover Publications, Inc., 1975. Most recent edition: Wellingborough, UK: Aquarian Press, 1983.

Briggs Myers, Isabel. *Gifts Differing.* 2nd ed. Palo Alto, CA: Consulting Psychologists Press, 1995.

Colquhoun, Ithell. *Sword of Wisdom, MacGregor Mathers and "The Golden Dawn."* New York: G. P. Putnam's Sons, 1975.

Crowley, Aleister. *Magick, Liber ABA, Book Four.* 2d ed., Edited by Hymenaeus Beta. York Beach, ME: Weiser Books, Inc.,1997.

———. *Magick, Liber ABA, Book Four.* 2d ed., Edited by Hymenaeus Beta. York Beach, ME: Weiser Books, Inc.,1997.

———. *The Book of Thoth by The Master Therion* (Aleister Crowley): *A Short Essay on the Tarot of the Egyptians.* London: O.T.O., 1944. *The Equinox* III (5). Reprint, York Beach, ME: Samuel Weiser, 1992.

———. *The Confessions of Aleister Crowley.* London, 1929. Abridged one-volume edition, edited by John Symonds and Kenneth Grant. London, 1969. Reprint, London and New York: Arkana 1989.

———. *The Equinox* I (5). Spring 1911, edited by Soror Virakam. London. Reprinted York Beach, ME: Weiser Books, Inc., 1992.

———. *The Equinox* I (6). Fall 1911, edited by Soror Virakam. London. Reprint, York Beach, ME: Weiser Books, Inc., 1992.

———. *The Equinox* I (8). Fall 1912, edited by Soror Virakam. London. Reprint, York Beach, ME: Weiser Books, Inc., 1992.

———. *The Equinox of the Gods.* London: O.T.O., 1936. *The Equinox* III (3). Corrected facsimile editions, Scottsdale, AZ: New Falcon Publications, 1991, and New York: 93 Publishing, 1992.

————. *The Heart of the Master*. First edition published in 1938 by Ordo Templi Orientis, London. Revised edition © 1992 Ordo Templi Orientis. Scottsdale, AZ: New Falcon Publications, 1992.

————. *Konx Om Pax*. Foyers, Scotland: Society for the Propagation of Religious Truth, 1907. Reprint, with an Introduction by Martin P. Starr, Chicago: The Teitan Press, 1990.

————. *Liber Aleph vel CXI: The Book of Wisdom or Folly*. Edited by Karl Germer and Marcelo Motta. Barstow, CA: Thelema Publishing Co., 1961. *The Equinox* III (6), rev. 2d, ed. Edited by Hymenaeus Beta. York Beach, ME: Weiser Books, Inc., 1991, and New York: 93 Publishing, 1991.

————. *The Law Is for All*. Scottsdale, AZ: New Falcon Publications, 1991.

————. *Liber LXV, Liber Cordis Cincti Serpente, sub fugura figura ynda*. from *The Holy Books of Thelema*. York Beach, ME: Weiser Books, Inc., 1983.

————. *Little Essays Toward Truth*. London: O.T.O. ,1936. Reprint, Scottsdale, AZ: New Falcon Publications, 1991.

————. *Orpheus, Liber Primus Vel Carminum*. Foyers: Society for the Propagation of Religious Truth, 1907. Reprint, Chicago, IL: Yogi Publications, 1978.

————. *The Qabalah of Aleister Crowley*. New York: Weiser Books, Inc., 1973. Retitled *777 and Other Qabalistic Writings of Aleister Crowley* in the fifth printing, 1977. Reprinted York Beach, ME: Weiser Books, Inc., 1990.

————. *Tarot Divination*. York Beach, ME: Weiser Books Inc., 1976.

————. (received by). *[Thelema]* Τηελεμα *The Holy Books of Thelema*, Edited by Hymenaeus Alpha and Hymenaeus Beta. York Beach, ME: Weiser Books, Inc., 1983. *The Equinox* III (9). Corrected second printing, York Beach, ME: Weiser Books, Inc., 1983 and New York: 93 Publishing, 1990.

————. *The Vision and The Voice—with Commentary and Other Papers*. York Beach, ME: Weiser Books, Inc., 1998.

DuQuette, Lon Milo. *Angels, Demons and Gods of the New Millennium*. York Beach, ME: Weiser Books, Inc., 1997.

————. *The Magick of Thelema*. York Beach, ME: Weiser Books, Inc., 1993.

————. *Tarot of Ceremonial Magick*. York Beach, ME: Weiser Books, Inc., 1995.

————. *The Chicken Qabalah of Rabbi Lamed Ben Clifford*. York Beach, ME: Weiser Books, Inc., 2001.

Eliade, Mircea. *A History of Religious Ideas*. Chicago: University of Chicago Press, 1984.

Fortune, Dion. *The Mystical Qabalah*. London: Ernest Benn Limited, 1976.

Friedman, Irving. *The Book of Creation*. York Beach, ME: Samuel Weiser, Inc, 1977.

James, William. *The Varieties of Religious Experience*. London: Longmans, 1910.

Jung, Carl G. *Man and His Symbols*. London: Aldus Books, 1964.

Kalisch, Isidor. *Sepher Yezirah: A Book on Creation, or The Jewish Metaphysics of Remote Antiquity*. New York: L. H. Frank & Co., 1877.

Kaplan, Aryeh, trans. *Sepher Yetzerah*.York Beach, ME: Samuel Weiser, 1990.

Kraig, Donald Michael. *Modern Sex Magick*. St. Paul, MN: Llewellyn Publications, 1998.

George M. Lamsa, trans. *The Holy Bible from the Ancient Eastern Manuscripts,* Translated from Aramaic. Trans. Philadelphia, PA: A. J. Homan Company, 1967.

Levi, Eliphas. *The Key of the Mysteries*. Translated by Aleister Crowley. York Beach, ME: Weiser Books, Inc., 1970; London: Rider & Co., 1969. Also as a special supplement to *Equinox* 1(10).

———. *The History of Magic.* Translated by Arthur Edward Waite. London: Rider, 1957; York Beach, ME: Weiser Books, Inc., 1970.

———. *Transcendental Magic: Its Doctrine and Ritual,* Translated by Arthur Edward Waite. London: Rider & Co., 1896; York Beach, ME: Weiser Books, Inc., 1974.

Mathers, S. L. MacGregor, trans. *The Kabbalah Unveiled.* York Beach, ME: Weiser Books, Inc., 1974.

Mordell, Phineas. *The Origin of Letters and Numbers According to the Sefer Yetzirah.* York Beach: Samuel Weiser, Inc., 1975.

Quigley, Joan. *Astrology for Adults,* New York: Holt, Rinehart and Winston., 1969.

Regardie, Israel. *The Complete Golden Dawn System of Magic.* Phoenix, AZ: New Falcon Press, 1984.

———. *The Eye in the Triangle.* Scottsdale, AZ: New Falcon Press, 1989.

———. *The Golden Dawn.* 6th ed. St. Paul: Llewellyn Publications, 1992.

Roberts, Susan. *Magician of the Golden Dawn.* Chicago, IL: Contemporary Books, Inc., 1978.

Rosengarten, Arthur. *Psychology and Tarot: Spectrums of Possibility.* New York, NY: Paragon House, 2000.

Stirling, William. *The Canon.* First Edition, London: Elkin Matthews, 1897. Second Edition, London: Research into Lost Knowledge Organisation in association with The Garnstone Press, 1974. Third Edition published in 1981 by Research into Lost Knowledge Organisation, 8 The Drive, New Southgate, London N11 2DY. Distributed by Thorson's publishers Limited, Wellingborough, Northamptonshire, England.

Suares, Carlo. *The Sepher Yetsira.* Translated by Micheline and Vincent Stuart. Boulder & London: Shambhala, 1976.

Townley, Kevin. *The Cube of Space, Container of Creation.* Boulder, CO: Archive Press, 1993.

Wang, Robert. *An Introduction to the Golden Dawn Tarot.* York Beach, ME: Weiser Books, Inc., 1978.

———. *Qabalistic Tarot.* York Beach, ME: Weiser Books, Inc., 1990.

Whicher, Olive. *Sunspace: Science at a Threshold of Spiritual Understanding.* London: Rufolf Steiner Press, 1989.

Zoroaster. *The Chaldean Oracles of Zoroaster.* Translated by Ruth Majereik. Leiden and New York: Brill, 1989.

PERMISSIONS